Creativity 101
James C. Kaufman, PhD

Genius 101
Dean Keith Simonton, PhD

IQ Testing 101
Alan S. Kaufman, PhD

Leadership 101
Michael D. Mumford, PhD

Psycholinguistics 101
H. Wind Cowles, PhD

Intelligence 101
Jonathan Plucker, PhD

Anxiety 101
Moshe Zeidner, PhD
Gerald Matthews, PhD

The Psych 101 Series

James C. Kaufman, PhD, Series Editor

Director, Learning Research Institute
California State University at San Bernardino

Moshe Zeidner, PhD, is Professor of Educational Psychology and Human Development at the University of Haifa, Israel. His main fields of interest are in the area of personality, emotions, and individual differences. He is the author or coeditor of 10 books and author or coauthor of over 200 scientific journal papers and book chapters. He received the lifetime achievement award for outstanding contribution to stress and anxiety research at the annual meeting of the Society for Stress and Anxiety Research in July 2003, in Lisbon, Portugal. His recent book, *What We Know About Emotional Intelligence* (MIT Press), with G. Matthews and R. Roberts, received the PROSE award for academic excellence from the Association of American Publishers, Inc., for the year 2009.

Gerald Matthews, PhD, is Professor of Psychology at the University of Cincinnati. His research focuses on the use of cognitive science models to understand the interplay between personality, emotion, and information processing. Specific interests include effects of anxiety on cognitive processes, the assessment of stress during task performance, and anxiety and vehicle driving. He is the author or coauthor, or the coeditor, of 13 books and more than 200 articles and book chapters. His coauthored book, *Attention and Emotion: A Clinical Perspective* (Lawrence Erlbaum), was the winner of the 1998 British Psychological Society Book Award. He was formerly Secretary-Treasurer of the International Society for the Study of Individual Differences.

Anxiety 101

Moshe Zeidner, PhD
Gerald Matthews, PhD

SPRINGER PUBLISHING COMPANY

NEW YORK

Springer Publishing Company, LLC
11 West 42nd Street
New York, NY 10036
www.springerpub.com

Acquisitions Editor: Nancy S. Hale
Senior Editor: Rose Mary Piscitelli
Cover design: Mimi Flow
Project Manager: Ashita Shah
Composition: Newgen Imaging

ISBN: 978-0-8261-0488-5
Ebook ISBN: 978-0-8261-0489-2

10 11 12 13/ 5 4 3 2 1

The author and the publisher of this Work have made every effort to use sources believed to be reliable to provide information that is accurate and compatible with the standards generally accepted at the time of publication. The author and publisher shall not be liable for any special, consequential, or exemplary damages resulting, in whole or in part, from the readers' use of, or reliance on, the information contained in this book. The publisher has no responsibility for the persistence or accuracy of URLs for external or third-party Internet Web sites referred to in this publication and does not guarantee that any content on such Web sites is, or will remain, accurate or appropriate.

Library of Congress Cataloging-in-Publication Data

Zeidner, Moshe.
Anxiety 101 / Moshe Zeidner, Gerald Matthews.
    p. cm.
  Includes index.
  ISBN 978-0-8261-0488-5
  1. Anxiety.   I. Matthews, Gerald.   II. Title.
  BF575.A6Z43 2010
  152.4'6—dc22   2010034557

Printed in the United States of America by Hamilton Printing

We dedicate this book to the person
who kindled our interest
in anxiety research—
Professor Charles Spielberger,
University of South Florida.

Contents

Preface

Anxiety is a ubiquitous and pervasive problem in modern society, as encapsulated by the popular depiction of the modern era as "the age of anxiety." The potentially crippling anxiety associated with the sundry dangers that adhere to our competitive postmodern technological society has created a massive body of knowledge focusing on the conceptualization, measurement, origins, and treatment of anxiety and anxiety disorders. The importance of anxiety as a core construct in both normal and abnormal behavior is highlighted by the central role ascribed to it in personality, counseling, and educational, occupational, and clinical psychology, shaping both theory and practice in psychology and psychiatry. In fact, anxiety is currently one of the most researched and discussed phenomena in the domain of Personality and Social Psychology, with well over 100,000 scientific papers published on various theoretical, assessment, research, and clinical facets of the construct.

Given the huge body of relevant research on anxiety conducted over the past few decades, the time has come for an up-to-date, integrative, and accessible introduction to the domain of anxiety for college students and other interested readers. *Anxiety 101* aims at filling this gap by providing a contemporary and comprehensive review and integration of what we know about some of the major facets of anxiety, including assessment, theory, development, research, and interventions. This introduction to the dynamic field of anxiety reflects the substantial progress made by researchers over the past few decades in concept differentiation, assessment techniques, theoretical models, empirical research, and clinical parameters and interventions. The theoretical and empirical body of research presented in this book is grounded in the work of scores of anxiety researchers working in a number of different areas, including differential psychology, personality and social psychology, stress, coping and emotion research, developmental psychology, psychological assessment, psychobiology and neuroscience, and clinical psychology.

Anxiety 101 is divided into seven broad chapters, briefly described as follows:

- Chapter 1—*Introduction*—presents a conceptual overview of the anxiety domain. The construct of anxiety is defined, its key components and facets delineated, and major conceptual advances highlighted. The key functions of anxiety are discussed and some of the real-life contexts for researching anxiety, including anxieties about evaluation, performance, and terrorism, are presented.
- Chapter 2—*How Do We Best Assess Anxiety?*—focuses on assessment and measurement of anxiety. Specific procedures for assessing the phenomenological, physiological, and behavioral facets of anxiety are presented. Major self-report inventories and alternative measures of anxiety (physiological, biological, performance, etc.) are described. Also, evidence for group differences in anxiety levels is presented.
- Chapter 3—*Theories and Perspectives on Anxiety*—presents and critically discusses major conceptual perspectives and theoretical models of anxiety in the literature. These include traditional models (psychoanalytic, learning theory, and drive) as well as more contemporary models (evolutionary, psychobiological, self-regulatory, and interactional) models.
- Chapter 4—*What Are the Origins of Anxiety?*—discusses the role of biology, primary socialization and family environment, school-related experiences, learning, and personal experiences, as key factors in the development of anxiety.

- Chapter 5—*How Does Anxiety Affect Cognitive Outcomes?*—selectively surveys the empirical evidence for the effects of anxiety on learning and cognitive performance. This chapter surveys empirical data on the magnitude of the anxiety-performance relationship, followed by the presentation of a number of causal models and mechanisms in the anxiety-performance interface. The effects of anxiety on various stages of information processing (input, storage and processing of information, retrieval, and output) are delineated.

- Chapter 6—*Does Intervention Help?*—reviews the role of coping as well as the effectiveness of various procedures and interventions, both cognitive-focused (e.g., cognitive-behavioral, cognitive skills training), and emotion-focused (e.g., relaxation, desensitization, and modeling) techniques in alleviating anxiety. Anti-anxiety drug treatment is also briefly discussed. Major clinical considerations in anxiety treatment are presented.

- Chapter 7—*Looking Ahead to a Cognitive Science of Anxiety*—concludes our treatment of anxiety. We will begin by arguing that the most satisfactory theory of anxiety has come from cognitive models of anxiety that relate the emotion to information processing and its regulation. However, a broader cognitive science is needed to integrate information processing models with neuroscience and with motivational aspects of anxiety. We will also feature some "anti-cognitivist" critiques of the approach.

The book should be of interest to undergraduate students taking basic courses in personality and individual differences, social psychology, educational psychology, and clinical psychology. The sheer volume of research on anxiety makes it virtually impossible to survey and do justice to all the significant facets of the construct. Thus, the coverage of various aspects was limited by the space constraints of a one-volume text. Although there is some overlap among chapters, this allows each chapter to stand on its own, and increases the accessibility of each one.

Dr. James Kaufman, *Psychology 101* series editor at Springer, has been most supportive, patient, and helpful in all phases required to bring this project to closure. Thanks to Nancy Hale, acquisitions editor at Springer, for her feedback and help in shaping up the manuscript. The University of Haifa and the University of Cincinnati provided congenial academic environments and physical resources necessary to undertake and complete this book.

Anxiety 101 should provide students with the foundations of knowledge, research, assessment methods, and clinical guidelines upon which more comprehensive understandings can be developed in future courses and learning experiences. For the authors, penning *Anxiety 101* has been a both a challenging and rewarding experience, and we hope readers will find it to be the same.

Moshe Zeidner and Gerald Matthews
June 2010

Anxiety 101

Introduction

> *To a man who is afraid, everything rustles.*
> Sophocles

magine the following. It is October 2008 and the global economy is collapsing. Your company is hard hit and the water cooler talk is all of job layoffs. You notice your coworkers seem to be avoiding you and your boss won't look you in the eye. You've always seen yourself as one of the top performers but now you start to worry. It doesn't help that your spouse was fired last week, and your retirement savings were mostly in company stock that is plunging in value every day. How will you keep up the mortgage payments and send your kids to a good college? As you reflect on your family, you feel extremely apprehensive, your heart pounds, and you feel physically sick. On the positive side, a Chinese organization is rumored to be interested in buying up the company.

The scenario here illustrates some key features of anxiety, an emotion with which we are all familiar. In lecture 25 of the *Introductory Lectures on Psychoanalysis*, Freud (1949), the noted founder of psychoanalysis, wrote: "I have no need to introduce anxiety to you. Every one of us has experienced that sensation, or to speak more correctly, that affective state, at one time or another on our own account" (p. 440). Indeed, anxiety is one of the most pervasive and ubiquitous of human emotions, in all cultures (Sarason & Sarason, 1990). It is safe to assume that readers of this text have experienced anxiety firsthand at some time throughout their lives and can readily resonate to the topic of this primer on a personal level.

Anxiety is considered to be a basic negative emotion, along with anger, sadness, disgust, and perhaps others. It should also be distinguished from fear, which may feel similar at a subjective level, but is focused on an immediate danger, such as encountering a snarling pit bull terrier. Anxiety, by contrast, corresponds to a state of uncertainty. In the aforementioned scenario, the employee suspects, but does not know for sure, that he or she will be fired. The signals of threat, such as the nonverbal behaviors of coworkers, are ambiguous; perhaps people are acting oddly because of their own anxieties. Anxiety is also often future-oriented; often, it accompanies concerns over possible disasters that the person anticipates, such as the various unpleasant consequences of becoming unemployed. Future disasters may seem overwhelming and outside the person's capacity to control, like an iceberg looming over an ocean liner.

A final feature of our scenario is that anxiety is experienced through both mental and physical symptoms. The state of anxiety is accompanied by feelings of nervousness and tension, as well as worries and intrusive thoughts. It is also typical to experience signs of bodily activation, sometimes described as the "fight-or-flight" response, such as a pounding heart, perspiration, and gastric disturbance.

Consider another scenario. Dan Levine was an 18-year-old freshman majoring in psychology at a major state university on the West Coast. As the deadline for the final exam in Psychological Statistics approached, he became progressively more preoccupied with anxious anticipation and worry. While taking the final exam in the course, he experienced heightened tension and apprehension, affecting his recall of the formulas and computational procedures he had memorized. He struggled to focus his attention during the exam, but by trying extra hard he managed to answer all the problems. After completing the exam, he anticipated failing and worried a lot about what kind of future he would have with poor grades. In the end, he received an above-average score of B+ on the exam.

Dan's experience is typical of moderate anxiety. Although he might have gotten a somewhat higher grade had he remained calm, he was able to manage his anxiety in the exam, and do reasonably well. In fact, his worries after the examination proved to be ill-founded. The scenario highlights a key research question: Does anxiety actually make a material difference to how well the person can perform mentally demanding tasks, such as taking an exam? As we will see, anxiety certainly can be detrimental, but this is not always the case. Indeed, there are circumstances in which anxiety may even be helpful in motivating the person to deal with some future danger. A little anxiety about grades may spur the student to prepare effectively for an exam.

Now consider a third scenario. Linda has been diagnosed by her psychiatrist as suffering from a clinical problem—social anxiety disorder. At the core of Linda's problem is excessive sensitivity to criticism and rejection. She is sure that she usually makes a fool of herself when she interacts with others in a social setting. Consequently, she tends to keep aloof from her coworkers at the office in which she is employed, and attending the annual office party is out of the question. It is all too easy for her to remember occasions where she said something really dumb, and she is convinced that she is a laughingstock. When she does talk to people, she is acutely aware of how anxious she becomes, and how her anxiety prevents her from expressing herself as she would wish. In fact, Linda's harsh view of herself is not objectively realistic. She has normal social skills, but lacks confidence to use them. Her tendencies to hide away from people are making her problems worse. Psychotherapy for Linda centers on gradually exposing her to social situations with the support and guidance of her therapist.

Linda's case illustrates how anxiety may be abnormal as well as normal. Excessive anxiety, based on unrealistic perceptions of the self and others, can be socially disabling. A key point is that clinical anxiety is more intensely felt than normal anxiety and it involves distortions in thinking. Anxiety patients often misinterpret events so as to perceive a threat where none actually exists. For example, the person might falsely see a negative comment as directed toward him or her, personally. As in Linda's case, they find it easier to recall their social failures than their successes. There is a sense in which the anxious patients live in a world of danger of their own imagining.

One of the starting points for psychological research on anxiety is its multifaceted nature. Anxiety may be mild or extreme, transient or long-lasting, and helpful or damaging. There are also a variety of ways of experiencing anxiety, which have differing consequences for the person's behavior and functioning in everyday life. Another key point is that anxiety is a response to external threats, sometimes realistic, sometimes exaggerated. Understanding anxiety requires us to look at how people manage threats, and how their attempts at coping are sometimes successful, and sometimes make the problem worse (Rachman, 2003).

In the remainder of this introduction, we will expand on the personal and environmental factors that contribute to anxiety. We will begin by describing anxiety in more depth, exploring its different components, as revealed by research. Then we will look a little deeper into the psychological function of anxiety; why have we evolved to experience this disquieting emotion? Answering this question requires us to unpack the different facets of anxiety. The final section of this chapter looks at some of the real-life contexts for researching anxiety, including anxieties about evaluation, performance, and terrorism.

WHAT IS THIS THING CALLED ANXIETY?

The concept of anxiety has a rather long and checkered history. The study and analysis of anxiety originated in the Classical Greek period and developed conceptually in parallel to the development of self-awareness in Western thought (Endler & Kocovski, 2001). The term *anxiety* seems to have been derived from the Indo-Germanic root, *angh*, which also appears in the Greek, and means a feeling of tightness, constriction, or choking under duress (Tyrer, 1999). The Roman statesman and orator Cicero (cited in Lewis, 1970) distinguished between *"anxietas,"* an abiding predisposition, and *"angor,"* a transitory emotional outburst or response.

Modern researchers have had a hard time building on the insights of antiquity. Although some early writings on the topic viewed anxiety as a unified concept, current work recognizes multiple facets of anxiety, which are not always well distinguished in research. We will now walk you through these sometimes subtle, but pivotal, distinctions.

Anxiety Versus Fear

We have already mentioned that anxiety and fear are distinct emotions. *Anxiety* refers to a psychological state in which the person's sense of uneasy suspense and worry is triggered by ambiguous circumstances. That is, *anxiety* refers to general feelings of uneasiness and distress about an unspecified, diffuse, uncertain, and often formless form of threat or danger. Because of the ambiguous nature of the anxiety-provoking stimulus, the person is uncertain how to act; because the nature and place of the threat are obscure, it is more difficult to cope with the ambiguous threat. The person's behavioral response to the ambiguous danger may be out of proportion to the actual threat. Anxiety often has a pronounced social element. As social beings, many of our concerns revolve around how others may view, and perhaps criticize, us.

By contrast, *fear* refers to an intense biologically adaptive physiological and behavioral response to the occurrence of a specific, identifiable stimulus (e.g., a dangerous animal). Because the danger is real and targeted, the person feels impelled to act, with fear being a "call for action" (flight, freeze, and fight). Along these lines, Freud (1949) wrote: "I think 'angst' [anxiety] relates to the state and disregards the object, while 'Furcht' [fear] draws attention precisely to the object" (p. 443). Research on fear has often studied individuals in dangerous environments such as parachutists and military combatants.

On paper, the distinction may seem clear enough, but in practice, there may be considerable overlap between fear and anxiety. They share a number of highly similar elements (Ohman, 2008). These include cognitive appraisals of a threat or danger in the surroundings; attributes of worry and apprehension; subjective feelings of uneasiness and tension; strong somatic manifestations and reactions of the autonomic nervous system; feeling that something bad is about to occur and we might be able to do something about it; and similar behavioral reactions (escape, attack, etc.). Also, both fear and anxiety are believed to have adaptive value for the organism, with evolution selecting for these emotions to help one attend to, identify, perceive, and react adaptively to potentially ominous or dangerous situations in the immediate environment. In addition, anxiety often follows fear, and when fear becomes activated, anxiety is frequently the emotional result (e.g., panic because of lack of perceived control). Also, repeated experiences of anxiety can generate fear reactions. Future research may show fundamental differences between fear and anxiety in terms of genetics, neuroanatomy, and psychophysiology (Ohman, 2008). Table 1.1

TABLE 1.1   DISTINGUISHING FEAR FROM ANXIETY

Criteria	Fear	Anxiety
Nature of threat or danger	Objective and clear danger or threat based on reality (or exaggerated perception of reality). Source of danger can be identified.	Subjective/symbolic danger—general expectation of diffuse and uncertain or formless threat or danger. Source of danger cannot be identified.
Time orientation	Present danger.	Future danger.
Causes or triggering mechanism	Specific objects or events (e.g., snakes, spiders, loaded gun, and sudden bolt of lightning) perceived as dangerous.	More general expectation that something bad will happen, without specifying or identifying any particular threat or danger. Difficult to identify cause of tension or nature of disruptive event. Source of danger is elusive.
Borders of threat	Circumscribed area of threat.	Devoid of clear borders.
Appropriateness of affective reaction	Generally proportional to threat.	Exaggerated reaction to actual threat.
Imminence of threat	Threat imminent.	Threat normally not imminent.
Intensity	Intense, with quality of emergency, and arousal sharply elevated.	Heightened arousal and vigilance, but not emergency; often at lower level of arousal.
Onset	Triggered by specific objects or events.	Onset unclear and difficult to time.

(Continued)

TABLE 1.1 DISTINGUISHING FEAR FROM ANXIETY
(CONTINUED)

Criteria	Fear	Anxiety
Degree of certainty of danger	High.	Low.
Duration	Brief, transitory, episodic, receding when danger is removed; rise and decline limited in time.	Long, lingering, present in the background. Uncertain points of onset and offset.
Globality	Circumscribed tension.	More global tension.
Context	Proximal.	Distal.
Controllability	High—great deal of certainty of specific danger and when it has passed.	Low—uncertainty of the specific danger or if danger has passed.
Subjective feeling	Unpleasant and tense emotional reaction.	Unpleasant apprehension and more difficult to tolerate than fear, being more pervasive and draining.
Rationality	Has rational quality to it.	Often of irrational quality.
Response	Tendency to act (flee, fight, and freeze).	Person feels uncertain how to act.
Coping	Organisms try to cope with the source of fear and use of rapid early information processing mechanisms, when coping options are available.	The situation does not allow effective means of coping and individual mobilizes resources to face a poorly defined threat. When coping options are not available the emotion may be turned into anxiety.
Neuroanatomical substrate	Central nucleus of amygdala.	Bed nucleus of the stria-terminalis.

presents a number of suggested tentative criteria for differentiating these two overlapping concepts. The topic of this book is anxiety, not fear, but it is important to point out that in practice, the distinction may become fuzzy.

Trait Versus State Anxiety

Cicero was correct: temporary feelings of anxiety are not the same as the person's more general tendencies toward anxiety. This distinction is critical to the trait-state theory of anxiety advanced by Spielberger (1966). *Trait anxiety* refers to being anxiety-prone, that is, a stable personality characteristic. Some individuals are more easily made anxious than others and are said to be high in trait anxiety. Trait anxiety is distinguished from *state anxiety*, which refers to the immediate feelings of being anxious, such as nervousness and bodily tension. As shown in Figure 1.1, depicting the state-trait model of anxiety, the person's experience of state anxiety depends on both his or her underlying personality—his or her stable vulnerability to anxiety—and the presence of situational stressors or threats. An external threat, like being criticized in front of a group of people, will raise state anxiety in most people. However, the level of state anxiety will depend on personality—specifically, trait anxiety. The highly trait-anxious person will probably experience intense state anxiety, whereas the more resilient individual, who is low in state anxiety, may only experience a moderate amount of tension. Thus, state anxiety reflects an *interaction* between trait anxiety and situational threat.

Two more points about Spielberger's trait-state theory are worth noting. First, it follows that people high in trait anxiety do not always experience state anxiety. In a relaxing setting,

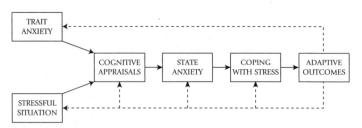

FIGURE 1.1 Transactional trait-state conceptions of anxiety.

even the trait anxious will often feel calm. Conversely, even low trait-anxious individuals may feel highly state anxious when confronted by a severe threat, like a man with a knife in a dark alley. Second, Spielberger claimed that state anxiety often has a more direct influence on thinking and behavior than does trait anxiety. As we shall discuss further in chapter 5, high state anxiety may interfere with concentration and performance of tasks. By contrast, trait anxiety has an indirect effect, which is dependent on state anxiety.

Facets of State Anxiety

Anxiety is currently viewed as a complex multidimensional construct embodying a series of interrelated cognitive, affective, somatic, and behavioral reactions. Let us unpack this perhaps rather jargon-ridden statement. What it means is that anxiety may be experienced in a variety of ways:

- *Disturbances of thinking (cognition):* When we are anxious, we often worry about our problems, focusing our attention inward. More subtle changes in cognitive processes include heightened awareness of the threat, and a focusing of attention on possible dangers.
- *Negative emotion (affect):* We feel anxiety as an emotion or mood—for example, feeling tense, nervous, and jittery.
- *Bodily (somatic) symptoms:* Anxiety is often accompanied by physical symptoms, such as racing heart and sweaty palms, as the body responds to a threat by preparing for a fight or flight.
- *Behavioral reactions:* Anxiety encourages us to respond in characteristic ways—for example, by seeking to escape the danger. In addition, anxious individuals may show characteristic nonverbal behaviors, such as fidgeting.

Our statement that anxiety is a multidimensional construct implies that we can measure these different facets of state anxiety separately, which has proved to be the case. The cognitive and emotional aspects of anxiety are often distinguished in questionnaire assessments. Somatic symptoms may be measured using the techniques of psychophysiology. For example, by placing electrodes on the chest (or other areas of the body) we can measure the small changes in electrical voltage that accompany the beating of the heart. Recording these voltages allows us to measure the increase in the rate with which the heart beats that may signal somatic anxiety.

When we take measures of these different facets of anxiety, we find that they are only loosely associated. There is a tendency for subjective tension to accompany somatic activation (e.g., racing heart), but the association between the two facets is only moderate in size. Some individuals appear to react more strongly through their emotions; others, via their bodily reactions. These *dissociations* between different anxiety responses are why we think of anxiety as being multidimensional, as further discussed in the following section.

Normal Versus Clinical Anxiety

Anxiety is a normal part of life, and it is an emotion that is familiar to all of us. However, much of the research on anxiety, especially in its early days, was driven by concerns about pathological anxiety, that is, anxiety which is so strong or disruptive that it interferes with normal living. Earlier in this chapter we described the case of Linda, who suffered from a socially debilitating anxiety disorder. Her problem was characterized by excessive anxiety, based on unrealistic perceptions of the self and others. Clinical psychologists recognize a number of different "anxiety disorders," each with a distinctive set of symptoms, as well as occurrences of strong state anxiety.

Generalized anxiety disorder (GAD) refers to intense "free-floating" anxiety, which is not tied to any specific threat or event. By contrast, phobias are defined by anxiety experienced in specific contexts such as open spaces (agoraphobia) or in response to specific stimuli such as spiders. Posttraumatic stress disorder (PTSD) describes long-lasting anxiety and other symptoms experienced by some individuals following a horrific event like being physically attacked or being trapped in rubble during an earthquake.

As further discussed in chapter 6 (Normative Versus Pathological Anxiety), clinicians work with a standard diagnostic manual for mental disorder, often the *Diagnostic and Statistical Manual of the American Psychiatric Association* (*DSM-IV*, 1994). The manual sets out specific diagnostic criteria, which must be present for each specific anxiety disorder. In effect, the clinician must be able to check off a sufficient number of distinct anxiety symptoms in order to make the diagnosis. Most simply, clinical anxiety is different from normal anxiety with respect to this diagnostic process. The feelings of anxiety we might experience in normal life simply would not match up to the clinical symptoms. For example, one common feature of GAD is significant difficulty in controlling anxiety and worry. The patients feel that their anxiety is out of control and they cannot cope with it. By contrast, in "normal anxiety" people typically feel that the anxiety is manageable. Another defining feature of GAD is that it causes significant problems for functioning in daily life. The patients may find that their anxiety prevents them from holding down a job or making friends with others. Again, nonclinical anxiety is not so disruptive. Clinical psychology gives us procedures for discriminating normal and abnormal levels of anxiety, which seem to work at least tolerably well in clinical practice. A number of these differentiating criteria are presented in chapter 6 (Normative Versus Pathological Anxiety).

General Versus Contextualized Anxiety

A final distinction is of particular relevance to understanding stable anxiety traits. The concept of trait anxiety might suggest a general proneness or vulnerability to anxiety, regardless of the nature of the threat. Perhaps, some people are just sensitive to threats in general. Indeed, current personality theory recognizes a major dimension contrasting emotional stability with negative emotionality (also known as "neuroticism"). Some people tend to show the full range of negative emotions, including anxiety, anger, and unhappiness, whatever situation they are in.

A contrasting view is that some people may be vulnerable to high anxiety only in specific contexts or settings. This view is included within the clinical perspective through the recognition of phobias associated with specific threatening objects (e.g., spiders), and through the existence of PTSD, relating to a specific traumatic event. For example, an army veteran might be especially sensitive to stimuli reminiscent of combat experiences, like reacting to a car backfiring as though it were a gunshot.

Theories of normal personality have also differentiated separate (though loosely interrelated) anxiety traits. Endler and Kocovski (2001) proposed that there are separate traits for social evaluation, physical danger, uncertainty, and daily routines. Other specific types of threat to which individuals may be vulnerable include health, work issues, and vehicle driving. For example, a person who is normally relaxed about life may tense up as soon as he or she has to drive, perhaps because of some bad experience in a vehicle. Research on "contextualized" traits has been most developed in relation to what are called "evaluative" anxieties, referring to concerns about being judged or assessed. These include the test anxiety experienced in academic tests and exams, sports anxiety, and the social anxiety that may be felt when the person feels "under the microscope" in a social setting.

ANXIETY: WHAT IS IT GOOD FOR?

Both fear and anxiety appear to have evolved as part of an organism's adaptive or defensive arsenal in times of threat or danger—a view that can be traced back to Aristotle and Darwin (1965/1872). Anxiety helps the person to adapt to environmental dangers and threats. It does so in several ways. First, it orients the individual toward anticipating dangers so that it acts like a kind of early-warning radar for threat. Beck and Emery (1985) described anxiety as an "attention getter," operating as a warning of an individual's vulnerability to social situations and physical dangers. Second, anxiety motivates the person to act in order to avoid events that might cause bodily harm or psychological distress. When anxious, we don't perceive threats as abstract problems to be pursued at our leisure; the emotion accompanies a sense of urgency to flee or otherwise preempt the perceived danger. Third, anxiety prepares the body and mind for such action. The physiological signs of anxiety such as a racing heart are elicited by increased arousal of the autonomic nervous system, in preparation for escape or confronting the danger. Changes in cognition serve to maintain the focus of attention on the threat.

As Darwin realized, our capacity for emotion, including anxiety, reflects natural selection, and we share much of our emotional apparatus with other mammals. The animal that fails to anticipate and act on threats is liable to end up as some other creature's dinner. More subtly, primates like us have evolved to live in social hierarchies, in which there is frequent social competition. Not to put too fine a point on it, the winners in these social contests improve their chances of finding a good mate (or mating at all), so that handling social competition becomes critical to the organism's chances of passing on its DNA to offspring. Social anxiety may help to attune the primate to threats to its place in the "pecking order." The low-life monkey that is sneaking around one's mate may be offering more than bananas, so that having some anxiety about the competition is essential.

Overall, anxiety evolved to promote evolutionary fitness— that is, survival and reproduction. Whereas a modicum of anxiety is functional and adaptive, a total lack of anxiety or fear might bring a person to walk straight into a dangerous or life-threatening situation, reducing one's chances for survival. From an evolutionary perspective, it is better to have a "wired-in" tendency to be somewhat oversensitive to threat. By "oversensitivity," we mean making a "false-positive" decision, by responding with anxiety when no danger is present. There may be minor costs to unnecessary alarm reactions and futile mobilization of somatic and cognitive resources. However, the cost of a "false negative," that is, failing to respond to a genuine threat, may be very high indeed. As noted by LeDoux (1996), it is better to have treated the stick as a snake than not to have responded to a possible snake. In fact, as succinctly phrased by Beck and Emery (1985), "One false negative and you are eliminated from the gene pool" (p. 4). Indeed, research shows that anxious individuals are inclined to overestimate the probability and seriousness of unfortunate events (Butler & Mathews, 1983).

The functional account of anxiety we have presented here contrasts with a view of fear and anxiety as dysfunctional emotions that compromise one's ability to respond and reason about events (e.g., Freud, 1959/1926). However, it is also the case that anxiety often seems to be detrimental to the person's best interests. As we shall see at various points in this book, anxiety tends to interfere with the person's capacity to plan and execute a rational strategy for dealing with threat.

Beck and Emery (1985) identified what they called the "anxiety paradox." On one hand, a central feature of anxiety is that a person is prewired or programmed to be vigilant to potential dangers in the environment and to quickly respond to these potential threats or dangers. On the other hand, the same cognitive-motivational systems that evolved to protect the individual from getting into harm's way may become twisted and misdirected so as to work against the person. In a nutshell, the anxiety paradox states that a person unwittingly brings upon himself or herself what he or she fears or detests the most (failure, inhibited behavior, etc.). For example, an anxious football quarterback during final playoffs may lose the ability to focus on the game plan; an apprehensive medical student partaking in his or her first invasive operational procedure faints on the spot; an accomplished pianist finds his or her fingers becoming stiff as he or she starts to play a sonata before an audience; a student who is taking his or her finals in physical chemistry finds his or her mind going blank.

There is at present no satisfactory explanation for why the universal emotion of anxiety, originally designed to assure survival of the organism, winds up producing inhibited behaviors and performance decrements—just those things we fear the most. A partial answer is that our cognitive processes may be especially sensitive to disruption of anxiety. As we discuss in the following, it seems to be especially the worrying aspect of anxiety that interferes with effective performance.

It is also important to stress that anxiety is not solely hardwired into us from birth. As the emotion theorist James Averill (1980, 1997) has argued, emotions are constructed by mental processes, reflecting our beliefs and motivations. We also have the capacity to regulate our emotions according to circumstances. Thus, anxiety reflects not just our evolutionary heritage but also our self-understanding, which, in turn, is shaped by the social-cultural influences that affect our development in childhood and into adulthood. When a novel threat like H1N1 influenza (swine flu) comes along, there is a sense in which we have a choice over how anxious we become (although not necessarily a conscious one). Depending on beliefs about personal vulnerability, we might variously write H1N1 off as a media-driven health scare, get vaccinated and forget about it, or become hypervigilant to threat and frantically disinfect possibly contaminated objects. One of these coping strategies is not intrinsically better than the other. How well they work will depend on the true, objective nature of the threat, which, as in the case of H1N1, is often hard to determine.

FACETS OF ANXIETY: UNPACKING THE ANXIETY RESPONSE

Thus far, we have made two separate cases. We said, first, that anxiety is multifaceted, and, second, that anxiety, taken as a whole, has adaptive functions. We can get a better sense of how anxiety influences behavior and adaptation (and sometimes maladaptation), by looking more closely at three of the key elements of anxiety: its cognitive, affective, and behavioral facets.

The Cognitive Facet

The cognitive components of anxiety relate to how information is processed in stressful situations. Anxiety is accompanied by changes in both the cognitive processes themselves (e.g., heightened attention to threat), and in the contents of cognition (i.e., the particular threats about which the person is thinking). Worry is currently viewed as the most powerful *cognitive* component of anxiety (Sarason, 1988). Worry refers to distressing concerns about impending or anticipated stressful events, when people feel "out of their depth." It is triggered by cues that indicate some undesirable event, such as failing at an important task that is imminent (cf. Deffenbacher, 1986; Eysenck, 1992a). Worry can interfere with cognition especially when it is prolonged, as the person mentally turns the problem over and over, without finding a satisfactory solution. Worried persons are often particularly preoccupied with *negative self-referential thoughts*, involving negative thoughts and doubts about oneself, one's competence, or one's ability to cope with challenging situations (Blankstein, Toner, & Flett, 1989). In particular, worry develops when a person perceives his or her ability

15

to cope with a task as unsatisfactory and is uncertain about the consequences of inadequate coping (Sarason & Sarason, 1990).

We can think of how a cost-benefit analysis might help us to understand the adaptive utility of worry (cf. Borkovec, Robinson, Pruzinsky, & DePree, 1983; Eysenck, 1992a, 1992b). Possible benefits are as follows:

● *Problem-solving function*: Worry may be a mental form of problem solving that helps to anticipate negative outcomes so that solutions might be found. The "work of worry" reduces anxiety by both identifying appropriate coping strategies and making them available, or by helping individuals learn to tolerate the situation.
● *Motivational function*: On the positive side, worry may activate effortful behavior, motivating task-oriented behavior. Worry may also serve a function in the regulation of unpleasant emotion by avoiding it. Focusing on the verbal act of worrying may reduce undesired physiological arousal and threatening imagery in the highly anxious (Borkovec et al., 1983).
● *Mastery (control) function*: Anxious persons may feel that as long as they worry about negative consequences, the less likely they are to happen. These individuals may worry excessively because they believe that it helps them achieve some degree of illusory control over the environment by preventing negative outcomes from happening (Freeston, Rheaume, Letarta, Dugas, & Ladouceur, 1994).

On the other hand, worry clearly has its costs. For one, worry tends to generate negative affect for an extended duration of time in anticipation of the stressful encounter (cf. Borkovec et al., 1983). Furthermore, worry may become reinforced because most of the threatening events that one is preoccupied with, say, totally bombing in a job interview or public presentation, seldom actually occur. This failure of negative events to materialize may be attributed falsely to the power of worry. Persistent worrying may serve to preserve deeply held beliefs about personal threats (sometimes called schemata; Meichenbaum & Butler, 1980), blocking the person from learning that he or she has overestimated the threat or underestimated his or her own abilities to cope effectively. In addition, the extra "cognitive load" of worry frequently serves to reduce task performance and efficiency (see chapter 5, Information Processing Models). Taken together, the afore-mentioned reasons reveal why frequent worry may be mal-adaptive in the long run.

The Affective/Somatic Facet

The affective or emotion facet of anxiety consists of both objec-tive symptoms of physiological arousal, as well as more sub-jective perceptions of bodily tension and emotions. Strong emotional arousal, such as that associated with anxiety, acti-vates the sympathetic nervous system, which readies the body for vigorous bursts of energy (e.g., fight/flight activity). This entails dilation of pupil of the eye, increased blinking of eyes, constriction of blood vessels and heightened contractibility of the heart, increased pulse and heart rate, heightened blood pressure, increase of blood flow to muscles, reduced blood flow to the skin (to reduce bleeding), increased rate of respiration and irregular breathing, inhibition of motility of the gastroint-ernal system and gastric sensations, scanty secretion of salivary glands, increased sweating, high conversion of stored energy to usable energy, secretion of epinephrine and norepinephrine, feelings of nausea, shaking, cold and clammy hands, and need to pass urine. It is currently held that physiological responses to anxiety are mainly sympathetic, with some *parasympathetic* manifestations (e.g., increase of gastrointernal track and bowel movement). This readying of the body, described by one of the pioneers of stress research, Walter Cannon, as the "fight-flight" response, is basic to stress (Gatchel, Baum, & Krantz, 1989). Although beyond the scope of this introductory text, consid-erable progress has been made in elucidating the various brain systems that control the physiological response. These include the limbic system in the medial temporal lobe (especially, the amygdala), as well as higher-level cortical brain activity (Caprara & Cervone, 2000).

The adaptive value of the "fight-flight" response is that it increases the vigor of the muscular responses required for escape from danger, while interrupting potentially distracting activities such as eating. One perspective, espoused by one of the authors of this book (see Zeidner, 1998), supposes that the response was undoubtedly adaptive to our hominid ancestors living in the savannas of Africa, but may be less so in modern times. It is not helpful in an exam or job interview to experience muscle tension, faintness, or sweating—somatic symptoms that may even distract the candidate from the task at hand. On the other hand, as previously indicated, even for early humans, threat may perhaps have been as likely to be social as derived from predators and other threats requiring immediate escape. The significance of the bodily signs of anxiety requires further investigation.

The Behavioral Facet

Defining anxiety in behavioral terms turns out to be more difficult than identifying emotional and cognitive expressions of anxiety. In animals, the most salient behaviors are defensive behaviors that typically involve avoiding or escaping threat. (Sometimes, the animal may freeze or fight back, if cornered.) However, people often have the capability to override such basic biological tendencies, through cognitive control of behavior. The test-anxious student might feel the urge to flee the examination hall, but, in practice, such behaviors are extremely unusual. Anxiety may not be rigidly related to any specific behavior.

Furthermore, recent work on the biological bases of emotion (Corr & Perkins, 2006) points to the need to distinguish fear and anxiety behaviors. These authors suggest that fear and anxiety are actually controlled by separate brain systems. Fear is generated by a fight-flight-freeze system that tends to produce classic defensive behaviors such as escape, depending on the organism's proximity to danger. Anxiety is a product of a separate system, the behavioral inhibition system (BIS), whose operations are more subtle. The BIS is activated by conflict, as when a mouse spots a crumb of cheese in the middle of the kitchen floor. The mouse brain must calculate whether the cheese is worth the risk of being exposed on an open surface. Anxiety, according to this model, encourages the evaluation of conflict situations (almost as though the mouse needs to worry about the cheese), and further exploration of the situation prior to action.

Research in humans has addressed the different ways that anxiety may be observed at a behavioral level. How can we tell, by observing a person, if he or she is anxious? Calvo and Miguel-Tobal (1998) performed one of the more thorough studies of this kind. They were able to measure the behavioral facet of anxiety through four types of indices:

- *Motor behaviors:* nonverbal indices of tension such as nail biting, touching hair, face, or clothes, and gratuitous head movements;
- *Facial behaviors,* including lip licking, swallowing, throat clearing, sighs, and grimaces;
- *Verbal* anxiety, including speech blocks, "ah…" sounds during speech, and avoidance comments;
- *Social anxiety,* measured by the single index of averting one's gaze while speaking.

Together, these measures seem to provide a good behavioral portrait of an anxious person. Interestingly, Calvo and Miguel-Tobal (1998) found that behavioral anxiety was unrelated to a standard measure of trait anxiety, which was more strongly associated with other components of anxiety. These findings fit with a more general view (Eysenck, 1997) that the different components of anxiety are often rather weakly related, especially when anxiety is relatively mild. The person's subjective sense of being anxious depends on a complex integration of the different components of anxiety, depending on the individual.

An interesting sideline to research on the multiple facets of anxiety is the so-called *repressor* personality, referring to individuals in whom the physiological and emotional facets diverge rather sharply. These persons show high levels of physiological responsivity (autonomic arousal) but do not seem to experience corresponding subjective anxiety. Derakshan, Eysenck, and Myers (2007) suggest that repressors have an unconscious vigilance toward threat, which triggers cognitive avoidance of anxiety, thereby suppressing conscious experience. The term "repressor" comes from Freud's idea of anxiety as neurotic repression of the urges of the libido. However, in this modern usage, repression is best seen as a style of coping, which can be effective in protecting the person from excessive anxiety.

MAJOR FORMS OF ANXIETY IN MODERN SOCIETY

In this section, we briefly survey a number of prevalent forms of anxiety in modern society. These ubiquitous forms of anxiety include test anxiety, math anxiety, computer anxiety, sports anxiety, social anxiety, and terror-related anxiety. Space does not permit us to cover other forms of anxiety, such as anxiety at work, health anxiety, and anxiety during vehicle driving. These different forms of anxiety typically resemble general anxiety in having multiple facets (i.e., emotional, cognitive, behavioral). At this point, our concern is simply to briefly introduce some of the main real-life contexts in which anxiety research is conducted. We will return to the important issue of how anxiety may disrupt performance—for example, in test situations (see chapter 5, Anxiety and Cognitive Performance).

Test Anxiety

Tests and evaluative situations have emerged as one potent class of anxiety-evoking stimuli in modern society, which bases many important decisions relating to an individual's status in school, military, college, and workplace on tests and other assessment devices (Puttwain, 2008). It is almost impossible to grow up in our modern test-consuming society without encountering some type of test, whether a classroom test in language or math or science, a standardized achievement test, a military placement or mechanical aptitude test, a scholastic aptitude test for college application, or an industrial occupational placement test. In fact, in most Western societies, there is an increasing emphasis on standardized testing in school, as mandated by the No Child Left Behind legislation in the United States. Students are taking more tests these days (i.e., classroom, district, international student assessment tests) than did students in the past (Wren & Benson, 2004). A negative outcome of this increased level of testing has been an increased level of test anxiety among students in the United States.

When one considers the many uses of tests in our culture, their high stakes, and the numerous ways in which they can determine the lives of people who take them, it comes as no great surprise that tests and testing situations often evoke anxiety reactions in many (Cassady, 2010). As noted by Powers (2001), test anxiety is one of the most oft-studied topics in all of educational and psychological assessment research, with anxiety running high for a nontrivial proportion of examinees who take so-called high-stake tests (college admissions, certification exams, etc.). Recent examinations of the prevalence for test anxiety suggest estimates close to 25–40% of the population. Higher prevalence rates have consistently been reported for females and ethnic minorities (Carter, Williams, & Silverman, 2008; Putwain, 2007). Early in life, many children in our culture become test-oriented and test anxious.

Test-anxious behavior is typically evoked when a person believes that his or her intellectual, motivational, and social capabilities are taxed or exceeded by demands stemming from the test or evaluative situation (Reeve, Bonaccio, & Charles, 2008). Test-anxious students interpret a wide range of situations as evaluative and react with cognitive concern and preoccupation with past failure and future negative consequences (Wine, 1980; Zeidner, 2010). These students have been reported to manifest a host of deficits in information processing during information encoding, processing, and retrieval (Cassady, 2004). During assessment sessions, test-anxious students are reported to suffer from heightened emotional arousal, worry excessively about exam failure, suffer from cognitive interference and task-irrelevant thoughts, and are highly susceptible to distraction (Zeidner, 2010). These self-related cognitions and interfering thoughts preempt the examinee's attentional resources, which could have been used for task-relevant mental activities. Also, due to their negative self-schemata, high test-anxious students constantly perceive a threat to their ego; they are said to be biased in processing more self-detrimental than self-enhancing information in test situations (Wong, 2008).

In addition, high test anxiety has been shown to accompany lower ability (Reeve et al., 2008). As the first author found, many test-anxious students are also reported to experience deficits in study skills and test taking, with poor preparation a major catalyst for anxiety in evaluative situations (Zeidner, 1998). Evaluative situations appear to be particularly detrimental to the performance of students low in perceived competence (Van Yperen, 2007).

Test anxiety is currently construed as a complex multi-dimensional construct embodying a series of interrelated cognitive, affective, and behavioral components and reactions (Zeidner, 2010). The fact that anxiety is such a complex construct, encompassing as it does both worry and self-preoccupation, physical upset, disruptive feelings, and maladaptive behaviors, makes it particularly difficult for researchers to sort out all these components. In our recent theorizing (Zeidner & Matthews, 2005), we emphasized the distinction between test anxiety as an attribute of the person and as a dynamic process. From the first perspective, dispositional test anxiety may be construed as a *contextualized personality trait*. Accordingly, test anxiety refers to the individual's disposition to react with extensive worry, intrusive thoughts, mental disorganization, tension, and physiological arousal when exposed to evaluative contexts or situations (Spielberger, Anton, & Bedell, 1976). The more transient state expressions of anxiety may be assessed separately from the more stable trait. From the second, process-oriented perspective, test anxiety depends on the reciprocal interaction of a number of distinct elements at play in the ongoing stressful encounter between a person and an evaluative situation (Zeidner, 1998). These elements include the evaluative context, individual differences in vulnerability (trait anxiety), threat perceptions, appraisals and reappraisals, state anxiety, coping patterns, and adaptive outcomes. Events that elicit test anxiety consist of a number of distinct temporal phases, including preparation, confrontation, anticipation, and resolution (Carver & Scheier, 1989; Zeidner, 1998). Accordingly, threat appraisals, state anxiety levels, and levels of task performance may change at different stages.

Test anxiety is frequently cited among the factors at play in determining a wide array of unfavorable outcomes and contingencies, including poor cognitive performance, scholastic underachievement, and psychological distress and ill health (Hembree, 1988). Indeed, many students have the ability to do well on exams, but perform poorly because of their debilitating levels of anxiety, particularly on difficult exams (Hong, 1999). Consequently, test anxiety may limit educational or vocational development, as test scores and grades influence entrance to many educational or vocational training programs in modern society. The loss to society of the full contribution of potentially capable students through anxiety-related underachievement and/or academic failure constitutes an important mental health problem in education. Indeed, it is difficult to communicate the pain, suffering, and misery suffered by high test-anxious subjects before, during, and after major evaluative experiences. Test-anxious college students, relative to their low-anxious counterparts, report suffering from poor mental health and psychosomatic symptoms (Depreeuw & De Neve, 1992).

Concomitant with the increased public concern with evaluative stress and test anxiety, test anxiety research has flourished over the years. The current widespread interest in helping student populations at all age levels achieve academic excellence, as assessed through high standards of academic and standardized test achievement, has further heightened public concern for reducing test anxiety, and its debilitating effects (Zeidner, 2008). Indeed, much of test anxiety research over the past half century has been conducted to help shed light on and ameliorate the aversive effects of test anxiety on examinee performance (Casbarro, 2005; Fletcher & Cassady, 2010). These concerns have stimulated the development of a variety of therapeutic techniques and intervention programs (see Zeidner [1998], and chapters in Spielberger & Vagg [1995a, 1995b]).

Math Anxiety

Math anxiety is a widespread phenomenon affecting student math performance across the globe (Jain & Dowson, 2009; Lee, 2009). The phenomenon appears to be prevalent across various groups—from elementary school children (e.g., Beasley, Long, & Natali, 2001) through high school (Lee, 2009) and college students (Davis, DiStefano, & Schutz, 2008). Burns (1998) estimates that about two out of every three adults in the United States "fear and loathe" math. Math anxiety is also quite pervasive among pre- and in-service teachers (Bursal & Paznokas, 2006).

Math anxiety refers to the aversive feelings of concern, tension, apprehension, mental disorganization, and associated bodily symptoms that are evoked in situations involving mathematical computations, problem-solving, and assessments (Ashcraft, Krause, & Hopko, 2007). Math's abstract nature, its exactness and hierarchical nature, and the high amount of mental energy often required to solve complex math problems become a challenging and often stressful experience for many math-anxious individuals (Richardson, & Woolfolk, 1980). As will be discussed in chapter 5 (see Anxiety and Cognitive Performance), math anxiety disrupts cognitive processing by compromising ongoing activity in working memory (Ashcraft & Krause, 2007).

Math anxiety is conceptually related to other forms of evaluative anxiety, for example, test anxiety, through a common theme of concerns about evaluation (e.g., Rosen & Maguire, 1990). However, math anxiety not only focuses on the evaluative nature of math tests but also concerns mathematical content, its distinctive features as an intellectual activity, and its meanings for many persons in our society (Richardson & Woolfolk, 1980). Thus, test-anxious persons are more likely to appraise exam situations as personally threatening, and math-anxious persons are likely to interpret situations involving manipulation of numbers and problems as threatening.

It is commonly recognized that in an increasingly technological and information-based society, mathematical literacy is crucial not only for the pursuit of many scientific and technical fields (e.g., engineering, computer sciences, and medicine) but is also increasingly important in business, the social sciences, and even the humanities. In fact, many intellectually capable individuals avoid taking math courses in high school and in college on account of high math anxiety, thus prematurely narrowing their career options and vocational choices. Thus, a review by Ashcraft and Krause (2007) indicates that high math-anxious individuals avoid elective coursework in math, both in high school and college, avoid college majors that emphasize math, and they avoid career paths that involve math. Because math success is a "major screening method and gate keeper" for many professions, math anxiety may have serious negative implications for a person's future career. An unfortunate consequence of the avoidance tendency is that, compared with people who do not have math anxiety, highly math-anxious individuals end up with lower math competence and achievement (Ashcraft, 2002). A deficit in mathematical competencies has been found to have a greater negative effect on employment opportunities than reading difficulties (Bynner & Parsons, 1997).

Math anxiety is more likely to occur among students with inadequate preparation and poor math training and background in high school (Betz, 1978), poorer academic orientation and interest in math (Resnick, Viehe, & Segal, 1982), and poorer math sophistication (Levitt & Hutton, 1983). One consistent and relatively powerful antecedent correlate of math anxiety is the degree of preparation and prior experience with mathematics. Overall, research supports the notion that a lack of foundation in math reinforces math anxiety (Benson & Bandalos, 1989; Ramirez & Dockweiler, 1987). A review by Ashcraft, Krause, and Hopko (2007) suggests that lower-than-average math abilities, susceptibility to public embarrassment (e.g., being called to the board to solve a difficult math problem, performing poorly, and being embarrassed by the teacher), and a nonsupportive or cold, emasculating teacher, may all be risk factors in developing anxiety (Ashcraft et al., 2007).

Math self-efficacy and self-concept are among the most powerful personal predictors of math anxiety in student groups (cf. Jain & Dowson, 2009; Lee, 2009). Specifically, students with higher math self-efficacy and confidence consistently report lower levels of math anxiety. Self-efficacy also mediates the effects of self-regulated learning on math anxiety (Jain & Dowson, 2009). A recent study (Hoffman, 2010) provides evidence that math self-efficacy mediates the relationship between math anxiety and cognitive efficiency in math performance. Furthermore, perceived math-related efficacy was shown to be a stronger predictor of college students' math anxiety relative to even prior achievement test scores in math (Betz & Hackett, 1983).

Furthermore, the level of math anxiety is shown to vary in intensity depending on the person's math ability. Thus, math anxiety is found to be inversely related to math ability or ability perceptions (Wigfield & Meece, 1988). Cooper and Robinson (1989) report that math ability and experience are even more predictive than is math anxiety on the selection of a mathematics-oriented major, such as economics or business administration (Betz & Hackett, 1983).

Math-related perceptions, appraisals, and expectancies are also powerful correlates of math anxiety. A 2-year follow-up study by Wigfield and Eccles (1990) in a sample of college

students suggests that positive expectancies of math performance have a strong, negative, direct effect on students' anxiety about math. Furthermore, the effects of math anxiety
were shown to be indirect, working through expectancies and
importance ratings (Meece, Wigfield, & Eccles, 1990). Perceived
importance of math may also interact with math ability in predicting math anxiety. Accordingly, data presented by Wigfield
and Meece (1988) show that students who have low perceptions
of their math abilities and do not value math may not report
as much math anxiety as students who have low perceptions
of their math abilities but think it is important to do well in
math.

Computer Anxiety

Computer-based technologies have expanded exponentially
over the past few decades, penetrating Western society on a massive scale. Because people are often required to use computers at
home, school, or work, computer literacy and computing skills
have become basic prerequisites for performing effectively in
various spheres of life, particularly in education and in the job
market. Whereas some people are fairly comfortable in using
computers, for others, the encounter with computers is viewed
as threatening and emotionally unsettling. In fact, a substantial
number of people express serious concerns and fears about living in a computerized society.

Computer anxiety (also termed "computerphobia," "technophobia," or "cyberphobia"; Choi, Ligon, & Ward, 2002) is a
relatively new form of anxiety, evolving rapidly after computer
usage became part of routine life in modern society. The construct of computer anxiety refers to apprehension, worry, fear,
and somatic arousal evoked in actual or imaginary interactions
with computers or computer-based technologies (Bozionelos,
2001). Computer anxiety may variously relate to (a) anxiety
about present or future interactions with computers or computer-related technologies, (b) worries and negative thinking
when interacting with the computer or when contemplating
future computer interaction, (c) difficulties in handling computer equipment, (d) negative global attitudes about computers, their operation, or their dehumanizing societal impact,
(e) lack of confidence in learning to use computers, (f) low

perceived control, competence, and efficacy in using comput-ers, (g) low expectancy of task success, and (h) low intrinsic goal motivation (Beckers, Wicherts, & Schmidt, 2007; Coffin & MacIntyre, 1999; Marsh & McInerney, 1999; Weil, Rosen, & Wugalter, 1990).

According to Thorpe and Brosnan (2007), the fear of tech-nology, in general, and of computers, in particular, constitutes a "real phenomenon." As reported by one fairly computer-anxious individual: "I believe I am absolutely, wildly, techno-phobic.... I do not know how to use a computer, I am absolutely terrified—don't even know what the mouse is" (cited in Thorpe & Brosnan, 2007, pp. 1261–1262). Prevalence rates for groups of employed individuals in Western society are estimated to range anywhere from about 14% to about 50%, varying as a function of context, age group, demographics, and method of assess-ment (Bozionelos, 2001; Thorpe & Brosnan, 2007). University students do not fare much better than the general population, with about 25% of students showing moderate to high techno-phobia (Weil & Rosen, 1995). In some cases, computer anxiety may reach clinical levels, which conform to *DSM-IV* criteria for specific phobias (Thorpe & Brosnan, 2007). The data currently available suggest that computer anxiety bears a negative impact on competence in using computers (Brosnan & Goodison, 2010), frequently resulting in the avoidance or minimizing of computer usage at home, the office, and in educational settings (Brosnan & Goodison, 2010). Because information technology is projected to be inextricably linked to economic survival in the years to come, computer anxiety may be an ever-increasing handicap in this technological age.

A meta-analysis of the computer anxiety literature synthe-sized results from 79 empirical studies in an effort to deter-mine the key correlates of this salient phenomenon (Rosen & Maguire, 1990). Computer anxiety was found to be positively related to math anxiety (and other anxieties, such as state, trait, and test), but these relationships rarely account for more than 10% of the variance in predicting computer anxiety. Although women were evidenced to be slightly more computer anxious than men, gender differences were minimal and not statisti-cally reliable (see also, meta-analytic conclusions by Chua, Chen, & Wong [1999]). These differences were attributed by the authors to differences in early computer experience or other experiential factors, rather than gender, per se. However, computer anxiety was correlated with sex-role identity, with "feminine" students being more computer-anxious and "masculine" students possessing a more positive attitude toward computers. Furthermore, age does not appear to be a reliable predictor of computer anxiety, with no consistent relationships found between age and any measures of computer anxiety in various populations.

The data currently available suggest that computer anxiety bears a negative impact on competence in using computers. Weil, Rosen, and Wugalter (1990) demonstrated that subjects high on computer anxiety felt more negative about their experience with computers, about themselves, about technology in general, and about their personal abilities than those low on computer anxiety. During an actual computer interaction, computer anxiety was reported to be related to lower expectations, poorer performance, more subjective anxiety and attention to bodily sensations, and a higher frequency of debilitating thoughts (Heinssen, Glass, & Knight, 1987). Accordingly, a study by Heinssen, Glass, and Knight (1987) showed that computer anxiety was related to poorer performance during computer interaction, possibly mediated by attention to bodily sensations and debilitating thoughts. Furthermore, computer-anxious students are reported to engage in more worry and off-task thoughts when using or when thinking about using computer than low-anxious computer users (Smith & Caputi, 2001). Similar to what has been found for test anxiety, the detrimental effects of computer anxiety is typically attributed to cognitive interference and self-preoccupation associated with loss of working memory capacity (Ashcraft & Kirk, 2001; Smith & Caputi, 2001).

Some data point to the importance of early negative experiences with computers or computer technology, particularly first experiences in computing, in the development of computer anxiety (McIlroy, Bunting, Tierney, & Gordon, 2001). Thus, early role modeling of technology by people who are not themselves comfortable with technology can be predictive of later technological discomfort exposed to these negative models. Furthermore, although prior computer experience, ranging from "touching a computer" to formal coursework, is inversely related to computer anxiety (Jay, 1981), the relationship between experience and lower anxiety is fairly weak. Indeed, it is untrue that experience alone will reduce or eliminate computer anxiety. Curiously, additional computer experience may actually exacerbate the problem and lead to further computer avoidance in high computer-anxious subjects (Weil et al., 1990). Thus, rather than alleviating their computer anxiety, additional computer experience strengthens their negative affective reactions and promotes further computer avoidance.

Computer anxiety overlaps with evaluative anxiety (Rosen & Maguire, 1990), but perhaps the predominant fear relates to the technological facet involved in interactions with computers. Computer-anxious persons may actually suffer from a more generalized technophobia, which itself is evident before adulthood (Weil & Rosen, 1995). For these individuals, each experience with computers is a sorrowful reminder that computers are intimidating, frustrating, and lead to acute discomfort and failure. As with evaluative anxiety, it is important in treating computer anxiety to understand the false beliefs about technology that may feed the condition—for example, that computer use is simply too difficult to accomplish. Working with a person who holds a positive attitude about technology and feels skilled and comfortable with computers may help build confidence in the computer-anxious individual (Weil et al., 1990).

Sports Anxiety

Athletes in modern society are regularly subjected to the stressful demands and pressures of competitive sports, where the adequacy of their athletic performance is evaluated against some external criterion of excellence. The setting of high standards in competitive sports appears to be an integral part of elite sports and believed to be beneficial for the athlete's performance (Koivula, Hassmén, & Fallby, 2002). Professional athletes have the capacity to earn millions of dollars for themselves, their team, management, and sponsors. From the late 20th century vast amounts of money have been invested in efforts to bring athletes to peak performance in order to maximize earnings of stakeholders. This investment in sports includes research in optimizing performance by management of sports performance anxiety. Indeed, various sources of threat and personal danger reside in the competitive sport situation, including the possibility of both short-term and permanent physical injury, but psychological threats may be especially acutely felt (see Woodman & Hardy, 2001, for a review). These include the possibility of failure and of disapproval by significant others who are evaluating the athlete's performance in relation to some standard of excellence, including coaches, teammates, other competitors, and spectators.

The effects of sports anxiety are readily observed in some international elite athletes, whose performances can seriously break down at crucial points in competition. In the 2009 Australian Open Tennis Championship, the Russian-born tennis champion, Dinara Safina, lost to U.S. champion Serena Williams, 6–0, 6–3. It is indeed surprising that Safina, with a world ranking of third before the tournament, could lose so decisively to Williams, who was ranked as second. In an interview following her loss, Safina told reporters that the critical importance of the match had simply overwhelmed her. As she lamented: "It was the first time for me to play not only for a grand slam, but also for Number One spot" ("Safina Sorry for Final Flop," 2009). In addition, Safina was also attempting to win the same title her brother Marat had earned in 2005—yet another potential source of stress and anxiety. Safina's breaking down at such a critical time is an outcome frequently observed in elite athletes, such as professional golfers, who may lead a tournament into the last few holes and then play poorly to lose a prospective major title.

Because of the potentially stressful nature of sports and the competitive surroundings, a good deal of research has been devoted to understanding the various antecedents, dimensions, and consequences of competitive sports anxiety (Martinent & Ferrand, 2007). Recent work (e.g., Dunn, Dunn, Wilson, & Syrotuik, 2000) has identified a number of key components of sports anxiety, including somatic symptoms ("My body feels tense," "My heart pounds before competition"), worry ("I have self-doubts," "I am concerned about doing well"), and cognitive interference ("I have lapses in concentration," "My mind wanders during competition"), as key aspects of state anxiety. The anxiety-performance association (i.e., linear and curvilinear) has been shown to vary as a function of the specific component under consideration (Chamberlain & Hale, 2007).

A review of the literature points to a number of situational and personal factors that are reliably associated with the level of athletes' state anxiety prior to competition (Smith & Smoll, 1990). Situational factors include the importance of the athletic contest, strength of opponent, presence of significant others, and degree of social support received from coaches, teammates, family, and the fans. Anxiety also rises sharply as the match approaches. Furthermore, a number of studies (Simon & Martens, 1979; Smith & Smoll, 1990) suggest that individual sports (e.g., gymnastics, track and field, and swimming) elicit higher precompetition state anxiety than do team sports (tennis-playing doubles, football, basketball, etc.).

As for personal factors, the cognitive appraisals of the degree of threat or challenge in the competitive situation, as well as the interpretation of one's cognitions and somatic arousal as "facilitative" versus "debilitative" have been shown to affect sports performance (Chamberlain & Hale, 2007). Also, anxiety symptoms in athletes are reliably predicted by ego-focused goal orientation (i.e., orientation toward outperforming others), coupled with low sport self-confidence (Voight, Callaghan, & Ryska, 2000). Overall, high-anxious athletes tend to focus more on the *outcome* rather than the *process* of performance and are more frequently and intensely distracted by task-irrelevant thoughts from their goals (Hodge, 2004). Performance success is also predictive of anxiety in sports situations, with the poorer performers having higher anxiety scores than the better performers (Smith, Smoll, & Schutz, 1990). Following competition, unsurprisingly, anxiety relates to the outcome of the match (Smith & Smoll, 1990). In addition, regardless of the outcome, postgame anxiety is inversely related to athletes' perceptions of how much fun they had. There is perhaps a lesson here for overcompetitive parents of young athletes.

Broadly, high levels of anxiety are detrimental to peak performance in competition, and sports psychologists typically work to build confidence in the athlete, but there are some subtleties also. Some psychologists believe that a moderate level of anxiety is best (Tenenbaum & Bar-Eli, 1995). If an athlete is either underaroused (sleepy, lethargic, and unmotivated) or overaroused (hyped-up, nervous, and distractible), performance will suffer in comparison to when the athlete functions within his or her optimal range of arousal. In addition, there is considerable individual variation; it appears that some athletes need to feel anxious to be adequately motivated, whereas others need to be relaxed to perform at their best (Raglin & Hanin, 2000). Thus, anxiety is not always debilitating; it appears that much depends on how the individual perceives his or her own mental state.

Social Anxiety

"Social anxiety" refers to feelings of tension, apprehension, self-consciousness, emotional distress, and increased autonomic arousal triggered in anticipated or actual social situations, particularly when a person perceives being exposed to negative evaluation by others (Crozier & Alden, 2001; Egloff, Wilhelm, Neubauer, Mauss, & Gross, 2002; Kashdan, 2007). Social anxiety may occur in response to immediate, "real" social encounters in which the individual is presently engaged (e.g., meeting new people, asking someone for a date, and speaking or performing before an audience) or in response to "imagined" encounters in which the individual contemplates an upcoming social interaction (Feldman, Cohen, Hamrick, & Lepore, 2004). The literature differentiates various affective constructs quite salient in modern society that are closely related to social anxiety, including speech anxiety, audience anxiety, stage fright, dating anxiety, shyness, shame, communication apprehension, social embarrassment, and so on (e.g., Bippus & Daly, 1999). Although these constructs are conceptually distinct from one another, social anxiety is seen as a central element of each one.

Two different classes of social anxiety have been differentiated in the literature, that is, "interaction anxiety" and "audience anxiety" (Schlenker & Leary, 1982). On one hand, shyness and dating anxiety are specific forms of interaction anxiety; these anxieties occur in *contingent interactions*, in which people must be continually responsive to the actions of others. On the other hand, stage fright and speech anxiety are specific forms of audience anxiety; these anxieties occur in *noncontingent interactions*, in which people are performing some preplanned material before others.

Social anxiety is currently viewed as existing on a continuum, or "social anxiety spectrum." Accordingly, social anxiety may range from absence of anxiety in social interactions, through ordinary shyness or awkwardness in social interactions and mild social anxiety, to more intense and functionally impairing social fears—including generalized social anxiety disorder. Moderate social anxiety may have an adaptive function, in that a realistic and proportionate concern about others' opinions and evaluations can inhibit behavior that is socially unacceptable. However, excessively high and inappropriate levels of anxiety are liable to interfere with social performance, and may be a concomitant of clinical conditions such as social phobia. According to Kashdan (2007), costs of excessive social anxiety are considerable. These include higher chances of being single or divorced, a wide range of sexual dysfunctions, smaller social networks and less social support, low self-reported quality of life and lower positive affect, and greater risk for suicide and comorbid psychiatric diagnosis. Also, high social anxiety relates to various difficulties in occupational adjustment (Bruch, Fallon, & Heimberg, 2003). In addition, scores on social anxiety measures tend to correlate with peer rating of social skills and with observational behavioral measures (Arkowitz, Lichtenstein, McGovern, & Hines, 1975). Specific deficits include inaccurate decoding of nonverbal cues; difficulties in communication (e.g., lack of fluency and expressiveness in conversational speech; Bruch, 2001); self-reported skill deficits relating to effective verbal discourse, and poor self-presentation and decoding of nonverbal information (Strahan, 2003).

Social anxiety is related to marked alterations in behavior during social interactions, with non-anxious people often observed to experience interactions with socially anxious people as "odd" or "off" (Heerey & Kring, 2007; Wenzel & Finstrom, 2005). Individuals high on social anxiety tend to be very concerned about the impression they make on others, and in particular, how anxious they might appear to others. They focus on their anxious feelings and experience self-related negative cognitions and appraisals of performance during anticipated or real social encounters (Abbott & Rapee, 2004). Their self-evaluation tends to be negative, and probably with good reason, as their social performance is rated negatively by other people as well (Cartwright-Hatton, Tschernitz, & Gomersall, 2005).

Socially anxious persons worry about social outcomes and attach fundamental importance to being positively appraised by others, yet experience marked insecurity regarding their ability to convey a favorable impression of themselves to others. As a consequence, they believe their social behavior will have disastrous consequences, such as public humiliation or rejection (Clark & Wells, 1995). Furthermore, when compared to their counterparts, who are less socially anxious, more socially anxious persons predict worse social performance for themselves, underestimate actual social performance in social situations, and engage in more negative postevent processing than persons who are less socially anxious (Dannahy & Stopa, 2007).

Socially anxious individuals tend to have a negative self-representational view of themselves (Vassilopoulos, 2008), and anxious arousal during social interaction stems largely from self-presentational concerns (e.g., negative evaluation of one-self is forthcoming, and signs of anxiety, such as shaking, fidgeting, or sweating, are noticeable). These concerns lead to increases in self-focused attention that may serve to increase social anxiety across interactions. As self-focused attention rises, the ability to concentrate on social interaction may further decline, leading to disjointed social performances (Heerey & Kring, 2007). During social interaction, the socially anxious person is likely to be in a self-focused mode, to expect failure, and to be less likely to notice any signs of being accepted or positively evaluated by others. Because the presence of social anxiety disrupts a number of important aspects of social behavior (e.g., communication of positive emotions, smooth and coordinated social interaction, and smiling), individuals with social anxiety may inadvertently provoke the negative perceptions they seek to avoid. Moreover, despite their desire to execute smooth social performances, socially anxious persons tend to engage in more self-focused attention and talk, seek more reassurance from others they interact with, and ask fewer questions (Heerey & Kring, 2007). These signals of anxiety seem out of place and uncomfortable, thereby serving to decrease the likelihood of future social interactions. By contrast, Bruch (2001) claims that at least some social skills deficits may reflect inadequate skill learning rather than disruption of performance by states of cognitive interference.

Some authors (e.g., Leitenberg, 1990) explicitly define social anxiety in social-evaluative terms. Socially anxious persons are typically self-devaluing of themselves, and worry often quite unrealistically about appearing physically unattractive, foolish, or boring. From this perspective, the essence of social anxiety is that the person is motivated to make a favorable impression on others, but fears that he or she will be found to be deficient or inadequate by others and therefore will be rejected (Leary, 2001). By contrast, Crozier and Alden (2001) indicate that some forms of social anxiety, such as fear of strangers or of exchanging pleasantries with the salesperson or bus driver, are not evaluative in nature. Psychometric studies have found distinct traits related to anxieties concerning evaluation, separation from significant others and self-disclosure (Endler, 2002). Also, akin to other social-evaluative forms of anxiety, social anxiety may be characterized by both trait and state facets. For instance, Crozier and Alden (2001) identify unfamiliar social situations, power and status differences, and large numbers of people as situational factors that elicit state anxiety in those individuals high in trait social anxiety. Furthermore, as was found for test anxiety, the distinction between affective and cognitive components of the anxiety state has also been identified for social anxiety (Sarason, Sarason, & Pierce, 1990).

As with other forms of evaluative anxiety, social anxiety may impair social performance via diversion of limited attentional resources to self-related processing (Sarason et al., 1990). In addition, cognitive models of anxiety highlight the importance of dysfunctional schema-driven information processing in the development and maintenance of severe forms of social anxiety. Indeed, several cognitive biases have been identified in social anxiety that contribute to negative self-statements and beliefs regarding dysfunctional behavior in social settings (Clark & McManus, 2002). Excessive self-focusing may be especially problematic since competence in social settings is linked to attending to other people in the environment.

Table 1.2 summarizes some common features of evaluative anxieties as discussed in the past sections.

TABLE 1.2 EVALUATIVE ANXIETIES:
SOME COMMON FEATURES

Dimensions	Description
Conceptualizations	State versus trait distinctions are cited.
Prevalent frameworks	Transactional or interactional models that link processing of situational demands to both stable personal dispositions and situational cues.
Facets	Three key facets: *cognitive* facet (worry, irrelevant thinking, negative self-referential thoughts, etc.), *affective* facet (tension, bodily reaction, perceived arousal), and a *behavioral* facet (deficient skills, procrastination, avoidance behaviors, etc.).
Temporal stages	Anxiety is viewed as process unfolding over time, with distinct stages (e.g., anticipation, confrontation, and resolution).
Subjective/personal antecedents	Appraisal of task difficulty, personal competence and future outcomes, subjective importance of situation, aptitudes and skills, self-concept, self-efficacy, metacognition, trait anxiety, personal-domain-relevant experience and skills.
Anxiety and performance	Meta-analytic studies show correlations of about $-.20$ between anxiety and performance, typically higher for worry than for emotionality.
Causal models and mechanisms underlying anxiety-related performance deficits	Cognitive-attentional deficit, limited working memory capacity, attentional bias, self-handicapping, avoidance coping lead to skill deficits, dysfunctional self-regulation.
Group differences	Females evidence higher levels of anxiety. Some cross-cultural and age differences are also reported.

Source: Based on Zeidner and Matthews (2005).

Terror-Related Anxiety and Trauma

A major arena for the study of severe anxiety is research on anxiety and stress responses to traumatic events such as physical attack (e.g., rape), natural disasters (e.g., earthquakes), and soldiers' combat experiences. High levels of acute stress typically follow these events, but subside in the absence of further trauma. However, a minority of individuals may continue to experience posttraumatic anxiety for years after the event. Psychiatrists recognize PTSD as a distinct anxiety disorder. Common symptoms include high anxiety and insomnia, "flashbacks" to the traumatic events, and disruption of normal relationships. We will illustrate the anxiety elicited by trauma, by focusing on a single research area that, sadly, has become increasingly prominent in recent years: anxiety provoked by terrorist attacks.

Terrorism is currently viewed as a ubiquitous and full-blown security problem and a grave global danger faced by mankind (Laqueur, 1999). Terrorism is defined as a politically, ideologically, religiously, and socially motivated form of violence, directed mainly against civilians (Higson-Smith, 2002; Hamden, 2002). To achieve strategic outcomes, acts of terror are designed to intimidate and create a paralyzing sensation of fear, anxiety, panic, unrest, uncertainty, and other paralyzing psychological emotions in the targeted population. Terror aims at demonstrating the ability of political or ideological factions to strike and create havoc and confusion in a society at any place and time.

The horrific nature of terrorism transcends our personal daily experiences and is therefore uniformly appraised as anxiety evoking in terms of threat to life, loss, and physical and psychological consequences (Zeidner & Ben-Zur, 1994). Through the use of psychological manipulation and intimidation, terrorists aim to create disproportionate anxiety in relation to the actual threat of injury and helplessness (Friedland & Merari, 1986). By creating an epidemic of fear and helplessness, terrorism often strips one's sense of personal safety and security of a familiar world. If one is apart from loved ones this can evoke intense separation anxiety (Raphael, 2007). The extreme portrayals of terror attacks in the media can aggravate anxiety and may intensify and prolong the stressfulness of mass trauma. Progress in media technology has created a channel for rapid dissemination of scenes of terror and violence as they occur in real time and in gory detail. Although the media do not deliberately set out to aggravate the fear, terror, and rage experienced by members of the community, neither does the media really see its major role as a calming agent in times of national trauma (Jone, Greenberg, & Wesseley, 2007).

Terror attacks are particularly stressful and anxiety evoking for a number of reasons (see Zeidner, 2006). To begin with, terrorism poses serious threats to one's life and personal security, confronting one with destruction, mutilation, and death. Research has been done in various specific contexts, such as the aftermath of the attacks on the Twin Towers on September 11, and attacks on the Israeli population during the Al-Aqsa intifada. Terrorism leads to a reduced sense of security in the population, intensifying psychological stress, anxiety, and demoralization. Concerns about terror attacks may come to dominate our social perceptions in everyday life. Terror attacks undermine the person's sense of resourcefulness, and frequently result in the loss of a sense of personal and community security and invulnerability. A sense of attacks as unpredictable, ongoing, and beyond personal control is especially anxiety-evoking (Baum, Singer, & Baum, 1981). Terrorism is also an existential threat, in that it challenges one's very worldview about the nature of man (Dunkel, 2002). Terror taxes our need to think the word is predictable and basically coherent. (cf. Van der Kolk & McFarlane, 1996). Thus, terror profoundly disrupts the sense of vital and cohesive selfhood that emerges in the context of normal relational experiences and betrays the experience of one's trust in one and in others (Brothers, 2003). Furthermore, the repugnant and malevolent intent of those who perpetrate terrorism can lock us into a perpetual cycle of fear and rage.

A study of the Israeli experience of the Palestinian intifada ("uprising") showed that close to 45% of the sample had been either directly exposed to terror or had friends and relatives exposed to terror attacks (Bleich, Gelkopf, & Solomon, 2003). This study showed more than 60% of the participants sensed that their lives were in danger and 70% of the sample reported at least one traumatic stress symptom. Interestingly, the prevalence of those with symptom criteria for PTSD was similar to that found after September 11 among residents in New York (Galea et al., 2002). Another Israeli study (Hobfoll et al., 2009) suggested that, although the majority of respondents lacked direct experience of a terror attack, the indirect exposure to stress and indirect trauma, including fear of being blown up on a bus or in a pizza parlor, might actually be as severe as direct exposure. It is also difficult to find effective ways of coping, given lack of personal control. Coping measures such as staying away from crowded shopping malls or restaurants tend to interfere with the pursuit of normal life goals and cause disruption of daily routines.

One major question of concern is: What are the cumulative effects of long-term exposure to terror? There are two dramatically opposed answers. One is inoculation—that is, persons are toughened by the traumatic experience and should be better off subsequently. Another possibility, based on Selye's (1956) notion of finite adaptive energy, is the depletion of resources in the long term. Accordingly, every person is expected to have a finite quantity of adaptive resources that are spent and are irreplaceable. Each exposure taxes these resources and by adding more and more stress, the individual eventually breaks down and exhaustion is expected. Because the pace at which the adaptive energy is used up is a function of the frequency and intensity and duration of stress, this does not bode well for the coping capabilities and resources for members of societies under chronic stress from political violence.

SUMMARY: KEY ISSUES IN ANXIETY RESEARCH

We suspect a 21st-century readership will not need much convincing that anxiety is a pervasive emotion that influences our ability to function effectively in a variety of settings. We hope this introductory chapter has provided a sense of the challenges facing the researcher who wants to dig deeper into the psychology of anxiety. Three challenges stand out:

- *Anxiety is multifaceted.* It may be experienced as a subjective emotion (a feeling state), as a bodily state of autonomic arousal, as disturbances in thinking, and in changes in expressive social behaviors. Researchers must tread a fine line in differentiating different facets of anxiety while also maintaining a grasp on the unity of the emotion.

● *Anxiety has multiple functions.* Evolutionary psychology tells us that anxiety is adaptive; we would not be here without its survival benefits derived from our human and prehuman ancestors. There is also a wealth of evidence to show that it may interfere with effective action, for example, during tests and evaluations. Excessive anxiety may be seriously maladaptive when it features in clinical disorders such as generalized anxiety, panic, phobias, and PTSD. It seems we should look further at the functional purposes of anxiety, and how they may be misapplied to our detriment.

● *Anxiety is experienced in different contexts.* We briefly surveyed some of the main arenas in which the anxiety process plays out in real life. Anxiety often arises in evaluative settings, where the person is formally tested or judged, including test anxiety itself, and math, computer, and sports anxiety. Normal social interactions may be perceived as a source of criticism and failure, giving rise to social anxiety. Physical danger initially elicits fear more than anxiety, but societies plagued by war or terrorism will also know anxiety over future attacks. General conceptualizations of anxiety can help us understand these different contexts. But each also has its own particular features. For example, it is easier for a student to take control of her own academic destiny than it is for a person to avoid society-wide threats such as terrorism. We need a general theory of anxiety alongside more context-focused accounts of the different forms of anxiety in real life.

A fairly brief, introductory volume such as this cannot hope to do justice to the ornate tapestry of anxiety research that has developed over the last century or so. We will try to set out some of the major themes and controversies of the field, as well as pivotal theories and research findings. Although there is a long tradition of using clinical judgment to understand anxiety, we will emphasize the importance of quantitative measurement of anxiety as the foundation for scientific research. Chapter 2 explores measurement strategies, introduces the questionnaire assessments that provide the most common measurement tools, and describes their strengths and weaknesses relative to other methods. Measurement allows for rigorous testing of theories, and the multifaceted nature of anxiety is reflected in a variety of theoretical perspectives.

In chapter 3, we will follow an historical overview of early theories with more detailed accounts of the biological and cognitive perspectives that predominate today. A good theory should help us understand both the causes and consequences of anxiety, and we will tackle these issues in chapters 4 and 5, respectively. Both psychobiologists and cognitive psychologists have compelling stories to tell about the origins of anxiety. The first narrative is one of genetic influences on the neural circuits controlling emotion within the child's development. The counternarrative is one of social learning processes that build internal cognitive structures and processes that provide the lens through which potential threats and dangers are understood and defended against. By contrast, we see cognitive psychological accounts as having accomplished more successful accounts of how anxiety influences behavior. (Full disclosure: both of us are cognitive psychologists.) Chapter 5 reviews the effects of anxiety and performance and looks at the cognitive models of information processing, executive control, and self-regulation that may explain these objective consequences of high anxiety and worry. In chapter 6, we turn to anxiety as a problem in living, causing distress to the normal individual, and clinical illness to those with anxiety disorders. Again cognitive psychological accounts have much to offer, in illuminating the coping strategies people habitually use to mitigate anxiety and its effects, and cognitive-behavior therapies for the clinically anxious. Nevertheless, the effectiveness of drug treatments signals that body may be as significant as mind.

Our final chapter will synthesize some of these major themes. We will present a case for cognitive psychological models as the dominant paradigm in the field, to date. Key accomplishments of this approach include evidence on the roles of cognitive appraisal and coping in the process by which anxiety unfolds, on the acquisition of stable self-beliefs as an enduring developmental influence on normal and clinical anxiety, and on the role of biases in information processing as a source of performance change in anxiety. At the same time, there is much about anxiety that the standard cognitive models fail to capture, not least its expressions in neural functioning. We will suggest that a broader cognitive science framework may provide a more comprehensive account. Such a framework may accommodate both a cognitive neuroscience of anxiety that integrates biological and cognitive explanations, and a deeper understanding of the motivational regulation of anxiety. We also look at some more radical challenges to the cognitive paradigm, including attempts to reestablish the primacy of physiological accounts of anxiety and the social-psychological perspective that emphasizes the study of individuals over broad trends evident in group data. We will leave the reader with the same question that we posed above: How do we reconcile the multifaceted nature of anxiety with its status as a unitary emotion?

How Do We Best Assess Anxiety?

When you can measure what you are speaking about... you can know something about it, but when you can not measure it... your knowledge is of a meager and unsatisfactory kind.

Lord Kelvin

In his classic book on methodology in the social sciences, *The conduct of inquiry*, Abraham Kaplan (1964) lamented that social scientists sometimes place too much emphasis on the quantification of constructs, instead of investing their intellectual efforts in interpreting the meaning and potential value of the constructs they are trying to measure. To illustrate this, he relates the frustration of one of the subjects who partook in Alfred Kinsey's well-known study of the sexual behavior of the human male in the 1930s. The participant complained bitterly about the fatal blow to his male ego because, in his words, "No matter what I told him (i.e., the interviewer), he just looked me straight in the eye and asked, 'How many times?'" The participant felt that in the eyes of the interviewer, *what* he had done between the sheets or elsewhere was incomparably less significant than the *frequency* of its performance. The respondent seems to have felt quite differently. Wouldn't you have?

Measurement, based on quantification, is a key pillar of scientific psychology. It is commonly held that advances in the sciences go hand in hand with advances in the measurement of its core concepts. In fact, as noted by the noted learning theorist, E. L. Thorndike, if a construct exists in nature, it is susceptible to measurement. If not, then for all scientific purposes we cannot make any tenable statements about the construct. In its broadest sense, measurement can be understood as an operation in the real world, in which a number or a symbol is assigned to objects or events according to an explicit rule (Stevens, 1946). Accordingly, measurement has been defined as a "rule for assigning numbers to objects in such a way as to represent quantities of attributes" (Nunnally, 1978, p. 3). This succinct definition includes three distinct components:

- A group of objects to be measured (albino mice, dogs, chimps, military inductees, college undergrads, and professors);
- A category or group of symbols representing various values of the scale employed (e.g., 0, 1, . . .);
- An explicit rule of correspondence relating elements of these two categories.

For a measure to be useful, the rules for relating objects to numbers or symbols must be explicit, clear, and practical to apply. Whereas this is implicit in the measurement of physical objects, such as a ruler used to measure width or length, these rules are not intuitively obvious in assessing most psychological attributes, such as anxiety. Since numbers or symbols assigned to objects according to an explicit rule designate the amount of an attribute present in an object, measurement is actually concerned with attributes or properties of objects, rather than objects themselves.

Table 2.1 displays a contrived anxiety test, presented to illustrate the elements of psychological measurement. Try taking this test. In this test, the objects to be measured are *feelings* of anxiety in students before an important exam; the symbols representing various values of the scale are numbered (from 1 to 4) responses to the items; and the rule of correspondence is the formula used to determine the score. The values are added to produce a score, which is then interpreted. Table 2.2 shows the responses of a hypothetical

TABLE 2.1   CONTRIVED STATE ANXIETY INVENTORY

Instructions. Please indicate how anxious you are at this moment, that is, right now, using the following response categories:
1 = not characteristic of you now
2 = somewhat not characteristic of you now
3 = somewhat characteristic of you now
4 = very characteristic of you now
There are no correct or incorrect answers. It is important you answer as honestly as possible.

1. I am worried.	1	2	3	4
2. My body feels tense.	1	2	3	4
3. I am frightened.	1	2	3	4
4. I can't concentrate.	1	2	3	4
5. I am breathing quickly.	1	2	3	4
6. I feel little control over my body.	1	2	3	4
7. I feel like I am in danger.	1	2	3	4
8. My palms are sweaty.	1	2	3	4
9. My heart is pounding.	1	2	3	4
10. I feel "butterflies" in my stomach.	1	2	3	4

student to the anxiety test. The responses are "scored"—that is, they are evaluated according to certain rules in order to adduce numerical values. The meanings shown in Table 2.2 are contrived sample results only.

In the sections that follow, we briefly survey current measures and assessments of anxiety. We begin by presenting some basic psychometric criteria for evaluating psychological measures. Since some of these psychometric concepts may be new to you, and even a bit daunting, feel free to gloss over the psychometric material and move on to the substantive content. What is important to remember is that any psychological measure needs to be both valid (it measures what it intends or sets out to measure) and reliable (consistent in measuring the desired attribute).

In chapter 1 (see What Is This Thing Called Anxiety?), we saw that anxiety is more complex than it seems at first glance, and researchers have made a number of distinctions between different forms of anxiety. Measurement is critical for showing

TABLE 2.2 SAMPLE RESULTS FOR COLLEGE FRESHMAN STUDENTS TAKING THE ANXIETY MEASURE DURING FINAL EXAM PERIOD

Items	Responses	Rules for Combining Values to Get a Score	Key for Final Score Interpretation
1. I am worried.	4	Sum Values (4 + 3 + 3 + 3 + 3 + 4 + 4 + 4 + 4) = 35	10–14 = not anxious 15–19 = very slightly anxious 20–29 = mildly anxious 30–35 = anxious 36–40 = extremely anxious
2. My body feels tense.	3		
3. I am frightened.	3		
4. I can't concentrate.	3		
5. I am breathing quickly.	3		
6. I feel little control over my body.	3		
7. I feel like I am in danger.	4		
8. My palms are sweaty.	4		
9. My heart is pounding.	4		
10. I feel "butterflies" in my stomach.	4		

these distinctions are actually meaningful. In fact, there are three pivotal issues for measuring anxiety as a multifaceted construct:

- *Reliability.* "Reliability" refers to the consistency of scores obtained by the same person when re-examined with the same test on different occasions, or with different sets of identical or equivalent items or under different examining conditions. In the context of anxiety assessment, each anxiety scale must be reliable and internally consistent; that is, it must measure "whatever it is that it measures" accurately. Simplistically, responses on the different items on the scale should be correlated. At a more sophisticated level, researchers typically calculate a quantity known as Cronbach's alpha to estimate internal consistency. The trait scale—but not state—measures need to be reliable in a different fashion also. They need to show high test-retest correlations across periods of months or years, because, by definition, the individual's personality should be stable across time.
- *Validity.* "Validity," the sine qua non of any scientific assessment, refers to the ability of a test to measure what it purports to measure. High reliability is a necessary condition for validity, but the converse is not true. Researchers distinguish several different kinds of validity, beyond the scope of this volume. One basic form is criterion validity; a test for anxiety should correlate with other, independent criteria for being anxious. These might include nonverbal behaviors such as averting the gaze, poor concentration under stress, and avoidance of performance-threatening situations. Establishing criterion validity requires multiple studies to explore how the test relates to a variety of different criteria. A more subtle form is construct validity, which means whether the "construct" measured (e.g., anxiety) can be related to a coherent theory. For example, having shown that anxiety relates to impaired performance under stress (criterion validity), we can then develop and test theories of why this relationship exists (e.g., worry uses up attentional capacity). Construct validity is always a work-in-progress, as theory and research evolve.
- *Discriminant validity.* Another form of construct validity, discriminant validity is especially important where we seek to distinguish multiple aspects of the same construct.

Discriminant validity is typically demonstrated by showing that measures of constructs that are conceptually unrelated do not correlate in the data. If we say, as we have done, that anxious emotion is different from anxious thought (worry), we need to show that we can measure these facets of anxiety as distinct qualities or attributes of the person. If our "emotion" ruler always gives the same number as the "worry" ruler, then we have failed to do this. Factor analysis, a statistical technique used to identify and analyze patterns of relationships among (many) different psychological variables, provides an initial way of discriminating multiple dimensions. However, it is vital to show that multiple dimensions differ in their criterion validity. A "cognitive" anxiety test should predict criteria related to thinking, such as performance impairment, whereas an "emotional" test should predict expressions of affect, such as facial expression. This form of validity is important even when we are measuring anxiety on a unitary basis, as a single dimension. One of the inconvenient properties of negative emotions is that they tend to occur together. The anxious person will often be sad and/or fearful as well, and so it is important that an anxiety scale specifically picks up anxiety rather than general negative emotion.

In reviewing anxiety scales, we will follow Lang's (1968) three-faceted approach to the assessment of anxiety. This framework distinguishes the following three subsystems for assessing anxiety:

- A *subjective subsystem*, composed of verbal reports of anxiety or anxiety phenomena (cognitions, sensations) during exposure to real or imagined anxiety-evoking situations. It lends itself to assessment using self-reports and questionnaires.
- A *physiological subsystem*, composed of autonomic nervous system (ANS) output, including heart rate, skin conductance, respiration, blood pressure, and muscle tension, together with longer-lasting hormonal responses such as cortisol secretion. Sensors such as electrodes may be used to record changes in these responses objectively.
- A *behavioral subsystem*, composed of observable behavioral signs of anxiety (facial expressions, fidgeting), performance

or behavioral deficits, and other overt indices for anxiety. In some cases, we can measure behaviors objectively, for example, by timing response speed on a performance test. Nonverbal expressions of anxiety are typically videotaped and coded by trained judges subsequently.

Under the heading of "subjective scales" we will, first, review the leading general measure of trait and state anxiety, Charles Spielberger's (1983) State-Trait Anxiety Inventory (STAI). We will then examine questionnaires that seek to accommodate the multifaceted nature of anxiety. We saw in chapter 1 (see Major Forms of Anxiety in Modern Society) that we can distinguish different forms of anxiety prevalent in modern society. We will present some examples of scales that aim to differentiate multiple forms, in relation to different contexts for experiencing anxiety, and in relation to the distinction between cognitive and emotional facets of anxiety. Next, we turn to physiological measures, covering both the classic ANS indices such as heart rate, and modern brain-imaging approaches. We will also discuss some reasons why these measures may be difficult to use in practice. The third member of Lang's (1968) trio of systems is the behavioral. We will survey some of the strategies that researchers have employed to identify behaviors that may be indicative of anxiety, including recent work on "implicit" tests that aim to assess unconscious behaviors. We finish the chapter with a quick look at age and gender differences.

SUBJECTIVE SCALES FOR MEASURING ANXIETY

Self-report questionnaires and procedures have been the most prevalent method for assessing the phenomenological facet of anxiety. On the one hand, the use of self-report methods and resulting data has had a long and controversial history. Self-reports can provide important data about both subjective aspects of anxiety (how worried or tense a person feels) as well as objective facets of anxiety symptoms (frequency of symptoms or anxious behaviors). On the other hand, many behavioral researchers hesitate to rely solely on self-report methods, given the historically prevalent position in scientific psychology that subjective reports of anxiety are inferior to more objective and externally valid behavioral measures. Furthermore, self-reports have prove to be the most effective means for discriminating *trait* and *state anxiety*—the enduring personality disposition (trait) and the immediate experience of anxiety (state).

General Subjective Measures

Dozens of anxiety measures have been developed for research and clinical purposes, including the *State-Trait Anxiety Inventory* (Spielberger, Gorsuch, & Lushene, 1970); *Beck Anxiety Inventory* (Beck, Epstein, Brown, & Steer, 1988); *Hamilton Rating Scale for Anxiety* (Hamilton, 1959); *Zung Self-Rating Anxiety Scale* (Zung, 1971); *Taylor Manifest Anxiety Scale* (Taylor, 1953); and *Endler's Multidimensional Anxiety Scale* (Endler, Edwards, & Vitelli, 1991). To give you the flavor of the development and attributes of a major anxiety assessment tool, we walk you through the key features of Spielberger's (1983) STAI, which has been used to assess anxiety more extensively worldwide than any other measure. The STAI has been adapted to more than 30 languages (e.g., Dutch, German, Greek, Hebrew, Russian, Spanish, and Turkish), with more than 2,000 publications appearing in the research literature on it since the STAI test manual was published in 1970 (Spielberger, 1989). Since its introduction nearly three decades ago, the STAI has been used in research and clinical practice in a wide array of populations (e.g., high school and college students, working adults, military personnel, psychiatric, medical, and dental patients), and it has been used for a variety of purposes, such as outcome measures to assess the effects of interventions for anxiety reduction; to investigate levels of anxiety in stress-related psychiatric and medical disorders; and to assess the effect of anxiety on learning and performance. The inventory is readily accessible to individuals with a sixth-grade reading level, with a special form available for 12- to 15-year-olds (Spielberger, 1973, *State-Trait Anxiety Scale for Children*).

The STAI was constructed on the assumption that in assessing anxiety there is a critical need to distinguish between anxiety as a transitory emotional state (i.e., state anxiety) and individual differences in anxiety proneness, as a relatively stable personality trait (i.e., trait anxiety). Accordingly, the STAI comprises two separate self-report scales for measuring both state and trait anxiety.

The *state anxiety* scale consists of 20 statements (e.g., *I feel jittery, I feel self-confident*) that evaluate how respondents feel "right now, at this moment." Respondents rate each item on a 4-point Likert scale (1 = not at all, 4 = very much so), assessing the intensity of the examinee's emotional reaction. The instructions are consistent with the definition of state anxiety, and the essential qualities evaluated by the scale are feelings of tension, nervousness, worry, and apprehension. The state scale has been extensively used to assess levels of state anxiety experienced by an individual at present, in the recent past, or how they will anticipate they will feel in a variety of hypothetical circumstances or situations likely to be encountered in the future. It has also been used to assess anxiety induced by stressful experimental procedures and real-life stressors (stress of dental procedures or job interviews) and as a sensitive indicator of changes in transitory anxiety experienced by clients and patients in counseling, therapy, and behavioral modification programs.

The trait anxiety subscale consists of 20 statements that assess how people generally feel. Examinees are presented with a statement (e.g., *I feel pleasant, I lack self-confidence*) and asked to indicate how they "generally feel" on a 4-point Likert frequency scale (1 = almost never, 4 = almost always). This subscale has also been used successfully for identifying persons with high levels of neurotic anxiety, for selecting participants for psychological experiments, and screening high school and college students and military recruits for anxiety problems.

Although designed to be self-administered, the STAI may be given individually or in groups, with no time limits. The state anxiety subscale is administered first, followed by the trait anxiety subscale. College students require about 6 minutes for completing each subtest, and about 10 minutes in total. It is noted that state anxiety and trait anxiety mean scores are approximately equal under normal testing conditions, but state anxiety scores are significantly higher than trait anxiety scores, on average, under stressful conditions. The median correlation between the trait and state measures is about .65, although the correlations are higher under conditions posing a threat to self-esteem. Individuals high on trait anxiety tend to be high on state anxiety, even in neutral situations.

Construction and Norming. Charles Spielberger began constructing the STAI in 1964, with the goal of developing a single set of items that could be administered with different instructions in order to provide an objective measure of state and trait anxiety. The item pool was developed by identifying items with a demonstrated relationship with other measures of anxiety. Most of these measures were trait anxiety measures, and the items with content related to the most widely used trait anxiety scales were rewritten to be used as measures of both forms of anxiety. Items were selected on the basis of the best psychometric properties for measuring either state or trait anxiety.

An important part of scale development is finding "norms"; that is, estimating the mean and standard deviation of the scale in the population in general, or within subpopulations. Norms are essential in psychological assessment for being able to evaluate a person's test score in relation to typical values. Effective norming requires administration of the scale to large, carefully selected samples. Two forms of the STAI were developed, that is, forms X and Y. More than 6,000 high school and college students and approximately 600 psychiatric and medical patients and 200 prison inmates were tested in the development and standardization and validation of the form X of the STAI; more than 5,000 persons were tested in the development and standardization of form Y of the STAI. Norms are available for a variety of different subgroups, including high school and college students, working adults, medical and neuropsychiatric patients, military recruits, and prison inmates. In the following sections, we present some of the data in support of the reliability and validity of the STAI.

Validity. The STAI test manual presents impressive evidence for the criterion and construct validity of this instrument, including correlations of the trait anxiety subscale with other trait anxiety scales (e.g., *Taylor Manifest Anxiety Scale*), along with other widely used personality and adjustment measures. The differential effects of treatments on state versus trait anxiety components provide further evidence for the scale's construct validity. Thus, state anxiety scores are highly sensitive to environmental stressors; it is easy to elevate state anxiety in laboratory studies, for example, by requiring the person to perform a difficult task or give a speech. By contrast, trait anxiety scores essentially remain the same before and after treatments of this kind and do not appear to be influenced by environmental stress. For example, state anxiety scores rise immediately before surgery and decline as patients recuperate, whereas trait anxiety scores are not influenced by stress of surgical procedures (Spielberger, 1983). High trait anxiety scores have been reported to be associated with a large number of self-reported problems in almost every area of adjustment and differences among contrast groups (neuropsychiatric patients vs. normal) on anxiety measures were also reported.

Factor analytic research also provided evidence in support of the validity of the conceptual distinction between state and trait anxiety. Factor analytic studies of the STAI items show that the most meaningful solution was a two-factor solution. All 20 state anxiety items show salient loadings on state anxiety and the majority (17 out of 20) of the trait anxiety items show salient loadings on trait anxiety. Based on both theory and factor analytic studies, STAI subscale scores may most aptly be interpreted as unidimensional measures of state anxiety and trait anxiety, with individual state anxiety and trait anxiety items consistently loaded on different factors.

Reliability. Both measures of internal consistency (alpha) and stability (test-retest) have been used to assess the reliability of the STAI subscales. With respect to internal consistency, across different normative samples (high school, college, working class, military recruits), alpha reliability coefficients range from .86 to .95 for state anxiety (median = .93), and from .89 to .91 for trait anxiety (median = .90). With respect to stability coefficients, whereas the test-retest reliability coefficients for the state form range from .16 to .62 (median =.33), test-retest coefficients are much higher for trait anxiety, ranging from .65 to .75 for high school students and from .73 to .86 for college students—as would be expected for a stable trait. Indeed, relatively low stability coefficients are expected for state anxiety because a valid measure should reflect the influence of the unique situational factor at the time of assessment.

Despite some of the attractive psychometric and practical strengths of self-report anxiety scales, such as the STAI, these do have their limitations and drawbacks, as briefly summarized in the next section.

1. *Threats to construct validity.* Most self-report measures, such as the STAI, are plagued with a number of threats to their construct validity, including faking good (or bad) responses, defensiveness, social desirability, response sets, acquiescence, and the like. Because respondents may be reluctant to endorse items with negative characteristics (e.g., feeling upset or tense or frightened), those high on defensiveness or social desirability may respond more positively to anxiety-absent items. Bias may be conscious or unconscious (Paulhus & Levitt, 1987). Persons applying for a stressful job, such as working as a police officer, might deliberately present themselves as being less anxiety-prone than they actually are. In addition, people have only limited insight into their own emotions, and may underestimate (or possibly overestimate) just how anxious they actually are. Greater effort needs to be made to construct scales that minimize these threats to the construct validity of current measures.

2. *Incomplete domain coverage.* The key content facets represented in current anxiety scales are rather limited and restricted in scope, with traditional scales failing to provide a detailed analysis of anxiety in specific situations. The subjective anxiety response, with the focus mainly on cognitive and emotional experience, is often the only content facet represented in most current scale items. Seldom do anxiety scales inform us about the various situational and personal antecedents eliciting anxiety (anxiety proneness, inadequate preparation, overstimulation), the full range of manifestations of anxiety (e.g., cognitive, affective, and behavioral), coping procedures and strategies, the consequences of anxiety, or the dynamic fluctuations in anxiety states across various phases of a stressful encounter. The restricted content scope can be improved by employing more systematic procedures for identifying the different facets of anxiety.

3. *Lack of scale differentiation.* Current anxiety measures need to be refined and differentiated. Thus, it might make sense to have one scale in an anxiety inventory sample in a range of potentially anxiety-producing stimuli (public speaking, job interview, computerized assessment, physical danger); another might deal with the particular response channel or style of reacting to anxiety (worry, arousal, hopelessness, etc.); another scale might assess the frequency and intensity of anxiety elicited; another would tap the styles of coping with anxiety (defensive reactions, avoidance, palliative coping, instrumental coping, etc.), and yet another would assess perceived consequences (decrements in memory, concentration, retrieval, etc.). A more refined and differentiated anxiety inventory would allow us to better delineate the profile of anxious subjects.

4. *Scales are not sufficiently relevant for clinical purposes.* When used for clinical purposes, current instruments only allow measurement of the overall level of anxiety or identification of a few of its key components. Prevalent measures are not very informative with respect to how anxiety is expressed in a client and in what situations. This limitation is another version of the problem of "incomplete domain coverage," discussed above. One of the key issues here is how to identify when anxiety is clinically significant. Is clinical anxiety no more than the frequent, intense experience of "ordinary" anxiety? Or is there some qualitative difference between normal and abnormal anxiety? For example, a clinical assessment might need to pay more attention to behavioral facets of anxiety in order to determine when the client's anxiety actually interferes with the activities of normal life. In addition, clinicians recognize a number of qualitatively different anxiety disorders, including generalized anxiety, panic disorder, various phobias, and posttraumatic stress disorder. Trait and state anxiety may all be elevated in these conditions, but they differ in other symptoms, in environmental triggers for anxiety, and in the behaviors characteristic of the disorder. Future scales need to be more relevant for planning, execution, and evaluation of clinical or educational intervention through specification of the various antecedent conditions, manifestations, and consequences of anxiety.

5. *Insufficient attention to the extreme manifestations of anxiety.* Current instruments are designed to measure the relative presence of anxiety, but do not inform us enough about the low-anxious individual. Thus, future measures need to cover specific manifestations of low anxiety, ranging from a total lack of concern about the threat and minimal motivation, to supreme self-confidence or high levels of self-efficacy. Overlapping with concerns about the clinical utility of anxiety scales, these measures may fail to tell us enough about the extremely high-anxious individual. Therefore, the coverage of items needs to be expanded to reflect the phenomenology of high-anxious individuals, including such manifestations as panic attacks, total blackout, and anxiety blockage when one is confronted with anxiety cues.

6. *Failure to distinguish between adaptive and maladaptive manifestations of anxiety.* Current scales do not provide sufficient evidence to separate adaptive and maladaptive effects of worry or anxiety in ego-threatening situations. Sometimes anxiety can be helpful in motivating the person to deal with a potential threat; perhaps, more commonly, anxiety is source of distraction that may interfere with successful goal-directed action. Future measures need to distinguish between the facilitating and debilitating forms of anxiety. It is important also to distinguish cognitive processes that are a rational response to threat (e.g., worrying about an imminent difficult exam in physics, which is prompted by a genuine threat) and those that are unrealistic (e.g., those prompted by an unlikely bombing of a straightforward job interview).

Anxiety in Context

Thus far, we have described general anxiety questionnaires. When anxiety is assessed as a trait, these scales are based on an assumption that people differ systematically in their proneness to anxiety across a variety of different situations or types of threats. Thus, the high trait-anxious person is assumed to experience high state anxiety in situations as varied as being overdrawn at the bank, being criticized by an acquaintance, being rejected for a job, and experiencing mysterious chest pains. In fact, personality theory generally recognizes that individual differences in emotional (and indeed, all) responses vary across situations (Funder & Ozer, 1983). Even if a person is generally anxiety prone, there will likely be some types of threats to which they are especially sensitive and others that do not bother them very much. Similarly, even low trait-anxious persons will probably be vulnerable to certain types of threats.

Some questionnaires for trait anxiety recognize the important role of context in individual differences in anxiety. We will discuss a number of these assessments in the following sections.

Multiple Dimensions of Anxiety. The first scale we will look at is *Endler's Multidimensional Anxiety Scale* (Endler & Kocovski, 2001). Like the STAI, it is based on an interactional model of anxiety that posits that anxiety is a function of the dynamic interactions between person and situation variables. Where it differs from the STAI is that it is assumed that trait anxiety (A-Trait) is multidimensional. The individual's propensity to become anxious varies from context to context, so that scales for anxiety should take into account the circumstances under which the person is vulnerable to threat. Specifically, the model posits that there are four distinct facets of trait anxiety, corresponding to four different types of contexts that may evoke state anxiety, as follows:

a. *Social evaluation* trait anxiety measures an individual's disposition to have increases in state anxiety in situations where one is being observed or evaluated by others (e.g., public speaking, competitive sports, test situations).
b. *Physical danger* trait anxiety measures an individual's predisposition to respond with increases in state anxiety in situations where one may be physically hurt (e.g., jumping out of an airplane, cleaning windows of a high-rise building).
c. *Ambiguous* trait anxiety relates to situations that are uncertain and novel to the individual (e.g., first day on a new job that has an ambiguous job description).
d. *Daily routines* trait anxiety is related to situations that involve an individual's daily routine and are generally innocuous (e.g., changing a flat tire, fixing a leaking valve in the kitchen sink, wearing a pair of nonmatching socks or shoes to work).

For a person, by situation interaction, to induce an increase in state anxiety, the threatening situation must be congruent with the facet of A-Trait being investigated. For example, consider how people might react to having to cross a busy highway with no crosswalk. Those high in physical danger A-Trait will experience a surge of high state anxiety, but persons vulnerable to social evaluation or ambiguity will not be especially unsettled (i.e., no more than average). Conversely, high social evaluation A-Trait persons would show exceptionally high state anxiety if performing in a talent show, but individuals high in other forms of A-Trait would not be disproportionately affected. The congruency hypothesis derived from this theory states that an interaction between person and state in impacting anxiety states is expected when the stressful situation is congruent with the facet of A-Trait under investigation. Person variables interact with situational variables to produce a perception of threat, which, in turn, evokes state anxiety and coping responses, defenses, behavioral and biological reactions, and physical illnesses. The vast majority of empirical studies testing the model (more than 80%) have provided support for the model (Endler & Kocovski, 2001).

Test Anxiety. Endler's model highlights social evaluation as a key context for anxiety. In fact, we can break down "social evaluation" still further into a number of separate arenas within which the person may be judged. These include formal testing, sports, social encounters, and math (Zeidner & Matthews, 2005). The most-researched of these "evaluative anxieties" is test anxiety, referring to concerns about failure on some formal assessment, which we introduced in chapter 1 (Major Forms of Anxiety: Test Anxiety). It is best known from studies of the discomfort, arousal, and anxiety that students often feel during examinations (Zeidner, 1998). We will introduce material from test anxiety research in various places in this book. Here we focus on the specialized measures that have been developed for its assessment. While test anxiety tends to correlate positively with general anxiety, it is a distinct construct. It is possible for a student to be generally calm in personality, but to react with strong anxiety to being tested.

Irwin Sarason, one of the doyens of test anxiety research, developed a general scale for trait test anxiety that assessed a range of symptoms of feeling anxious during tests and exami-nations. Later on, he came to see the value of discriminating different elements of anxiety and especially the cognitive and emotional facets that we have already described. Sarason's (1984) questionnaire has four scales, assessing the following inter-related but separate aspects of vulnerability to test anxiety:

- "Bodily reactions" refer to the physical symptoms of anxiety, such as a racing heart and an upset stomach.
- "Tension" refers to negative emotions such as feeling nervous and jittery.
- "Worry" is a cognitive dimension that refers to being con-cerned about failing during tests.
- "Test-irrelevant thinking" refers not to thoughts, of the test, but to other personal concerns.

Together, bodily reactions and tension describe trait test anxiety in relation to the affective (emotional) aspect of anx-iety described in chapter 1 (Facets of Anxiety: The Affective/Somatic Facet), whereas the other two scales—that is, worry and test irrelevant thinking—define the cognitive aspect of test anx-iety. Sarason (1986) developed a companion measure to the RIT scale, the *Cognitive Interference Questionnaire*, which measures state rather than trait test anxiety. It focuses on the worry states that can divert attention from effective test performance, includ-ing separate scales for test-related worries and test-irrelevant interference. Sarason's scales have proven to be especially useful in investigating the cognitive consequences of anxiety, as further discussed in chapter 5 (Anxiety and Cognitive Performance).

Another luminary in the area of test anxiety assessment, Charles Spielberger, developed the *Test Anxiety Inventory* (TAI—Spielberger, Gonzales, Taylor, Algaze, & Anton, 1978), by far the most widely used TAI around the globe. The TAI, designed to measure individual differences in test anxiety as a situation-specific personality trait, is a 20-item self-report scale based on a two-dimensional (i.e., worry and emotionality) concep-tualization of test anxiety. The instrument has been translated into over a dozen languages including Arabic, Chinese, Dutch, German, Hindi, Hebrew, Hungarian, Italian, Japanese, Korean, Norwegian, Persian, Portuguese, and Spanish. The scale has been reported to have excellent psychometric properties and has been employed in various populations, ranging from students in elementary school (e.g., Zeidner, Klingman, & Papko, 1988) through college student populations (e.g., Zeidner & Nevo, 1992).

Driving Anxiety. Our final example of a context-linked anxiety scale relates to vehicle driving. Moderate anxiety over driving is not uncommon and in extreme cases can be expressed as a phobia. Given that motor vehicle driving has been common only for a little over a century—and has no evolutionary basis—the existence of a distinctive anxiety trait shows how anxiety may be attached to almost any significant human activity.

The Driver Stress Inventory (Matthews, 2002) has multiple trait scales for different forms of vulnerability, but includes a Dislike of Driving scale that relates to vulnerability to anxiety and other negative emotions. Its validity is shown by its capacity to predict negative emotions, including tension, in both real-life driving and experiments using a driving simulator. It is also distinct from general personality, correlating at about .4 with neuroticism in the Five-Factor Model. Personality may indeed change when the driver gets behind the wheel. Vulnerability to driving anxiety appears to have a cognitive basis, related to perceptions of lack of competence and control as a driver. Interestingly, driving anxiety is neutral in regard to safety. High anxiety does seem to increase the likelihood of driver error, but anxious drivers compensate by driving more slowly, so that there is no net effect on crash risk.

PHYSIOLOGICAL MEASURES OF ANXIETY

Anxiety often feels as though it permeates the whole body. We feel sweaty, our hearts race, and our muscles tense. We may even feel like throwing up or urinating. Some theorists believe that this "embodiment" of anxiety is crucial to the development of the subjective emotion. The measurement techniques of psychophysiology provide a means for precise measurement of these "fight-or-flight" responses of the body. A body of data attest that individuals often show substantial increases in a variety of indices of physiological arousal and other autonomic activity when they are exposed to ego-threatening situations (Holroyd & Appel, 1980). These include Galvanic skin response (GSR), respiration (rate/volume), somatic activity (muscle tension), cardiovascular system (pulse rate, heart rate, blood pressure, etc.), electrical brain activity (electroencephalogram), and metabolic activity of specific brain areas (functional magnetic resonance imaging [fMRI], positron emission tomography). The GSR is an example of an electrodermal measure, based on the increasing electrical conductance of the skin as the person perspires. From the mid-1970s, physiological measures gained considerable currency in anxiety research for the purpose of gauging changes in somatic activity shown to accompany the subjective and behavioral components of anxiety.

The use of physiological measures to gauge anxiety in stressful situations would seem to have a distinct advantage over self-report measures. Because it is fairly difficult (though sometimes possible) to voluntarily control ANS responses, physiological responses would presumably be immune to a number of problems endemic to self-report measures of anxiety (e.g., faking good or bad responses, defensiveness, social desirability). However, despite some important advantages, physiological indices suffer from a number of formidable methodological problems, briefly summarized as follows.

Questionable Construct Validity

Using physiological measures of autonomic reactivity to gauge anxiety raises serious concerns relating to the construct validity of these measures. The extent to which static measures of peripheral autonomic reactivity (e.g., pulse rate samples or finger sweat prints) validly reflect central emotional changes that occur as a result of stressful situations has not been decisively determined. Furthermore, autonomic arousal may not necessarily be synonymous with anxiety but instead may be considered a measure of *state* anxiety alone, as people tend to cognitively label arousal in a particular state as anxiety (Holroyd & Appel, 1980). Additional problems impacting on the validity of physiological measures involve defensiveness and autonomic co-awareness. Defensiveness occurs when some subjects short circuit the threat through the use of defenses, while "autonomic co-awareness" refers to individual differences in the degree to which people can accurately perceive their own autonomic activity. Thus, some individuals tend to overestimate their physiological activity while others underestimate their physiological activity. In addition, some folks can control their ANS responses, via biofeedback, more than others can.

A major concern with respect to construct validity is that physiological measures generally fail to converge with self-report measures of anxiety, even though common experience suggests a close relationship between these two classes of measures. Whereas anxious individuals frequently report a variety of autonomic symptoms as well as subjective feelings of anxiety, the relationship between how a person reports feeling and how she responds physiologically is very complex (Hodges, 1976). In fact, one of the most curious and puzzling aspects of research in anxiety is the failure for these two different kinds of dependent measures to correlate significantly when a person is under some kind of stress.

At best, physiological measures provide information about overall emotional arousal but fail to provide information about the unique significance of anxiety or differences between anxiety and cognate emotions. If high-anxious individuals are compared physiologically with generally low-anxious subjects, some of the low-anxious ones are affected by stress and are indeed anxious but handle it in a defensive manner. Researchers need to identify those who both score low on self-report anxiety measures and manifest low levels on physiological measures, that is, truly low-anxious ones, versus those individuals who score low on anxiety self-report measures but show high autonomic activity.

Low Convergence of Physiological Measures

Another serious problem relates to the low convergent validity of physiological indices. Thus, one cannot assume that the various measures of physiological arousal used in anxiety research (heart rate, respiratory rate, skin resistance level, etc.) are entirely comparable measures. As further noted in the following discussion, people appear to differ in the responsiveness of different physiological responses (described as *response stereotypy*—Lacey [1967]). Thus, one person might express anxiety primarily through increased heart rate, whereas another might display increased perspiration (increasing skin conductance). A growing literature has indicated significant differences in response patterns across the three response systems in both normal and clinical subjects when confronted with anxiety-provoking situations (Lawyer & Smitherman, 2004). For example, electrodermal and cardiovascular responses may provide very different indices of arousal because each of these measures reflects complex and specific physiological processes sensitive to many internal and external influences. Indeed, research suggests that these indices suffer from a lack of convergence with other physiological measures (see Lang, Rice, & Sternbach, 1972).

Poor Reliability

Virtually all physiological measures have problems of reliability. Given that anxiety may not be a unitary phenomenon, and that the cognitive, physiological, and behavioral components of the construct are loosely coupled, it is hardly surprising that the measures of the various components of the anxiety construct do not always correspond (Rachman, 2004). In fact, some people experience subjective anxiety but remain outwardly calm and show none of the expected physiological concomitants or make no attempt to avoid the threat or escape from the dangerous context. The fact that the various components of anxiety don't always correspond makes it imperative to specify which component one is describing.

Not only are measures of different channels of anxiety expression only partially dependent, but correlations between measures of the ANS (heart rate, blood flow, blood pressure, GSR, respiration rate, etc.) tend to be very low, so that no one measure could be used as an indicator of anxious arousal. Clearly, a one-to-one correspondence between anxiety and physiological arousal in a particular situation may not be assumed and physiological measures should not be used as an independent criterion for state anxiety.

Most physiological indices reflect a wide range of differences among individuals, unrelated to specific stressor conditions. Thus, as pointed out by Rachman and Hodgson (1980), within any person, anxiety response systems may be relatively different at any one time (discordance) and may change at different rates (desynchrony) during exposure to anxiety cues. Also, physiological measures reflect an equally wide range of differences within the individual, related to diurnal cycles or other temporal or environmental conditions orthogonal to specific stressors. These problems require elaborate design controls and counterbalancing, as well as careful calibration of the instruments themselves.

In addition, physiological indices evidence low temporal stability, and appear to be sensitive to a variety of situational influences (Allen, 1980). Some physiological measures (GSR, pulse rate, perhaps others) are probably vulnerable to testing or reactivity effects; that is, the measurement procedures themselves may alter the levels of measured state anxiety in stressful situations.

Response Specificity

One major determinant of the low correlation among autonomic nervous measures is response specificity. Specifically, it is well documented that individuals have specific response patterns in autonomic functions—that some are high heart rate responders and others are respiratory responders or perhaps responders both with increased GSR and heart rate. These response patterns are reliable over time and occur regardless of the type of stress to which the subject is subjected. There is also "stimulus specificity" in the sense that different people may be sensitive to different stimuli. Then there is also stimulus-response specificity—that is, the characteristic of the stimulus (e.g., physical or ego-oriented threat) may affect the physiological pattern obtained.

Threshold and Ceiling Effects. Threshold and ceiling effects may make the choice of a physiological measure difficult. For example, in an experimental study, if the person's anxiety is high to begin with, the heart might already be beating fast, prior to exposure to a stressor. Because it is difficult for heart rate to increase still further, the person might show only a small response to the stressor (a "ceiling effect"), falsely suggesting that he or she was not experiencing much anxiety. Indeed, resting levels are frequently ill-defined and can be powerfully influenced by uncontrolled pre-experimental variables. A more general problem is that we can take a number of different measures of a response, which may give us different information.

If we take the electrodermal response as a measure of anxiety, we could use a number of different parameters (e.g., size of response, latency [delay] of response, duration of response [i.e., time to return to baseline]) as our response, each of which may provide different patterns of effects and correlations.

Lack of Norms. A related psychometric difficulty involves a lack of normative information against which to judge high levels of emotional arousal in stressful situations. In contrast to well-developed standardization data reported for a number of anxiety questionnaires, as demonstrated earlier for the STAI, little information is available about how individuals with high and low anxiety distribute themselves on physiological indices. To be maximally useful, these data would have to be collected in a variety of situations, ranging from experientially relaxing to highly stressful (Allen, 1980). Furthermore, the purely physiological effects of factors such as age, gender, health, physical fitness, smoking, and other influences mean that different norms would have to be obtained for different subject populations.

Low Practicality in Naturalistic Settings. Psychometric issues aside, physiological measures also have a number of inherent technical problems when used as measures of anxiety in true-to-life or applied contexts. Clearly, locating a complex physiological apparatus (e.g., a physiograph) in a true-to-life-situation (classroom, boardroom, study, airport, outdoor military drill) is challenging. Imagine implementing physiological assessment procedures during an artillery exercise in the U.S. Marines. Electrodes need to be attached to soldiers in the field under simulated combat conditions, who then need to engage in the long waiting periods needed to obtain steady baseline measures, often under heavy fire. Aside from possible reactivity of these measures, the cost of using such equipment and of obtaining the necessary technical staff to operate may be prohibitive, particularly in field settings.

However, recent developments in the field of "ambulatory monitoring" are beginning to tackle the practical difficulties (Ebner-Priemer & Trull, 2009). Technological developments in physiological sensors and wearable computers are making the "online" measurement of anxiety responses in real-life settings more feasible. Alpers (2009) reviews work of this kind in relation to clinical anxiety disorders, which, of course, tend to provoke stronger responses than those that accompany normal anxiety. It is possible to mention the cardiovascular responses and hyperventilation that accompany panic attacks, for example. Researchers are also investigating the cortisol response that accompanies activation of the hypothalamic-pituitary-adrenal axis during anxiety and fear.

One of the limitations of ambulatory monitoring of this kind is that it may fail to pick up the critical cognitive elements of anxiety. Indeed, Alpert cautions that physiological responses are often less distinct than expected on the basis of anxiety patients' experiences. This particular limitation may be overcome by integrating ambulatory monitoring with another assessment technology for emotion, *experience sampling* (Christensen, Barrett, Bliss-Moreau, Lebo, & Kaschub, 2003). This approach prompts the person to report his or her emotional state and thoughts episodically, so that changes in emotion during normal activities can be recorded. Its use in concert with physiological monitoring may allow the cognitive context for the anxiety response to be understood.

Limitations of Brain-Imaging. Neuroscientific studies of emotions, including anxiety, have been revolutionized by brain-imaging techniques such as fMRI. Researchers can now map those specific brain areas that are active while the person is feeling anxious, or while he or she is processing and responding to a threatening stimulus. We address the neuroscience theories of emotion that explain these findings in chapter 3 (see Biological Perspectives: Functional Neurobiological Perspectives), but broadly such research converges with other lines of evidence in pinpointing structures in the subcortical "limbic system" of the brain, notably the amygdala, as being critical for anxiety.

We might then hope that we could measure anxiety, directly and physiologically, as the level of activation of the "anxiety centers" of the brain. Barrett and Wager (2006) have reviewed studies in this area. On the one hand, they conclude that the link between fear and activation of the amygdala is the most robust within emotion research; it has been substantiated by two major reviews. On the other hand, they caution that the fear-amygdala association is not fully replicable; only about half the relevant published studies obtained it. Individuals also vary in the extent to which amygdalar activation accompanies fear. (It is also unclear whether we can distinguish fear and anxiety in these studies.) Another issue is that the amygdala does not activate *only* in response to threat; it may respond to other emotions, including positive ones, and it seems especially responsive to faces. Thus, while imaging technology will undoubtedly continue to improve, it is not yet ready for prime time as a tool for assessing the individual's level of anxiety.

Indeed, the blood flow responses measured by fMRI do not necessarily reflect the emotional significance of a stimulus, its meaning, unexpectedness of stimulus, or its properties (Kagan, 2007). The current popular practice of describing brain profiles of anxiety states from MRI scanners as if they were equivalent to anxiety is problematic for several reasons. First, machines reveal changes in blood flow to brain sites several seconds after presentation of an emotive stimulus, whereas some anxiety reactions occur immediately (i.e., in less than 2 seconds, which is the time it takes for the scanner to detect any changes in blood flow). Also, the particular profile of brain activity in response to a stimulus or any incentive can vary with both the immediate context as well as the individual history and psychological state of the person being scanned. Because the causes of change in blood oxygen level remain an enigma, the psychological meaning of any alteration is necessarily ambiguous. The use of fMRI is also a good example of an important principle: that psychological measures can only be interpreted in the context of a theory that tells us what the measure actually means. As we shall see in the next chapter, theories of anxiety can be broadly divided into those that see anxiety as a reflection of the level of activity in brain systems that react to threat, and those that see anxiety as attached to the personal meaning attributed to threat, which is only indirectly related to neural processes. An fMRI measure of anxiety makes more sense in the context of a neurological theory than a cognitive one.

BEHAVIORAL MEASURES OF ANXIETY

Another approach to the assessment of anxiety has involved the use of behavioral measures of performance. Behavioral observations are an extremely valuable source of information on anxiety, permitting great accuracy and more objectivity than self-report or interview procedures. Thus, probably the most direct and least inferential way to assess anxious behaviors is to observe relevant behavioral manifestations of the construct in ego-threatening situations in which they occur (King & O'llendick, 1989). Specific behaviors reflective of anxiety (distress, distraction, avoidance) are operationally defined and recorded. Instead of having examinees rate or rank themselves on a series of items reflecting the anxiety experience, or hooking up the participant to a polygraph, an alternative approach would be to have a trained observer (experimenter, teacher, therapist) rate the client's level of anxiety (Suinn, 1990). Accordingly, the observer utilizes some standard set of observation categories in documenting anxious behavior, though sometimes cameras, tape recorders, or other devices are used.

Mandler and Sarason (1952) were the first to employ performance measures involving direct observation of behavioral manifestations of anxiety, such as observed perspiration, excessive body movement, and inappropriate laughter, when subjects were engaged in exam situations. Individuals with high and low anxiety scores were discriminable by these criteria. Horne and Matson (1977) conducted observations behind a one-way mirror, with 1-minute time samples of 24 mannerisms related to anxiety (chewing on nails or a pencil, hand wringing, "fidgety" trunk movements, etc.) gathered from a group of students who were taking a test. Adequate interobserver reliability of the duration of anxious behavior was reported ($r = .78$). Observations are often touted as the most desirable form of obtaining data and as being more "objective" than alternative methods—presumably not subject to the kind of human biases necessarily involved in self-reports. However, the use of observational procedures for measurement of anxiety is rare and the psychological processes considered to be relevant to anxiety (or coping with anxiety) are not very amenable to direct observation. To do so requires that someone monitor people in ego-threatening situations continuously, and somehow have access to their ongoing psychological processes.

Early behaviorists tended to accept behavioral observation data on the basis of their surface validity, but a variety of problems related to their use have been identified over the years. Among these are the complexity of the observation code, observer bias and reliability, "observer drift" in coding behaviors, the reactive nature of the observation process itself, and the high costs of conducting observational procedures. Finally, even a relatively ingenious researcher may be hard put to construct observational procedures or instruments that yield reasonable indirect assessments of all processes related to the anxiety construct. Furthermore, depending upon how the observations are obtained, this procedure may well introduce some element of artificiality in the setting. The very nature of being observed can produce changes in the target behaviors. Several types of behavioral sampling methods might be considered for use, including role-playing, simulations, and naturalistic observations.

Researchers have seldom used unobtrusive measures (Webb, Campbell, Schwartz, & Sechrest, 1966) to assess anxiety. One notable exception is a study by Johnson and Sechrest (1968), in which two trace indices of evaluative anxiety were employed. The first was a measure of "paper messiness," under the assumption that anxious and tense subjects would produce messier and more disorganized papers. The second unobtrusive measure consisted of nonessential marks on the margin (letters, symbols, punctuation marks), assumed to be reflective of increased tension and emotional ventilation. The potential of using these measures has not yet been fully realized in contemporary anxiety research. It may also be challenging to establish validity; for example, disorganization might simply be a function of low motivation or lack of subject knowledge.

Implicit Anxiety Measures

The behavioral assessment of anxiety has been given new impetus by progress in "implicit" measurement of personality. The assumption is that people are often unaware of their own attitudes and emotions. Interest in implicit assessments began with studies of prejudice. Behavioral measures can identify the "unconscious racist" who believes himself or herself to be free of prejudice but would hate to live next door to a person of different race. One of the standard measures in this field is the Implicit Association Test (IAT; Schnabel, Asendorpf, &

Greenwald, 2008). It requires the person to press one of two keys so as to classify stimuli into different groups (e.g., "good" vs. "bad"). In studies of prejudice, the critical condition requires people to perform two classifications within a single block of trials. For example, in a study of anti-Semitic prejudice, the person might have to classify objects as "Jewish" or "non-Jewish," and emotive stimuli as good or bad. The anti-Semite betrays himself by responding slowly in classifying "Jewish" stimuli such as a Star of David or Hebrew script. The assumption is that slow response reflects a person's unconscious (or "implicit") association between Jews and badness. The assessment is objective because it is based solely on the reaction times for the different categories of stimuli, and self-assessment plays no part in it.

The technique can be adapted to measuring personality traits. In this case, what is of interest involves the qualities the person unconsciously associates with "me" (as opposed to "others"). Implicit anxiety can be assessed in relation to the person's association of "me" with qualities relating to anxiety. Egloff and Schmukle (2002) showed that an IAT for anxiety predicted nonverbal expressions of anxiety better than a standard "explicit" questionnaire did. Generally, there is reasonable evidence for the validity of IATs for personality (Schnabel et al., 2008).

Another way to assess anxiety is by orally (via an audio channel) presenting subjects with ambiguous words (e.g., *pain/pane; bury/berry*), which can be variously interpreted. At the same time, anxiety-related words are presented on the screen (Blanchette & Richards, 2003). This is a subtle and implicit measure of anxiety. Anxiety does not bias someone toward perceiving everything as dangerous; it simply heightens people's attention to context and increases the response to whatever is present.

Explicit and implicit measures are only modestly correlated (often about .3), suggesting that there is a shadow personality, which may include anxiety, of which the person is unaware. On the other hand, the psychometric properties of implicit measures, such as their stability over time, sometime fall short of those of conventional measures.

Performance Measures

Performance measures of anxiety (e.g., interview protocols, examination scores, semester grade point averages, course grades, measures of decrements in cognitive functioning, latency and errors in recall of stress-relevant stimulus materials, etc.) assess a wide array of cognitive and academic performances. Most measures in this category are indices of performance designed to provide data about the types of cognitive disruptions that anxious individuals experience in ego-threatening situations when engaged in particular types of cognitive tasks involving learning, complex problem-solving, and short- and long-term memory. Performance measures pose a number of difficult conceptual problems. First and foremost, they focus only superficially on the experience of anxiety. At best, they may be considered to index the effects of anxiety on cognitive behavior. Second, it is hard to determine what are the psychological functions (e.g., encoding, reasoning, short-term memory, judgment) that, when impaired or otherwise affected, are evidence of anxiety or of its effects. Third, it is likely that there are vast individual differences in these psychological processes, quite apart from the effects of anxiety on them.

GENDER AND AGE DIFFERENCES

In the following section, we briefly sketch some gender and age differences in anxiety. Gender, as a correlate of many developmental trends, is commonly claimed to impact upon the development and manifestation of anxiety in a wide variety of situations. Thus, women, compared with men, are said to be more sensitive to a wide array of threatening stimuli (evaluative, ambiguous, and physically harmful) and consequently show more anxiety in the face of these stimuli than men.

Developmental theory and some empirical evidence might lead us to predict an increasing incidence of anxiety with age. As is commonly held, older people are bombarded with manifold life events, transitions, and other external stressors (health crises, decline in physiological functions, loss of social roles, financial insecurity, relocation, loss of mobility, altered social roles, feelings of inadequacy, and loss of self-esteem; diminishing sources of social support, loss of loved ones, awareness of proximity of death, etc.) that threaten their socioemotional, physiological, and economic integrity. Thus, given the greater predominance of negatively evaluated life events experienced by older people, likely to elicit anxiety and other aversive emotional responses, heightened anxiety in old age may be viewed as a natural response to stressful events.

However, we could reasonably make an alternative prediction that age is accompanied by increasing learning and accrued expertise in handling threats, and perhaps some more generic wisdom that supports acceptance of life's ups and downs. In addition, older people may be free from some stressors such as those inherent in pursuing a career and raising children. In fact, the research findings are not consistent and not all studies point to heightened anxiety as a function of advancing age in adulthood. Now, let us turn to the empirical evidence.

Gender Differences

With respect to evaluative anxiety, research has consistently pointed to gender group differences, with female students evidencing higher evaluative anxiety levels than males (Hembree, 1988; Seipp & Schwarzer, 1996). Gender group differences in test anxiety begin to emerge during the middle years of elementary school, with females consistently reporting higher levels of test anxiety scores than males from elementary school through high school and college (Hembree, 1988; Hill & Sarason, 1966). Meta-analytic findings (see Hembree, 1988; Seipp & Schwarzer, 1996) indicate that gender group differences in test anxiety are quite modest, amounting to slightly less than a third of a standard deviation. Furthermore, gender group differences are shown to be of considerably greater magnitude on the Emotionality than on the Worry component of test anxiety. These data support the notion that the affective component of test anxiety is a significant differentiating factor for the sexes.

Recent cross-cultural research among college students (e.g., Baloglu, Abbasi, & Masten, 2007) shows that gender differences vary by nationality. For example, whereas no gender differences on either state or trait anxiety were found among Philippine students, American college women scored higher than men, on average, on trait but not state anxiety. By contrast, Turkish and Mexican females scored higher, on average, than their respective male counterparts on both state and trait anxiety. Ben-Zur and Zeidner (1989) reported higher trait and state anxiety levels among Israeli females as compared with males. They concluded that women are more vulnerable to stress and anxiety than men, even when given exposure to similar stressors.

A meta-analysis of the computer anxiety literature (Rosen & Maguire, 1990) found that women show slightly more computer anxiety than men, although gender differences were minimal and not statistically reliable. These differences were attributed by the authors to differences in early computer experiences or other experiential factors, rather than gender, per se. However, computer anxiety was correlated with sex-role identity: "Feminine" students had more computer anxiety, whereas "masculine" students possess a more positive attitude toward computers.

Math anxiety has received considerable attention for its role in explaining sex-related differences in math achievement and course enrollment patterns (Meece, Wigfield, & Eccles, 1990). However, research bearing on the relationship has not yielded consistent results. Research suggests that it is not gender per se that determines math anxiety, but rather it is the amount of prior experience and interaction with math that predicts level of math anxiety in college students (Richardson & Woolfolk, 1980). Thus, women students with strong math backgrounds who have chosen careers in the science are no more anxious than most men students, and they are less anxious than both male and female students of lesser math sophistication. In fact, the size of gender group differences tends to drop drastically, or may vanish altogether, when math background is controlled for (Betz, 1978; Cooper & Robinson, 1989; Fennema, 1977; Resnick, Viehe, & Segal, 1982). Overall, current research suggests that gender differences in math anxiety may exist (cf. Hembree, 1990), but they are probably much smaller than has been suggested previously, and are probably mediated by math background, course work, and sophistication.

Women are also reported to obtain higher scores than men on measures of social anxiety and public self-consciousness administered during actual testing situations (Sowa & Lafleur, 1986). Endler and his coworkers (e.g., Flett, Hewitt, Endler, & Tassone, 1994/1995) reported that Canadian females tend to be significantly higher on trait anxiety in social evaluations than their male counterparts. The increased degree of public self-consciousness in women may cause them to become more concerned about their personal inadequacies then men and consequently to feel more apprehensive and uncomfortable in social evaluative situations. Systematic and large-scale research on additional demographic correlates of social anxiety is much needed.

Silver et al.'s (2006) Web-based national probability sample of adults 2 months after September 11 reported higher levels of distress anxiety among women than men. He hypothesized that women, who tend to indulge in emotional outlets and use elevated levels of emotion-focused coping, may prolong the ensuing negative state feelings. Furthermore, these results may be perhaps suggestive of some unsatisfactory emotional processing of the traumatic events on the part of females.

How can these gender differences, observed for both social evaluation and physical danger situations, be accounted for? The most prominent account attributes gender group differences to differential patterns of socialization and styles of child-rearing for boys and girls in our culture (cf. Maccoby & Jacklin, 1974). Accordingly, women may be socialized to express and acknowledge anxiety because anxiety is perceived as a feminine trait (Deaux, 1977). Thus, society's reaction to anxiety in women tends to be more of a supporting and reassuring nature, which allows them to admit rather than to hide their anxiety. By contrast, anxiety in modern society is regarded as being incongruent with "masculinity," with males expected to repress or deny anxiety. Furthermore, males may be socialized to view some stressful situations as presenting a challenge to be instrumentally coped with and overcome, whereas for females it may present a threat which requires mainly emotion-focused coping or escape behaviors (Deaux, 1977). The socialization hypothesis also explains cross-cultural differences, given that cultures may differ in their standards for the appropriate ways for anxious males and females to behave. Evidence for generational change, discussed in the next section, also highlights the role of culture.

In view of the findings presented earlier, some researchers have concluded that the observed gender group differences in anxiety do not reflect a real difference in actual levels of anxiety as much as a gender difference in self-presentation and in the willingness to openly admit anxiety (Hill & Sarason, 1966). Although both sexes may actually experience anxiety to a similar degree, the higher level of anxiety among females may be due to males' greater defensiveness about admitting anxiety. Whereas it is regarded as more "socially acceptable" for females to express anxiety, males may be more defensive because manifestations of anxiety show more ego alienation for them; admission to being anxious would be socially disapproved as "unmasculine," particularly during the school years.

A potential challenge to such perspectives comes from evolutionary psychology. It might be argued that it is adaptive for women to be more anxious. Because women are universally the primary caretakers of infants and young children, it might have been particularly adaptive for them to develop particular sensitivity and reactivity to cues of threat and danger in their immediate surroundings, in order to keep their families out of harm's way.

However, although intriguing, it is difficult to obtain conclusive evidence for or against such propositions.

Age Differences

Reviewing the literature, Lowe and Reynolds (2005) report that there is little consensus among researchers on age trends. A large-scale epidemiological study conducted in Scandinavia (Kata, 1975) reports age to be one of the best demographic predictors of anxiety, with positive anxiety-age correlations observed in each of the countries studied. Similarly, a study by Zeidner (1988), based on a probability sample of Israeli adults, reported that trait anxiety means increase linearly by age. Other authors have reported age-related decline in anxiety, whereas work by Lowe and colleagues shows a curvilinear relationship. Anxiety may decrease from childhood and adolescence into adulthood, and then increase again in the elderly.

Much research has also addressed the neuroticism trait that is strongly correlated with trait anxiety and is said to be one of the "Big Five" traits that define personality. The majority of studies using large, representative samples have found that neuroticism declines between the teenage years and old age, although the size of the effect is often modest, and may vary from culture to culture (Lucas & Donnellan, 2009).

Some believe that anxiety in the elderly is qualitatively different from anxiety in younger persons, while others downplay the difference. Some say that current diagnostic criteria do not adequately capture the nature of anxiety in older adults. In community samples, feelings of anxiety are quite commonly reported, by up to 24% of participants, with anxiety disorders much rarer, varying from about 2 to 15%. Thus, key controversies as to the prevalence and nature of anxiety in adults remain unresolved (Bryant, Jackson, & Ames, 2007).

A new twist to the issue is provided by research demonstrating "cohort" differences in anxiety. The idea is that, because of cultural changes, children may be socialized to become more or less vulnerable to anxiety. If we measure anxiety in individuals of the same age, we may find differences in scores between individuals of different generations—that is, baby boomers, Generation X, and so forth. We can examine this possibility by examining the mean scores obtained by people in different years during a given historical period. If we know the birthdates of these individuals, we can separate the influence of year of birth from the influence of the person's age.

A provocative study of this kind (Twenge, 2000) found that Americans shifted substantially toward higher anxiety during the period 1952–1993. The average American child in the 1980s was apparently more anxious than the typical child psychiatric patient in the 1950s. A later study (Twenge et al., 2010) also found evidence for substantial increases in clinical anxiety and psychopathology in American college students, between 1938 and 2007. This generational change should be seen in the context of other cohort changes, toward greater assertiveness, self-esteem, and individualism. Jean Twenge sees these personality changes as reflecting (and perhaps contributing to) the replacement of social connectedness with consumerism as a core value. One of the most striking generational changes is rising narcissism: Twenge has referred to the current generation of young adults as "Generation Me." Thus, rising anxiety is not just some generic threat sensitivity; it may reflect increasing personal insecurity born from unrealistic self-expectations shaped by Western culture.

Generational change is also relevant to the gender differences previously described. The changes described are generally in the direction of a more "masculine" personality, with a devaluing of the emotionally expressive and communal traits traditionally ascribed to women. These changes may be challenging for young women.

SUMMARY AND CONCLUSIONS

We have seen that researchers use a multiplicity of measures to assess trait and state anxiety. Stressful situations typically have effects on various response systems, and so there are potentially several different methods for assessment (i.e., subjective experience, physiology, behavior). Each measurement method possesses unique advantages for anxiety assessment as well as specific and unique limitations. At present, most anxiety measures assess only single facets of this multidimensional construct, failing to assess all the different components of anxiety—that is, subjective experience, physiological changes, self-related cognitions, and behavioral responses (e.g., attempts to avoid or escape).

In questionnaire-based research (and probably research in general), the "gold standard" for the field has been Charles Spielberger's STAI, and a huge amount of research attests to its validity. While it is often appropriate to measure anxiety as a single, unitary construct, there are occasions where a more fine-grained approach is needed. We described how we can discriminate anxiety traits that are geared to different types of threat and context, such as test anxiety, and even motor vehicle operation. Measures for test anxiety have been especially important in discriminating emotion and worry as related but separable facets of anxiety.

While self-report anxiety questionnaires provide the most direct assessment of the subjective facet of anxiety, they may be open to a variety of response biases, including deliberate distortion and defensiveness. By contrast, physiological measures of anxiety are less transparent in terms of being susceptible to conscious distortion, but we saw too that there are various methodological difficulties in using such measures to assess anxiety. It is reasonable to hope that advancements in recording technology, especially in the field of brain imaging (e.g., fMRI), will lead to better objective indices of anxiety. However, it remains debatable whether we can truly say that a measurable brain state *is* anxiety; the psychological aspect is elusive but critical. Objective behavior-based measures tend to be relatively stable measures and less susceptible to distortion, but they are somewhat more "remote" indices and tend to be influenced by numerous other factors apart from anxiety. Because data derived from the various observational domains are relatively independent and frequently exhibit failure of agreement (Eysenck, 1997), it is desirable to obtain measures from all three systems and "triangulate" any observed effects by means of converging operations (Allen, Elias, & Zlotlow, 1980).

Theories and Perspectives on Anxiety

The only thing we have to fear is fear itself.
Franklin D. Roosevelt
There is no terror in a bang, only in the anticipation of it.
Alfred Hitchcock, Attributed to

n chapter 1, we described anxiety and its various facets in general terms. In chapter 2, we surveyed the different measures of anxiety that researchers use. The ability to measure trait and state anxiety, along with all the other facets of anxiety we described, allows researchers to investigate the prevalence, nature, dimensionality, and consequences of anxiety in various experimental studies. In fact, anxiety scales relate to a wide variety of other psychological measures including emotional responses, changes in attention and performance, and real-life outcomes, such as job satisfaction and vulnerability to mental illness. The next step in research is to develop theories that explain how anxiety is generated, how it impacts behavior, and its role in human life. Next, we examine different theories of anxiety in some depth. What are the key neurological and/or mental processes that provoke the various symptoms of anxiety? What are the causal factors that lead to anxiety? Why do individuals differ in their susceptibility to anxiety? What are the consequences of anxiety in terms of psychophysiological, behavioral, and social functioning? Over the years, psychologists have provided a variety of answers to these questions, ranging from analysis of the interplay between id and ego in psychoanalysis, to modern cognitive neuroscience accounts.

This chapter surveys a number of salient theories of anxiety, focusing on models that have been broadly influential. A number of more specific or restricted models of anxiety are treated elsewhere in this book (see chapter 4 for developmental models and chapter 5, Theoretical Perspectives, for models of the anxiety-performance relationship). Each model's unique contributions to understanding the multivariate and complex nature of anxiety will be discussed.

Theories of anxiety are highly diverse, but, for convenience, we will group them into three categories. First, we will look at theories that have been historically influential but have faded into the background of contemporary accounts. These include Freudian psychoanalysis and two models inspired by animal research. Learning theory supposes that anxiety reflects basic conditioning processes. Drive theory proposes that anxiety contributes to the organism's overall strength of motivation ("drive"). Second, we will review modern psychobiological theories which build on the initial insights of learning and drive theory, in the context of a much deeper understanding of the neural systems that regulate anxiety. Third, we will discuss cognitive theories, in which it is biases (or even faults) in the processing of information that produce anxiety and its behavioral correlates.

OF HISTORICAL INTEREST

The Psychoanalytical Model

The psychoanalytical model is one of the earliest and most influential models of anxiety. This model has had an enormous impact on Western thought and modern civilization, contributing to both clinical nomenclature and practice (Pervin, Cervone, & John, 2005). Sigmund Freud, the founder of psychoanalysis, was the first to draw attention to the pivotal role of anxiety in personality dynamics and developmental theory (Freud, 1949). In fact, Freud considered anxiety to be one of the cornerstones of psychoanalytical theory, identifying this emotion as the fundamental symptom in clinical practice. It is interesting to note that Freud may have been informed, in part, by his own experiences, as he personally experienced anxiety attacks, phobias (fear of trains), and bouts of depression. He also used cocaine to calm down his agitation and tension.

For Freud, anxiety appeared automatically whenever the psyche is overwhelmed by an influx of stimuli too great to be mastered or discharged. Anxiety is such an uncomfortable feeling that the individual experiencing it seeks to reduce or eliminate it, just as one would seek to reduce similar drives, such as hunger, thirst, or pain. Freud believed that anxiety can be adaptive if the discomfort that goes with anxiety motivates people to learn new ways of approaching life's challenges. However, it would be generally considered abnormal to feel strong chronic anxiety in the absence of any obvious source of threat, danger, or harm in the environment. As Freud (1949) points out in his introductory lectures to psychoanalysis, only by evaluating one's coping resources—that is, one's strengths in comparison with the magnitude of threat—can one decide whether flight, defense, or even attack is the best way to handle anxiety. These notions remarkably presage Lazarus's (1966) cognitive model of stress and emotions that views coping as the delicate interplay between primary (degree of threat) and secondary (availability of coping resources) appraisal processes (see below).

Types of Anxiety. Freud distinguished three types of anxiety (1959/1926): (a) objective (reality) anxiety, (b) neurotic anxiety, and (c) moral anxiety. This distinction helps to clarify when anxiety is adaptive, and when, as in neurotic anxiety, it is psychologically harmful.

1. *Reality anxiety* is rooted in the real world and refers to the fear and apprehension of a stimulus that is objectively dangerous. This is the kind of fear you experience when there is a realistic danger present, of various kinds: being approached

in an alley by a suspicious panhandler wielding a shining knife, being attacked by a rabid fox, crashing into your father-in-law's new Porsche, or botching up an important assignment at work or school. The danger impinges on the ego and it is basically the ego's job to deal adaptively with the physical environment. Unlike reality anxiety, the next two forms of anxiety originate within the person.

2. *Neurotic anxiety*, the historical root of the trait anxiety concept (Reiss, 1997), is a signal that unconscious material is threatening to enter consciousness. Neurotic anxiety arouses when the ego feels it is going to be overwhelmed by libidinal urges and impulses stemming from the basic impulses of the id (sex, aggression). When libidinal excitation is aroused, the ego attempts to restrain the impulse and repressed anxiety erupts. Neurotic anxiety does not involve fear of the id's urges per se but, rather, fear of punishment that may result from expressing them. The generation of anxiety is the ego's reaction to internal turmoil and conflict and is designed to signal the ego that there is a threat of a breakdown of defenses.

3. *Moral anxiety* refers to people's experience when they are about to violate, or when they have already violated, internalized values or moral codes. Moral anxiety is generated by the conflict between the biological urges of the id and the moral and ideal standards of society represented by the superego. For example, if the moral code forbids cheating (on one's partner or on an examination), and one in fact cheats or is tempted to cheat, the person will feel moral anxiety, where one's conscience is in conflict between the biological impulses of the id and prohibitions of the superego. The impulses are in opposition to moral and ideal standards of society and are subjectively experienced as shame or guilt. The punishment by the superego is at the root of moral anxiety. The three types of anxiety are graphically depicted in Figure 3.1.

Neurotic and moral anxiety tend to provoke defense mechanisms: unconscious ego processes that keep the disturbing and unacceptable impulses from direct expression, often distorting reality. Freud described various defense mechanisms, of which repression is the most fundamental. The dangerous impulse is actively excluded or removed from consciousness. These two forms of internal anxiety can't be easily escaped and

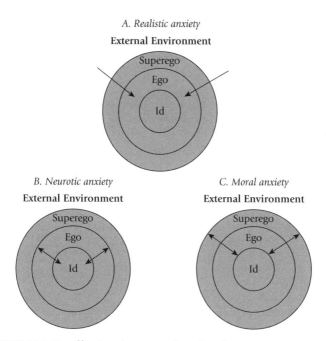

FIGURE 3.1 Freud's tripartite conception of anxiety.

the repressed experiences don't go away but continue to exert a powerful influence on personality. When anxiety increases and defenses are not working, neurotic symptoms are developed. Symptoms are the symbolic representation of the traumatic experience, which is no longer consciously available to the patient (Breuer & Freud, 1955/1895). Figure 3.2 graphically depicts the role of external and internal threats in normal and neurotic anxiety, respectively.

Differing Conceptualizations of Anxiety. Freud revised his conceptualization of anxiety several times throughout his career. In his early writings in the 1890s, Freud initially conceptualized anxiety as a way of relieving libidinal energy that had been blocked or dammed up from direct release. It should be mentioned that Freud and his fellow psychoanalysts were preoccupied with anxiety as a symptom of sexual conflict. Accordingly, anxiety was thought to be largely sexual in origin, with the repressed sexual ideas or libidinal impulses

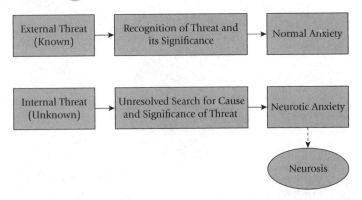

FIGURE 3.2 Freud's view on the role of anxiety in neurotic disorders, graphically depicting the role of external and internal threats on normal and neurotic anxiety, respectively. (Adapted from Tyrer, 1999.)

then transformed into a symbolic representation in the form of anxiety. As Tyrer (1999) remarked: "When Freud looked through the convoluted tunnels of possible explanations for his patient's condition, he always seemed to finish up in the tunnel marked 'sex.' To be more specific, the direction over the tunnel read 'sexual anxiety'" (p. 50).

Accordingly, Freud put forth a "transferred libido" theory of anxiety, theorizing that anxiety is the end product of repressions of unfulfilled or unacceptable sexual impulses. Thus, the development of anxiety is the reaction of the ego to danger from demands of its libido, and the internal danger is converted into an external one, with somatic accompaniments of palpitations, shaking, increased rate of breathing, sweating, and so forth. (Freud, 1949). Interestingly, Galen, the second-century Greek physician, anticipated Freud by 18 centuries, by suggesting that anxiety is due to blocked sexual outlets (Zuckerman, 2005).

Later, Freud came to believe that his original explanation of anxiety as displaced libidinal drives was wrong. Consequently, in the 1920s Freud (1936/1926) revised his theory to state the reverse: Anxiety is the cause of repression and leads to suppression of unsavory thoughts. It signals impending danger, threat, or internal conflict and serves as a call for action and a warning signal to the ego that something bad is about to occur. Whereas normal anxiety could be expressed when there was a known threat, neurotic anxiety was created when there was an unknown threat to the ego. This explained why pathological anxiety was so much more distressing to the person than normal anxiety, as the source of the anxiety could not be identified and therefore became more ominous.

One general guideline in handling anxiety that may be garnered from the psychoanalytic perspective is to try to avoid, whenever possible, both external dangers and internal conflicts; if unavoidable, one should try to deal with them as effectively as possible. It is adaptive to attempt to release libidinal impulses in acceptable ways and measures and at appropriate times. Also, one should probably avoid doing things that run counter to one's conscience, as this might result in superego punishment (Kalat & Shiota, 2007). When anxiety becomes severe enough to generate neurotic symptoms, the person is advised to seek psychoanalysis in order to make the unconscious material conscious and deal with it rationally.

If the truth be told, Freud's theory of anxiety is intriguing, engaging, and extremely rich in theorizing, but it is deficient and lacking in methodological rigor, with little solid empirical evidence to support its basic tenets (Rachman, 2004). In addition, because this theory is drawn primarily from case histories, there is a paucity of reproducible evidence. It provides no systematic way of assessing anxiety, which is critical for testing hypotheses from the theory. Psychoanalysis relies on the subjective judgment of the clinician, which is vulnerable to a variety of biases. Furthermore, in contrast to the basic assumptions of the psychoanalytical model, focusing on a person's sexual urges and sex life, anxiety can be reduced without undertaking a major analysis of a person's sexual life. In fact, most people who suffer from anxiety have satisfactory sexual lives. Freudian theory is generally rejected by modern psychological science, because of its lack of methodological rigor and consequent difficulties in deriving and testing hypotheses that can be falsified by empirical data (Grünbaum, 2001). Perhaps its greatest contribution is to highlight the potential importance of unconscious processes beyond the person's immediate awareness of being anxious. As we saw in the previous chapter, there is increasing interest in measuring unconscious or "implicit" traits through objective, behavioral measures.

Learning Models of Anxiety

Human learning involves long-lasting changes in cognition or behavior due to environmental experiences. According to learning theorists, anxiety is best viewed in terms of behavioral response tendencies learned as a result of the person's cumulative experience with environmental threats over time (Hill, 1972, Pekrun, 1985). It seems reasonable that a person might learn through a series of unfortunate experiences that places, people, and events around which their life revolves are threatening, and, in consequence, become prone to anxiety responses. The scientific principles and models of human learning may be useful in accounting, in part, for an individual's acquisition of anxious behaviors in response to certain environmental stimuli. We look briefly at both classical learning theory and the role of modeling in social-cognitive learning.

Classical Conditioning of Anxious Behaviors. Principles of classical learning may account for both the initial acquisition of anxiety reactions to certain cues or stimuli as well as the maintenance of these reactions over time. The essence of learning theory models of anxiety is that anxiety and fear are acquired by conditioning or other learning processes, and these, in turn, generate escape or avoidance behaviors. The anxiety or fear persists in part because it is at least partly successful in leading to escape or avoidance behavior, followed, in turn, by a significant reduction in anxiety or fear. Such ideas have a long and fruitful history in psychology (Rachman, 2004).

According to one of the original statements of learning theory, any neutral stimulus is potentially capable of being converted into an anxiety-evoking stimulus, via conditioning to an unconditioned anxiety-evoking stimulus, thus acquiring the ability to evoke fear or anxiety subsequently on its own. In the terminology of classical conditioning, an *unconditioned stimulus* is an automatic and unlearned stimulus which elicits an *unconditioned response* (an automatic response). A *conditioned stimulus* is a neutral stimulus which is paired with the unconditioned stimulus and eventually comes to elicit a *conditioned response*, quite similar in nature to the unconditioned response. This would occur if a neutral stimulus (e.g., a social gathering at work) impacted on the individual at about the time the fear reaction was evoked (e.g., following a nasty remark by a superior). Once established, conditioned anxiety reactions take on motivating properties. In an attempt to reduce anxiety, people engage in escape or avoidance behavior (e.g., avoiding a social gathering at work). If this is followed by reduction in anxiety, the behavior becomes strengthened and the anxiety reactions preserved from extinction. Figure 3.3 schematically depicts classical "Pavlovian conditioning." In this example, the sound of a bell (conditioned stimulus) is conditioned to food (unconditioned stimulus), eventually eliciting a salivation response (conditioned response) in a canine.

According to classical conditioning theory, as the pairing of conditioned stimuli (e.g., party contexts) and unconditioned stimuli (e.g., critical remarks) increases in frequency, so does the strength of the conditioned response increase (i.e., social anxiety reactions). Thus, the individuals who are repeatedly exposed to aversive experiences surrounding social situations should learn to associate social contexts with threat and danger and be readily conditioned to respond to such social situations with elevated levels of anxiety. As the intensity of the unconditioned stimulus (e.g., mild rebuke vs. cruel mockery) increases, so does the strength of the conditioned stimulus and the speed in which it appears. Furthermore, anxiety responses may be generalized to a variety of other social stimuli, such

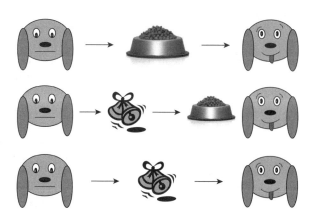

FIGURE 3.3 A graphical depiction of Pavlovian conditioning.

as invitations to attend any social event. Some conditioned anxiety responses may be the result of single traumatic events or a series of subtraumatic events, involving strong nervous system reactions. These conditioned responses that are reinforced are strengthened; those that are not are extinguished and fade away.

Modeling appears to be a particularly promising mechanism for understanding the relationship between an individual's interpersonal relations and behaviors and the development of anxiety proneness and reactions in social contexts. Every family at times faces threats and dangers. Do the parents model a cool, problem-solving demeanor in the face of threat, or do they flap, fuss, and display visible fear? Research attests to the important role which direct observation and modeling of behaviors of significant human models (e.g., parents, siblings, teachers, peers, coworkers, supervisors, and mentors) may play in the learning of social and affective responses (Bandura, 1965). In fact, much social learning is made possible by exposure to real-life models that perform, intentionally or unwittingly, patterns of behaviors that may be imitated by others. Bandura's (1997) theory supposes that the child's sense of self-efficacy (being able to perform the actions necessary to pursue its goals) derives from modeling as well as from direct experience and instruction in challenging contexts. Self-efficacy is represented as a cognitive structure that shapes the child's reactions to challenges, fostering a "can-do" attitude.

Similarly, complex emotional response patterns, such as elevated anxiety reactions in physical danger or socially threatening situations, may be acquired observationally by witnessing the arousal, tension, concern, and expressed worry of relevant models (real or symbolic) undergoing a physical challenge or an evaluative encounter. Modeling may, in part, explain gender differences in anxiety; fathers are perhaps less likely to model anxiety for their sons than mothers are for their daughters. Cross-cultural differences in emotional expression, such as the restraint in emotional displays typical of East Asian cultures, may also reflect modeling. In addition to modeling of others' behaviors, anxiety reactions may be further shaped and strengthened by observing one's own anxiety-related reactions in stressful encounters (Pekrun, 1985).

Learning theory is more soundly based than psychoanalysis, and it continues to contribute to contemporary theory. Evidently, people can learn to associate fear or anxiety with intrinsically harmless stimuli that signal danger, and their history of conditioning may persistently affect current emotions. However, learning theories in their original form have fallen out of favor for two reasons. First, we appear to be biologically prepared to condition fear more readily to some stimuli than to others. Many more people are afraid of spiders than of electrical outlets. Contemporary biopsychological theories reject the idea of an essentially arbitrary conditioning process in favor of accounts that accommodate our evolutionary heritage. This perspective requires that we look more closely at the brain structures that regulate response to threat stimuli, as we will discuss shortly. Second, cognitive theorists have argued that learning is often mediated by internal cognitive representations. Thus, social anxiety is much more than a set of conditioned reflex responses to social stimuli. The socially anxious person builds an internal model of how social situations develop, and how such situations pose threats that are difficult for him or her to manage. The impact of social stimuli is filtered via this internal belief system, even though it may be unrealistic. Cognitive models have been especially influential among researchers on social learning processes. Bandura's observations of the importance of modeling continue to provide an important pillar for social-cognitive perspectives on learning. In sum, learning is important in anxiety, but we cannot satisfactorily explain human anxiety on the basis of a single learning mechanism.

Drive Theory

Another influential learning theory of anxiety, Spence and Spence's (1966) drive theory, was based on Hull's (1943) learning theory. Hull was concerned with how motivation influenced the execution of learned responses. He began with the obvious point that conditioned behaviors are more likely to be performed if they meet an immediate motivational need. A person may have learned that inserting a dollar bill into a vending machine will deliver a Coke, but if he or she is not thirsty, he or she will feel no compulsion to perform the behavior. In detail, Hull's theory is rather complex, but we will touch upon a number of basic drive theory concepts. To begin with, *drive* (*D*) refers to the various need states of an individual that combine to determine his or her total level of motivation at a particular time. Drive is viewed as a global energizer resulting from motivational states within the person. Another important concept, *habit strength* (*H*), is defined as the strength of the tendency to make a particular response to a specific stimulus, based on previous conditioning (the frequency of past reinforcement of a particular response). Turning to response, *excitatory potential* (*E*) is defined as the statistical probability that a particular response or set of responses will occur. Essentially, Hull's formulation was that response strength = motivation × strength of conditioning of the response. More exactly, we can write Excitatory potential = Drive × Habit strength, or, succinctly, $E = D \times H$. Thus, a person would be most likely to feed a bill into a vending machine (high *E*) if (a) he or she is extremely thirsty (high *D*), and (b) he or she had successfully used vending machines many times previously (high *H*).

Spence and Spence's (1966) version of drive theory broadly equates anxiety with Hull's concept of drive: anxiety is essentially motivation. The consequence of anxiety is then a broad activation of responses, including those that are not directly relevant to the task at hand. Loosely, drive theory sees the anxious person as being in a kind of hyperactive state, spraying out responses of various degrees of relevance to the current situation, including verbal responses. (Our older readers may recall Woody Allen in his early comedies.) The theory makes a basic, testable prediction that anxiety should impair performance in situations where there is high response competition—that is, various incorrect responses are available that may compete with selection of the correct response (Spence & Spence, 1966). For example, recalling the largest city in Illinois probably evokes only a single response (Chicago), whereas recalling the largest city in Texas is liable to evoke two competing responses (Dallas and Houston). Anxious individuals should be especially prone to pick the wrong response in the latter situation (high response competition). Spence and Spence (1966) were able to find evidence from studies of memory and learning in favor of this hypothesis.

Another way of deriving testable predictions from the theory is to link drive to the different but related concept of general arousal, referring to the overall level of activation of the cerebral cortex of the brain. As further discussed in chapter 5 (Anxiety and Cognitive Performance), the so-called Yerkes-Dodson Law proposes that there is a curvilinear relationship between arousal and performance, resembling an inverted-U shape. That is, moderate levels of arousal are best, whereas performance is impaired when arousal is low (e.g., sleepiness) or high (e.g., emotional agitation). Excessive arousal is particularly damaging to difficult tasks, which, from a drive theory perspective, may be those that activate multiple competing responses. It follows that anxious individuals should be prone to high arousal and should perform badly across a range of difficult tasks. Conversely, on easy tasks, anxiety may actually be an advantage, because the single dominant response is energized strongly. Again, there is some evidence that on difficult tasks anxious subjects perform at a lower level as compared with their less anxious counterparts (Eysenck, 1982), although data showing enhanced performance of easy tasks in anxiety states are less consistent (Tobias, 1985). Another prediction that has received some support is that anxiety should be detrimental early in learning, where the person has not strongly conditioned the correct response, but facilitative later in learning, where there is only a single dominant response (e.g., Lekarczyk & Hill, 1969).

Drive theory performed a valuable service in highlighting the motivational side of anxiety; certainly, anxiety states often seem to add urgency to behavior. Unfortunately, the theoretical underpinning of the theory, Hull's drive theory, has been largely abandoned. Its central proposition that motivational strength can be captured by a single "drive" factor is untenable: $E = H \times D$ is no $E = mc^2$. Hull himself was obliged to add various terms to his equation, such as variables reflecting the presence of incentives, in order to deal with snowballing empirical problems. Modern motivational theory typically separates positive and negative motivations rather sharply, although, as we shall see, it retains the idea of a system dedicated to regulating the impact of punishment stimuli on behavior. Anxiety is related not to "drive" but to escape and avoidance motivation.

Although the Spence and Spence (1966) theory broadly predicts the vulnerability of anxious individuals to error when performing difficult tasks, it has turned out to be a rather weak basis for predicting behavioral effects of anxiety. Understanding the impact of anxiety on both social behaviors and task performance typically requires understanding of the cognitive structures that mediate anxiety effects. Indeed, the model is limited in scope by the fact that it best applies to those kinds of learning that are of least interest in academic or practical settings—that is, relatively simple tasks whose respective habits and strengths and competing response tendencies could be well specified. In fact, this model can only make definite predictions about the effects of anxiety on performance provided there is detailed information available about the relative strengths of all relevant responses and the location of response thresholds; such an analysis is difficult, if not impossible, to conduct in typical social or performance situations.

BIOLOGICAL PERSPECTIVES

Evolutionary Perspectives

Over a century ago, Charles Darwin (1872) discerned that the communication and expression of emotions has considerable survival utility. Accordingly, emotional expression (facial expressions, posturing, action tendencies, etc.) serves to signal messages to others in the social group so that behavior and action can be smoothly coordinated and imminent danger avoided or circumvented. Darwin discerned that facial expressions associated with anxiety, which are universally recognized, alert others to the situation (potential future threat, danger, prospects for loss), and inform others of the threat. Anxiety is a functional emotion with deep evolutionary origins, reflecting the fact that the earth has always been a hazardous environment to inhabit and humans have always needed to be on the watch for dangers in the environment (Ohman, 2008). Thus, since the beginning of mankind, predators, competitive and aggressive humans, and unhealthy toxins in the environment have been a source of danger. Given that fitness involves survival and passing on genes, organisms have developed certain mechanisms—that is, fear and anxiety—to deal with threat in the environment. Hence, in order to stay alive, thrive, avoid danger in the environment, and pass on one's genes to the next generation, anxiety and fear are central to mammalian evolution.

In modern evolutionary psychology (Ohman, 2008; Panskepp, 1998; Rachman, 2004), emotions are universal hard-wired affect programs designed to serve as barometers of ego functioning. Thus, emotions such as anxiety serve as an "online" indicator of how successful, or not, we are in adapting to the threats and challenges in our immediate environment (Keltner & Haidt, 2001). A functional view of "anxiety as information" suggests that this emotion represents and signals to the individual relevant information concerning danger in the face of uncertainty. Thus, if we do get anxious and upset, this is *prima facie* evidence that something important is at stake and we perceive that our personal resources are being endangered or threatened. Often, the threat is social in nature—for example, the dangers of losing physical resources (e.g., food) to others, social status, or the affections of a loved one.

According to Ohman (2008), basic fears and anxieties reflect evolutionarily shaped behavioral systems. Social anxiety is hypothesized to originate in a dominance-submissiveness system; the adaptive function was to promote survival within such a social order. Also, fear of animals originated in prehistoric humans' fears of predators. Indeed, modern man may react with fear to stimuli that once threatened the survival of his ancestors (e.g., open spaces, loud noises, heights) but have little if any threat value at present. A factor analysis of common fears by Arrindel, Pickersgill, Merkelbach, Ardon, and Cornet (1991) identified four classes of fear: (a) interpersonal events (e.g., evaluation, fear of criticism, rejection, conflict, interpersonal aggression), (b) fear related to physical injury (death, illness, etc.), (c) fear of animals (domestic, creeping, crawling), and (d) fear of open spaces (agoraphobia). Of course, whether anxiety can be associated with specific fears is debatable.

Anxiety disorders may also be explained by evolutionary accounts. Thus, in order to guarantee effective defense when life is at stake, the system is programmed in a biased fashion to "play it safe" by activating defenses to what may turn out to be nondangerous situations. An organism that tends to be jumpy will more likely survive than one that is oblivious to danger.

Anxiety disorder may reflect an extreme case of the "better safe than sorry" principle.

Functional Neurobiological Perspectives

If the evolutionary perspective is correct, the brain must have evolved to contain one or more neural systems that help orchestrate and coordinate perceptual, physiological, and behavioral channels that promote survival in the face of danger. Neurobiologists in fact have several ways of approaching anxiety. Whereas some researchers feel that the natural place to seek understanding is to look at the molecular biology in analyzing the genetic mechanisms that transmit biological propensities, others believe that neural circuits are the place to seek understanding of anxiety, while others favor investigating the specific neurotransmitters and hormones subserving anxiety and fear. Before reading this section, the student is forewarned that some of the material is advanced and quite challenging at times. If you feel cognitively overwhelmed by any of the sections below, feel free to gloss over the material and return to it at some later time.

Just over a century ago, Freud lamented that we know practically nothing about the functional neurobiology of anxiety in the brain (Panksepp, 1998). Fortunately, recent decades have seen dramatic progress in research on the neurobiological substrates of anxiety and fear. Current research suggests that anxiety is not localized in one specific brain structure. Instead, researchers typically seek to identify brain systems that react to threat stimuli and modulate other brain circuits so as to affect physiological and behavioral response. Linking anxiety to a system or circuit within the brain matches the functional perspective suggested by evolutionary theory. Anxiety is a sign that the brain is *doing* something—more specifically, to analyze and respond to threat or potential punishment.

One of the pioneering theories in the field, put forth by Eysenck (1967), was compatible with the learning and drive theories already discussed. Anxiety was said to be generated by what Eysenck rather quaintly termed the *visceral brain* (hippocampus, amygdala, septum, and hypothalamus), which today is more commonly termed the *limbic system,* shown in Figure 3.4. These limbic structures (amygdala, entorhinal cortex, hypothalamus, hippocampus, fornix, etc.) are commonly linked to emotion and

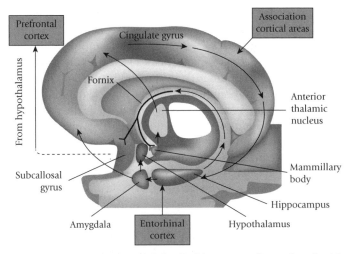

FIGURE 3.4 Key structures of the limbic system. (Reproduced with permission from Springer Publishing Company.)

motivation, and, in evolutionary terms, are more primitive than the cerebral cortex, which is the site of higher cognitive functions, such as language and thought. The limbic system controls subjective experience and autonomic emotional response, particularly in potentially stressful environments. Its activation by emotive stimuli was associated with increases in both cortical arousal, and the autonomic nervous system, as reflected in the elevated tonic levels of heart rate, skin conductance, and blood pressure. Individuals of anxious or "neurotic" personality were said to have a visceral brain that was readily activated.

Attempts at empirical vindication of Eysenck's model represent a rather confused picture (Eysenck, 1992b), although most theorists would agree on the importance of the limbic system for anxiety (as well as other emotions). Zuckerman (1994) argued that we should not confine our search for biological determinants of anxiety to the limbic system, because it is likely that multiple neurotransmitters and brain pathways are implicated in anxiety. The slower responses of the endocrine system are also significantly involved. Anxiety is related to the activity of the HPAC (hypothalamic-pituitary-adrenal-cortical) system activated during stressful encounters, which leads to cortisol secretion from the adrenal cortex.

Sapolsky's (1992) seminal work on the role of the HPAC in stress suggests that the hippocampus may play a role in anxiety by processing more explicit memories from higher cortical areas and modulating the amygdala responses and output of the HPAC system, originating in the hippocampus. Prolonged emotional stress can kill neurons in the hippocampus and alter trait anxiety, sometimes irreversibly. Prolonged stress and anxiety has also been found to be related negatively to entire brain volume relative to the remainder of intracranial volume. Thus, stress and trait anxiety over time can decrease brain volume and can produce deficits in memory processing and functional ability to inhibit emotional reactions.

How can we move beyond the position that anxiety corresponds to some (rather generic) negative emotion system in the brain? More recent neurobiological work takes two rather different tacks. One perspective looks backward, in an evolutionary sense, to research the brain systems in lower mammals. The assumption is that anxiety is much the same in all mammalian species, and that studies of rats, for example, can serve to identify the key brain structures and their functional role in handling threat. The amygdala, a small structure within the limbic system, is attributed a central role. A second perspective is more human-centric and is concerned with how the brain regulates as well as generates anxiety. A central concern is how areas of the cerebral cortex (traditionally linked to higher-order cognition) regulate the activity of the lower-level limbic system structures. Indeed, recent research links anxiety to brain areas that are seen as interfacing emotion and higher-order cognition including the cingulate cortex (supporting executive control of cognition) and insula (supporting awareness of body states). In the next sections, we will describe research that illustrates these perspectives.

The Amygdala: A Key Structure for Anxiety. Aggleton and Mishkin (1986) have described the amygdala as the "sensory gateway to the emotions." It is the amygdala, it appears, that has received the lion's share of interest and systematic research on the neural underpinnings of anxiety (LeDoux, 1996). Brain-imaging studies using functional magnetic resonance imaging suggest that the amygdala "lights up" or becomes activated when such threatening stimuli as angry faces are presented.

Indeed, Kubota et al. (2000) found that exposure to pictures of a threatening face evoke amygdala response, even when the viewer does not report consciously seeing the face at all. The amygdala is believed to be "hard-wired" by evolution to respond to natural threats such as predators.

One of the key functions of the amygdala is to interrupt ongoing activity in order to enhance processing of threats and support quick responses to dangerous situations. The amygdala may also be responsible for unconscious emotional learning, which is automatic and impulsive, as opposed to more conscious processing and memories, which are processed in the hippocampus and parts of the prefrontal cortex. Furthermore, the amygdala stores emotion memories and may modulate memories in other areas as well and helps retrieve them rapidly and efficiently in times of need. A final function of this small but mighty organ is to activate many of the various components of fear behaviors, including increased respiration, heart rate, behavioral "freezing," and analgesia. (We may note that the amygdala is made of various different nuclei that perform different functions.)

Intriguingly, genes that relate to amygdala function may also relate to individual differences in anxiety. Hariri and Holmes (2006) review research on a gene known as 5-HTTLPR, which influences the serotonin neurotransmitter. The gene exists in different versions, or *alleles*, which vary from person to person. The version known as the S allele is reliably related to trait anxiety or harm avoidance, as well as impaired capacity to cope with stress. Function-imaging studies pinpointed the amygdala as a brain region with exaggerated reactivity to emotionally provocative stimuli in S allele carriers, paving the way for future research to elucidate the precise neural mechanisms underlying the behavioral abnormalities associated with this gene variant. Overall, a single gene variant such as the 5-HTTLPR would be expected to contribute only a small amount of the overall interindividual variance within the milieu of other genetic and environmental influences.

A systemic view is provided by Panksepp (1998). He has posited the existence of a separate fear circuit of the brain mediating fear and anxiety, coursing between the central amygdala, the periaqueductal gray, and the mesolimbic system (Panksepp,

1998). More specifically, this system extends from the temporal lobe (central and lateral amygdala), through the anterior and medial hypothalamus. It projects to the lower brain stem, through periventricular gray substrata of the diencephalon and mesencephalon. It then continues down to activate the various autonomic and behavioral outputs produced by fear. Minor tranquillizers may exert their anti-anxiety effects by decreasing arousal in this system.

As Gray (1990) pointed out, the theory assumes that human anxiety is equivalent to unconditional escape behaviors (fight or flight). It also has little use for higher-level cognition and language processing. These assumptions may be problematic. One of the features of human anxiety (by contrast with fear) is indecisiveness and reflection on alternative courses of action, experienced as worry. Worrying is often supported by verbal processes and it is unclear that it can be effectively captured by an animal model.

An other relevant theory assigns a kind of secondary support role to higher-level cognition in anxiety. Research in LeDoux's lab demonstrated that there is both a *high road* and a *low road* to processing of incoming sensory stimuli, providing an outline of the fear reaction system (see Figure 3.5). The amygdala receives two parallel inputs supporting threat processing. The "low road" is a "quick-and-dirty" system for fast detection of threat without the need for cognitive processing. The thalamus receives sensory input and projects directly to the amygdala, which in turn can activate the fight-or-flight response. Although this quick circuit can't tell the amygdala exactly what is out there, it can provide a fast signal that warns that something dangerous may be there. We can thus begin to respond to potentially dangerous stimuli before we fully know what the stimulus is. The thalamus also transmits sensory information to the cerebral cortex, which can perform a more detailed analysis, taking into account contextual factors. The cortex in turn has connections with the amygdala, which modulate its activity. This indirect, "high road" provides a second pathway which, on occasion, can override the influence of the direct connection from thalamus to amygdala.

LeDoux (1996, 2006) gives the example of flinching away from a "snake" in his backyard at night, which turned out to be

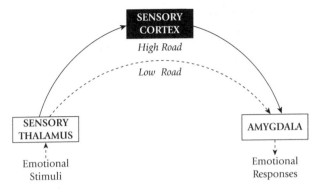

FIGURE 3.5 Parallel circuits in processing emotional information: low and high roads. (Adapted from LeDoux, 1996.)

a garden hose. The low road rapidly processes the coiled shape as a snake and initiates the escape response, before the person has much conscious awareness of the event. The "high road" correctly identifies the object as harmless but takes longer to do so before it eventually suppresses activation of the amygdala and the experience of activity. In fact, LeDoux's studies of rodents suggested that the thalamic-amygdala pathway is very fast indeed, taking about 12 ms, compared to 40 ms or more for the high-road circuit.

However, it should be remembered that the brain's reaction is always a function of the person's mental set, expectations, and private interpretations of an event and that these processes recruit activity in neural circuits that are not the same across individuals. Popular opinion in the behavioral neuroscience literature posits that activity in the amygdala mediates any overt behavior regarded as unfamiliar or aversive or symbolic of threat, with the amygdala contributing to the acquisition and experience of behaviors presumed to be signs of fear in animals (e.g., body immobility, increased startle response, reluctance to explore unfamiliar areas).

Finally, it is of interest that the amygdala may be the only neuroanatomical structure that has a rock band named after it—the *Amygdaloids*—with neuroscientist Joseph LeDoux as guitarist and vocalist. Their original songs are all about mental life and mental disorders ("A Trace," "Memory Pill," "An Emotional Brain," "Inside of Me," and "Mind-Body Problem"). Their latest album (see album cover in Figure 3.6) contains such potential hits as "Fearing," "Brainstorm," and "Crime of Passion." Curiously, the Amygdaloids call their music "Heavy Mental."

Reinforcement Sensitivity Theory. Another "systems" model of anxiety is the Reinforcement Sensitivity Theory (RST) developed by Gray, and subsequently modified by Corr (2009). In its current form, it distinguishes three brain systems for motivation and emotion. The behavioral activation system regulates response to reward stimuli (and signals of reward). The fight-flight-freeze system (FFFS) is activated by all aversive stimuli and regulates escape and avoidance behaviors. Anxiety is mediated by a distinct, second system, the behavioral inhibition system (BIS) of the brain. The BIS is activated by

FIGURE 3.6 Cover of latest album of the Amygdaloids, titled "Theory of My Mind" (J. LeDoux, second from left; reprinted with permission by J. LeDoux).

conflicts between competing goals, such as approach-avoidance conflicts—think of a snarling pit bull standing over a $100 bill. In conflict situations, the BIS inhibits ongoing behavior, increases vigilance for potential threats, and increases arousal. The BIS has a rather more "cognitive" nature than the brain systems discussed in the previous section, in that it initiates risk assessment scanning of memory to resolve goal conflicts, an activity experienced as worry and rumination. Anatomically, it is based on frontal areas as well as the limbic system. Figure 3.7 graphically depicts key inputs and outputs of the BIS.

Four major types of stimuli activate the BIS and serve as primary *inputs* to the BIS system (Gray & McNaughton, 2003). These are: (a) signals of punishment, (b) signals of nonreward, (c) novel stimuli, and (d) evolutionary salient innate fears (e.g., fears of loud noise, heights, insects, rodents) and threatening social encounters of stimuli (Gray & McNaughton, 2003). According to Gray's theory, these stimuli are basically functionally equivalent, in that they each activate the BIS and evoke anxiety. The *outputs* of the system involve various forms of conflict resolution, including (a) behavioral inhibition, where all ongoing behavior, whether innate or instrumental or classically conditioned, is inhibited; (b) orienting response; and (c) elevated arousal and increased attention. Corr (2009) argues, from animal models, that fear and anxiety tend to have different behavioral consequences, with fear promoting defensive avoidance (including flight) and anxiety eliciting a defensive approach (e.g., cautious exploration). Behavioral effects of the FFFS and BIS also depend on "defensive distance," the proximity of the threat. A rat cornered by a cat may fight back, whereas

FIGURE 3.7 Gray's model of the behavioral inhibition system, showing inputs and outputs of the system. (Adapted from Gray & McNaughton, 2003.)

it will run from a cat at a greater distance. RST also provides an explanation for individual differences in trait anxiety, which reflect the sensitivity of the BIS to the various inputs listed earlier (Corr, 2009). In this theory, the anxious person is not necessarily highly fearful, but is someone prone to conflicts between competing goals, a definition that captures the uncertainty and indecisiveness that often accompany anxiety.

However, like other psychobiological theories, the RST raises the issue of the extent to which animal models of emotion can be generalized to humans. As aptly pointed out by Eysenck (1992b), any realistic model of anxiety would need to consider the complex, independent functioning of cognitive, physiological, and behavioral systems, and not rely on neurobiological systems alone. Specifically, although the model incorporates constructs such as goals and expectancies, it does not provide a detailed account of the cognitive aspects of anxiety that are critical for its effects on performance, and for understanding how anxiety relates to distorted perceptions of the self and environmental threats. Zuckerman (2005) takes issue with theories such as those of Eysenck and Gray because they assume a one-to-one mapping (isomorphism) between anxiety and focal brain systems. Anxiety is no more than the state of excitation of the BIS, in the RST. As Zuckerman sees it, the complexity of the brain is such that a key personality trait, such as anxiety, most likely relates to several brain systems, and any given brain system may contribute to two or more personality traits. Brain systems are typically functionally interdependent. Also, associations between activity of systems and traits may be nonlinear.

Regulation of Emotion. Another strand of psychobiological research is concerned with the "top-down" regulation of emotion by higher-level cognitive processes. LeDoux's "high road," through which the cortex projects to the amygdala, represents a simple mechanism of this kind, but recent research, often using brain-imaging techniques, provides more sophisticated models of control. The interplay between brain centers for cognition and emotion also matches current psychological research on the self-regulative processes that allow us to avoid being "carried away" by our emotions or otherwise act stupidly or impulsively.

As previously mentioned, some of the key structures are located in the frontal lobes of the brain, specifically structures known as the prefrontal cortex and the anterior cingulate. Brain-imaging studies suggest that the prefrontal cortex is activated when the person is trying to actively reappraise some emotive stimulus—that is, rethinking its personal significance (Ochsner & Gross, 2005). Reappraisal may indeed influence emotional experience and the activity of the amygdala. (To the extent that reappraisals depend on what the person makes of his or her own emotion, the process is a two-way street.)

The prefrontal cortex may also be involved in the persistence of emotion over time. One of the salient features of anxiety and worry states is that they tend to hang around, even when the stimulus that initially provoked anxiety has disappeared. Persistent activity in a neural circuit connecting the amygdala and prefrontal cortex may maintain one's attention to one's concerns, which is experienced as rumination or worry. Consistent with this hypothesis, highly neurotic individuals show more sustained activation of the prefrontal cortex following presentation of sad facial expressions (Canli, 2009). Like the other structures we discuss here, the prefrontal cortex can be divided into several smaller, more specialized nuclei. Interestingly, the specific structure in which activation was sustained in the research described by Canli (2009) was the medial prefrontal cortex, which is believed to relate to self-referential emotional processing. Perhaps the neurotic individuals in the experiment saw some personal significance in the sad faces they viewed. It is important to note that the prefrontal cortex supports a variety of other cognitive functions in addition to emotion regulation, notably working memory. Discriminating these multiple processes and their interaction is a considerable challenge for research.

The anterior cingulate is directly connected to the prefrontal cortex and is also believed to play a central role in cognitive control. However, it is believed to function as an error detection system that supports effortful performance when tasks are difficult. Canli (2009) suggests that the anterior cingulate has a "tuning" function so that responsiveness to negative stimuli is enhanced when the individual is in a negative mood. Studies reviewed by Canli (2009), based on the emotional Stroop test, broadly confirm that anxiety may be associated with the response of this structure to emotional conflict.

The focus on cognitive regulation of emotion has also inspired studies focusing specifically on the cortical processes that may support regulation. Negative emotion has been related to asymmetry in the activation levels of the two cerebral hemispheres. Specifically, negative emotions including fear and anger appear to be associated with right hemisphere dominance (Carmona, Holland, & Harrison, 2009). These authors also describe some complexities in the literature, such as differences between patients with generalized anxiety and those with panic disorder. For example, high arousal tends to provoke right hemisphere activation, especially in generalized anxiety disorder patients. Verbally mediated worrying may also be associated with left hemisphere activity. According to Davidson (2002), whereas the right prefrontal cortex potentiates fear reaction, the left prefrontal cortex is involved in inhibition of anxiety through extinction; the lateralization extends down to the amygdala. Right amygdaloid reactions predicted trait anxiety, with the right side involved in unconscious processing of anxiety, whereas the left side serves more conscious emotional learning. Furthermore, individual differences in anxiety may be more a function of prefrontal regulation of emotion than of amygdalar activation.

Overall, the entire brain appears to be involved in the generation of anxiety. A number of systems contribute jointly to the brain's overall emotional response of anxiety, including Panskepp's fear system, the amygdala and extended amygdala, the hippocampal-septal system, and numerous others. It is, however, still unclear how these various brain systems create the phenomenal experience of anxiety, as they do, leading to widespread manifestations of anxiety in the human psyche.

COGNITIVE MODELS

Appraisal Theories

The core idea of cognitive models of anxiety is that feelings are expressions of thinking (though not necessarily conscious thinking). A widely accepted view in the cognitive theory of emotion is that emotions reflect *appraisals*—evaluations of the personal significance of stimuli and events. A classic study was performed by Richard Lazarus (Lazarus & Alfert, 1964).

He had participants watch a gruesome film of a tribal rite involving bodily mutilation (we will spare our male readers, in particular, the gruesome details). He also manipulated appraisal by giving different groups of subjects different orientations to the content of the film. Instructions that emphasized denial or intellectual detachment from the pain experienced by the protagonists not only lowered subject distress in the viewer, but also physiological signs of anxiety such as skin conductance.

Broadly, anxiety is generated by appraisals of events as personally threatening. Appraisal theorists (e.g., Lazarus, 1991; Scherer, 2009) go beyond this commonsense point of view to specify in some details the information processing that supports cognitive appraisal. For example, uncertainty over threat may be a key appraisal process in anxiety. Scherer's theory also posits multiple levels of appraisal operating in parallel, ranging from low-level stimulus analysis performed by neural circuits that respond to "biological" threats such as snakes, to conscious evaluation of stimulus meaning. Thus, anxiety emerges from a complex and dynamic sequence of processes that extract the personal significance of each stimulus. Figure 3.8 depicts the key appraisals components of the transactional model proposed by Lazarus.

Cognitive models do not deny the importance of brain processes. However, they assume that working with the "virtual" information processes of the mind is more informative than working directly with neurophysiology. The idea is similar to understanding how a computer application like a word processor functions by examining the program as software, rather than in terms of current flowing through a silicon chip.

Current cognitive models go beyond identifying anxious emotion with appraisal processes and address the dynamics of cognition. Anxiety is not like a pop-up window that appears in consciousness briefly before being closed down again. Instead, there is an internal flow and sequence of processing geared toward accomplishing personal goals, of which the threat appraisal is only a limited part. External dynamics involve how anxiety arises in the context of the person's interactions with the outside world. External pressures require the person to find ways of coping with events that may change the nature of those

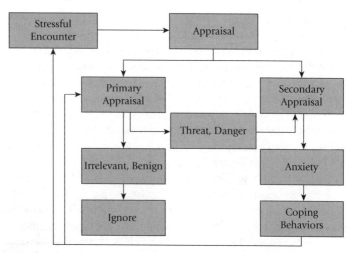

FIGURE 3.8 Transactional model of stress and anxiety. (Based on Lazarus & Folkman, 1984.)

pressures (reducing them if coping is effective). Anxiety may then describe a style of interaction between the person and the external environment, characterized by a sense of one's being overwhelmed by events, and uncertainty over the best coping strategy.

Internal dynamics are characterized by self-regulation models that describe how goal-directed behavior is regulated by feedback signals. Anxiety corresponds in part to a certain type of negative feedback signal that tells the person that accomplishing significant goals are under threat. This feedback elicits coping efforts that are intended to counter threats and maintain progress toward personal goals. Unfortunately, anxiety often leads to counterproductive coping efforts such as protracted but ineffectual worrying about problems. In this section, we look briefly at interactionist models of person-situation interaction and at self-regulation models that focus on the internal cognitive dynamics of anxiety.

State-Trait Interactional and Transactional Models of Anxiety

Lazarus's (1999) transactional model of stress and emotion is a landmark cognitive model, which continues to shape much contemporary research. Emotions are *relational* constructs that, so to speak, tell us how the person stands in relation to external demands, pressures, and opportunities. Thus, stressful encounters, including those that elicit anxiety, typically unfold over extended periods of time. Anxiety over losing your job may, over several months, be driven initially by negative comments from your boss, followed by a formal firing process, loss of salary and health insurance, criticism from your spouse, and uncertainty over future job prospects. At each stage, you may try different strategies to cope (pleading with your boss, acquiring new job skills, drinking heavily), which, in turn, have a varying impact on the pressures experienced. Appraisal is thus a continuing process which drives coping efforts, and is itself shaped by feedback on the perceived success of coping efforts, as well as changes in external circumstances beyond the person's own control. Thus, anxiety depends on both the external events themselves and how the individual appraises them and copes with them over time.

There are substantial individual differences in these cognitive processes. Individuals differ in their appraisals; for example, pessimism about the eventual outcome will tend to elevate anxiety. They also differ in self-appraisals. People with the positive, can-do attitude, described as self-efficacy, will anticipate successful coping, mitigating anxiety. People also differ in their actual coping skills and resources. Losing one's job is much less threatening if you are confident that you have sought-after skills that will be attractive to other employers.

Several theorists have developed interactional models that represent these basic principles. As we discussed in chapters 1 and 2, Spielberger's (1972a, 1972b, 1972c) *State-Trait Model* of anxiety made the useful distinction between anxiety as a stable personality trait (A-Trait) and anxiety as a transient emotional state (A-State). Building on the transactional theoretical framework of stress proposed by Lazarus (Lazarus & Folkman, 1984), and his own state-trait theory of anxiety, Spielberger proposed that anxiety is a dynamic process (Spielberger, 1972a, 1972b; Spielberger & Vagg, 1987, 1995a, 1995b). His model emphasizes the interaction between personality traits and environmental stressors in determining anxiety states and underscores the crucial role of cognitive appraisals as mediating factors

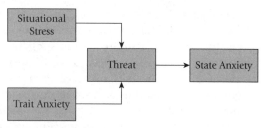

FIGURE 3.9 Spielberger's interactional state-trait model of anxiety. (Based on Spielberger 1972b, 1972c.)

between persons and situations in impacting upon state anxiety. Accordingly, the model differentiates between the objective properties of ego-threatening situations that are potentially stressful, the subjective interpretation of a particular situation as more or less threatening for a particular person (threat), the emotional states that are evoked in stressful situations (such as state anxiety), the coping reactions and responses to the aversive emotional state (defensive behaviors, palliative and instrumental forms), and adaptive outcomes (see the graphical depiction of the model in Figure 3.9).

Spielberger further emphasized how the different components of anxiety may come into play during the temporal sequence of events unfolding in a stressful encounter. Accordingly, the affective and cognitive concomitants of anxiety may provide additional negative feedback that further alters the appraisal of a situation as more or less threatening. For instance, a person who reacts to an important competitive sports situation with heightened degrees of tension, hyperventilation, profuse sweating, stomach cramps, and worries about choking, may assess the event as being uncontrollable and even more threatening than at the outset, thus elevating state anxiety levels. Feedback from increased anxiety, in turn, may lead an anxious athlete to reappraise the sports event as more threatening, resulting in a further elevation of state anxiety, with the athlete caught up in a vicious cycle of negative appraisal and spiraling anxiety reactions.

Self-Control (Regulation) Model of Anxiety

Spielberger's model starts with the individual's appraisals of potentially threatening stimuli. As we have described, it also accommodates the person's internal responses to feedback from emotional and somatic states, but the main focus is on the interaction between the person and the external situation. Another leading cognitive model (Carver & Scheier, 1984, 1991) provides further insights into the internal self-regulative processes that shape the person's understanding of the external threat and his or her attempts at coping. Carver and Scheier proposed a *control process* self-regulation model of anxiety in order to better understand the nature of anxiety in ego-threatening contexts and its impact on human performance. We begin by briefly sketching the basic concepts and principles of Carver and Scheier's model and then attempt to show its applicability to anxiety theory and research. Figure 3.10 presents a schematic description of part of this complex and elaborate model.

This model is based on the assumption that intentional goal-directed behavior in humans displays the functional characteristics of a feedback control system (Carver & Scheier, 1988a,

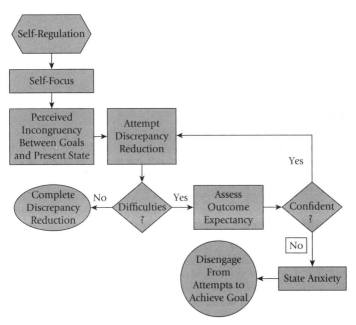

FIGURE 3.10 Carver and Scheier's self-regulation model. (Based on Carver & Scheier, 1988a, 1988b.)

1988b, 1990; Carver, Scheier, & Klahr, 1987). Accordingly, people establish goals and standards for themselves, which they use as reference points in guiding and monitoring their behavior. Present behaviors are continuously sensed and brought to mind and then compared against situationally salient reference values and goals. Any observed discrepancies encountered between present behaviors or states and salient reference values or behavioral standards are handled by adjusting behavior in the direction of the latter.

The basic unit in this suggested cybernetic model is *a feedback loop.* A feedback loop involves to a sensed value ("It's Tuesday, February 10, and I'm only halfway through my end-of-year report for the executive committee"), which is compared to a reference value or standard ("Have the report sealed and delivered by Monday, February 16"). Whenever people consistently move toward salient reference values they use to guide behaviors, they manifest the functions of a *negative feedback loop,* which is designed to bridge the gap between intended and actual qualities of behavior. The control system makes adjustments, if necessary, to reduce the discrepancy by shifting the sensed value in the direction of the standard ("Finish up the company tax returns in 3 days"). However, a great many circumstances exist in which people encounter impediments and are therefore unable to make desired adjustments in their behavior in order to match behavior to goals. These impediments toward reaching the goal, such as skill deficits, serious doubts about self-adequacy or efficacy, and situational constraints, tend to be anxiety evoking (Carver & Scheier, 1990). Curiously, anxiety states are also viewed as a common obstacle to goal attainment, thus generating further anxiety.

When difficulties are encountered in moving toward whatever goal one has taken up, a second control process kicks in. Accordingly, people remove themselves momentarily from the monitoring of their present behavior and assess their future prospects. More specifically, people form expectancies of whether they can actually perform the actions necessary to attain their goals (similar to self-efficacy). Evidently, if you don't believe that you can actually accomplish some necessary action, you are likely to become demotivated. Research reviewed by Carver and Scheier (1990) shows that unfavorable behavioral expectancies yield mental disengagement, non-task-related rumination, and lowered performance. Conversely, favorable behavioral expectancies yield behavioral conformity to salient standards, increased on-task effort, and thus lead to performance facilitation (Slapion & Carver, 1981). Anxiety is viewed as a coping process that is frequently maladaptive or counterproductive.

The model proposes that ego-threatening conditions, particularly social evaluative pressures, make everyone anxious. The crucial difference is in how different people respond to the arousal and the situation as a whole. Loss anxious individuals retain confidence in being able to perform well despite the anxiety, whereas highly anxious persons are tormented by doubts over their performance. Furthermore, in highly ego-threatening circumstances anxious persons tend to be focused primarily on avoiding the experience of anxiety, rather than on performing well (Carver, Peterson, Follansbee, & Scheier, 1983). Anxious persons are likely to have strong chronic doubts about either performing adequately, being evaluated favorably by significant others, or being able to control their feelings so that they don't feel overwhelmed by them (Carver & Scheier, 1984). Thus, when undergoing events that are of critical importance for them, anxious persons engage in self-deprecating ruminations and neglect or misinterpret readily available cues.

Carver (1996) theorizes that a person who is working on a task (e.g., painting a picture) often needs to deal with setbacks in the effort to do well on the task. However, an artist who is working exceptionally hard on an original piece of art as a way of trying to maintain self-esteem, as is often the case in anxious individuals, has a bigger job when performance falters. The greater the implications for the overall self-image, the bigger are the potential threats. Following Carver's (1996) line of reasoning, anxious persons may tend to generalize from a single bad occurrence of failure to the broader sense of self-worth. Thus, when they perform poorly or below expectations, it means a failure of the self. Generalization in response to poor performance outcomes would be reflected in cognitions about broad personal inadequacy, rather than inadequacy pertaining to some particular domain of academic performance. These cognitions, by their very nature, interfere with further efforts to perform. As aptly put by Carver (1996): "The more a task matters to the sense of self, the more the person is immersed in the phenomenology of being stuck in a behavioral loop that's not moving forward but can't be let go of" (p. 40).

SUMMARY AND CONCLUSIONS

In sum, this chapter surveyed key models of anxiety, both old and new. At present, no single theoretical perspective on anxiety can readily account for the complex and multifaceted nature of this construct, including: phenomenology, developmental antecedents, correlates and consequences, and therapeutic interventions. Current explanatory models seem capable of subsuming only parts of available research, but no one model is capable of encompassing all of the current research. Given the multivariate nature of anxiety, its various channels of expression, and its myriad causes, and consequences, it is reasonable to assume that several mechanisms, not just one, are needed to account for anxiety. Yet, there is an urgent need for more comprehensive and integrative models of anxiety that cover a larger number of facets of the anxiety domain and synthesize many of the conceptual frameworks presented in this chapter.

The models we have reviewed suggest some key themes and components for future theorizing:

1. *Anxiety is both conscious and unconscious.* The most obvious feature of anxious emotion is the familiar *feeling* state, often accompanied by awareness of bodily and thought disturbances. However, going back to Freud, theorists have also recognized that both the sources and the manifestations of anxiety may be unconscious. A hidden side to anxiety is recognized in both biological and cognitive theories. From the biological perspective, the operation of the neural circuits that support anxiety is frequently unconscious. Cognitive models, such as Scherer's appraisal theory, incorporate both unconscious and conscious analysis of stimulus meaning.

2. *Anxiety is both learned and innate.* Modern biological theories highlight brain circuits for anxiety as part of our evolutionary

heritage, tuned to the major threats facing primates, including both physical dangers and the pressures of living within a dominance hierarchy. Molecular genetic studies are beginning to substantiate such a perspective. However, as the classic learning theories emphasized, anxiety also reflects the person's past experience of threats and the associations formed to threat stimuli. Cognitive theories, likewise, see anxiety as reflecting the self-beliefs shaped by personal history, and expressed in self-regulative processes.

3. *Anxiety is both biological and cognitive.* The evidence is persuasive for a central role for brain structures such as the amygdala, embedded within wider functional systems for regulating responses to threat stimuli. Modern neuroscience is continuing to make rapid progress in mapping the relevant brain circuits. At the same time, purely neurobiological theories fail to capture essential aspects of the psychology of anxiety, notably the roles of personal meaning and dynamic self-regulation. In terms of a computer metaphor, we need to understand both the neural "hardware" and cognitive "software" that support anxiety and its behavioral consequences.

What Are the Origins of Anxiety?

No passion so effectually robs the mind of all its powers of acting and reasoning as fear.

Edmund Burke (1757)

regor Mendel, the noted pioneer and founder of classical genetics, was the son of peasant farmers and lived in what is now Slovakia. Early on, Mendel was recognized by his teachers as an extremely talented and promising student. With his sterling academic record, he gained admission to the renowned University of Vienna to pursue his interests in the natural sciences. While he was there, he received a first-class education from some of the academic luminaries of his time. Unfortunately, however, Mendel evidenced a rather severe case of anxiety: Every time he had to face an important university examination, he became physically ill, taking months to fully recover and get back to his academic work. As a result of this serious and debilitating condition, he was unable to complete his academic work and was forced to leave the university, without completing his degree. To subsist, he joined a monastery in the city of Brno, where he continued to pursue his interest in inheritance and to conduct experiments on plants to help uncover the mechanisms in the inheritance of physical traits in plants. Although his theory and results were at first discredited by key members of the biological community, his work eventually gained worldwide recognition and acclaim. As attested by Mendel's experience, anxiety can have serious consequences for one's physical and mental health, as well as for one's educational achievements and occupational career. At the same time, not everyone with anxiety will also necessarily fail in life's tasks (Zeidner, 2007).

Mendel is an example of a person with high *trait anxiety*, an enduring disposition to experience intense anxiety states. In this chapter, we consider the origins of high trait anxiety. The issue is brought into focus by the growing awareness of the serious persistent problems that anxiety presents to people in modern society. Epidemiological studies indicate that a sizable proportion of the population suffers from anxiety disorders, with anxiety found to be the most common psychological disorder of both childhood and adulthood. A body of evidence suggests that anxious children are at increased risk of having social and academic difficulties, at risk of becoming anxious adults, and are also at increased risk of developing serious secondary psychological disorders, particularly major depression and substance abuse. A variety of processes may elaborate anxiety in the brain, including causes that have become associated with aversive stimuli, painful events, and stimuli that have indicated danger in the evolutionary history of species (Panksepp, 1998). When confronted with all the discomfort, cognitive problems, and suffering experienced by anxious children and adults, the question arises: How does anxiety arise and what are its origins?

Even children may show anxious personality, and so we must look to the processes of child development to identify its sources. We have already touched on different views of the origins of trait anxiety in biologically based dispositions or learned self-beliefs. A basic observation is that high anxiety tends to run in families (Beidel & Turner, 1997), with children nearly five times more likely to be diagnosed with anxiety disorder when parents meet criteria for anxiety disorder (Beidel & Turner, 1997). However, the "transmission" of anxiety from parents to children might reflect either the genes they have in common, or the role of anxious parents in providing an anxiety-inducing environment for the child. We will look at how genes and environment may interact, during child development, to affect anxiety.

In addressing the developmental origins of anxiety, it is useful to distinguish between *distal* and *proximal* antecedents of anxiety (Phillips, Martin, & Meyers, 1972; Stein, 2006). *Distal* factors would include biological givens and early environmental factors that impinge on children (e.g., specific patterns of the parent-child relationship; preschool and early school experiences, cumulative success and failure experiences, etc.), which contribute more indirectly to anxiety reactions as responses to stressful or threatening conditions. They are "distal" or indirect in the sense that they are the factors which have their major initial impact as antecedents of anxiety in the early years of life, although their influence continues to be felt throughout life.

By contrast, *proximal* antecedents are those factors which are specific to the stressful situation and more directly responsible for anxiety reactions in specific settings. For example, in the case of evaluative anxiety, contextual factors, such as test atmosphere, task difficulty, perceived face validity of the test, and time pressure, are possible proximal factors in evoking evaluative anxiety. By contrast, in the case of community disaster situations (e.g., political violence, a ballistic missile attack, a tidal wave, a tornado, and an earthquake), the intensity or magnitude of the disaster, its scope, amount of damage done, degree of preparation for the stressor, and its predictability and controllability are proximal antecedents. Whereas distal factors are believed to shape anxiety, as a personality *trait* or disposition, proximal factors are expected to impact upon anxiety, primarily as an emotional *state*. In this chapter we focus mainly on distal antecedents. We will also primarily be concerned with the influences of these factors on "normal" trait anxiety, rather than clinical anxiety disorders, although we expect that many of the factors that elevate trait anxiety will also increase vulnerability to clinical anxiety.

SOME BASIC ISSUES

Typically, when psychologists investigate the development of anxiety, they are concerned with individual differences in trait anxiety (or related variables). If we have some measure of the individual's trait anxiety, we can run longitudinal studies that track how anxiety changes over periods of years. One of the first issues that comes up is whether, in Freud's (rather sexist) phrase, the "child is the father of the man." Do anxiety-prone children grow up to be trait-anxious men and women? Or does childhood anxiety reflect juvenile fears that have little bearing on anxiety in adulthood?

In principle, we can straightforwardly answer this question by measuring anxiety at regular intervals in a sample of children followed into their adult years. There is an immediate problem here, however—how to measure anxiety in younger children who cannot complete standard personality questionnaires. In fact, there is a subfield of personality research, referred to as *temperament* research, which is concerned with just such issues. Temperament involves basic features of character with a strong biological basis that are evident in very young children, such as emotionality and activity.

Temperament in Children

Researchers have developed a variety of means for measuring temperamental qualities that are based on *direct observation* of the child (e.g., Rothbart & Bates, 1998). In the laboratory, the child can be observed in standard conditions, and its behaviors observed and coded systematically. Clusters of behaviors that commonly occur together then define temperamental traits. For example, researchers might infer that the child is high in anxiety or fearfulness if it cries frequently, hides behind its mother, and shows a fearful facial expression—all behaviors that can be directly observed. Researchers may also have parents or teachers code the child's behaviors in more naturalistic settings.

Observational data support several dimensional models of childhood temperament. One of the best known was developed by Rothbart (e.g., Rothbart, Sheese, & Conradt, 2009), which discriminates three broad dimensions—extraversion (including positive emotionality), negative emotionality, and effortful control (e.g., inhibition of impulses). Even in infancy, these dimensions can be distinguished. Anxiety is one of several emotions that may relate to negative emotionality, much as adult trait anxiety may be seen as a facet of the broader neuroticism dimension. It seems to be harder to distinguish fear and anxiety in children than in adults, perhaps because the cognitive elements of anxiety, such as worry about personal concerns, develop later in childhood.

At a theoretical level, temperament is often seen as closer to basic biologically formed dispositions than is personality. Researchers such as Rothbart, Sheese, and Conradt (2009) have explored the individual differences in brain systems that may underlie childhood temperament. We should note that these systems continue to develop throughout the childhood years, so that changes in temperament during the childhood years may partly reflect the continuing maturation of the brain. Negative emotionality (and anxiety) is typically related to the childhood equivalents of the brain systems for fear and behavioral inhibition that we discussed in the previous chapter. The anxious or distress-prone infant may already possess limbic system structures that are highly sensitive to potential threats and negative reinforcers in the environment.

Longitudinal Studies

Reliable and valid measurement of temperament allows researchers to explore how much continuity actually exists between childhood temperament (measured by observation) and personality in later childhood, adolescence, and adulthood (measured by questionnaires). Longitudinal studies that track a single sample of children are most easily run over periods of a few years, although we will soon discuss an example of truly comprehensive longitudinal studies that have tracked children from infancy into the adult years.

Several general conclusions are supported by these studies (Asendorpf, 2008). First, Freud was correct in supposing that there is continuity between childhood and adult personality. Children who are above average in temperamental qualities, such as fearfulness and inhibition, will indeed tend to be elevated in trait anxiety as adults. Indeed, measurements of distress in response to laboratory stimuli taken in infants of only 6 months of age predict an anxious temperament later in childhood (Rothbart et al., 2009); the roots of anxiety are evident very early indeed.

Second, although childhood temperament predicts adult personality, the association is not very strong (Lewis, 2001). Child-adult correlations may only be around .2 or .3 (depending on the exact length of the time interval). Asendorpf (2008) argues that *plasticity* of personality is one of its key features. The individual's personality changes throughout the life span. Thus, an anxious child has an elevated probability of becoming an anxious adult, but some such children will grow up to be calm and stable (and some calm children will become anxious as adults) as a function of their unique family and social environment.

Third, personality does become more stable as the person becomes older; we can predict future personality in adults with more confidence than we can with children. Asendorpf (2008) lists several factors that tend to stabilize personality:

- As physical brain development ceases, the influence of genetic factors on personality becomes a more constant one.
- Adolescents and adults tend to gravitate toward environments that reinforce their personality characteristics (e.g., socially anxious students may avoid challenging social interactions on campus).
- People develop a stable identity and sense of self that filters through their life experience. If you believe yourself to be anxious or inhibited, you will often behave accordingly— and communicate anxiety to others.
- People tend to become more resilient with age, so that personality becomes less sensitive to changes in external circumstances.

Early behavioral inhibition is related to an increased risk for symptoms of anxiety and anxiety disorders (Hirshfeld-Becker et al., 2007; Kagan, Snidman, Arcus, & Reznick, 1994). Earlier work on inhibition (Kagan, Reznick, & Snidman, 1988) linked this feature of temperament to excessive reactivity of the sympathetic nervous system in response to novel stimuli. A longitudinal study by Rende (1993) demonstrated that higher levels of negative emotionality in infancy and early childhood were significantly related to mothers' reports of their children's anxiety and depression at age 7. Follow-ups of inhibited toddlers and young children into late childhood and adolescence suggest that early behavioral inhibition is more specifically related to social anxiety (Biederman et al., 2001).

One of the more comprehensive studies in the field is the remarkable Dunedin Study (http://dunedinstudy.otago.ac.nz/aboutus.html). The researchers began with a sample of 1,037 babies born in Dunedin, New Zealand, during 1972 and 1973. As children, the participants in the research were evaluated first at age 3, and then at 2 yearly intervals. The study is continuing to follow the participants as adults, and it is hoped it will follow their children as they grow older. Of interest here, the researchers assessed temperament at age 3. The model of temperament they used differed somewhat from those previously described. The closest temperamental attribute to anxiety was *inhibition*, defined as fearfulness, social hesitancy, and emotional vulnerability to new people and situations.

The Dunedin Study researchers were then able to show that inhibited 3-year-olds tended to grow up to be unassertive, socially disengaged adults (at age 26), who took little pleasure in life (Caspi, Moffitt, Newman, & Silva, 1998). As previously noted, correlation magnitudes were modest; personality is certainly not set in concrete at age 3! Another temperamental trait that related to adult negative emotionality was described as "undercontrolled" (impulsive, restless, and emotionally unstable). However, this "externalizing" group was more prone to antisocial behavioral problems, including criminal and delinquent behaviors, as adults. A later analysis showed that inhibited temperament is also linked to later symptoms of clinically generalized anxiety and depression in adults (Moffitt et al., 2007).

Research suggests that the specific developmental period during which children and their families are exposed to a wide array of risk factors, and the complex interplay between these factors, may affect the development of internalizing problems (Essex, Klein, Cho, & Kraemer, 2003). Some research suggests that children are more vulnerable to maternal distress, family adversities, and lack of social support in the period of early childhood, which stands out as a vulnerability developmental period for anxiety.

A recent Norwegian prospective study set out to identify early predictors and pathways of anxiety and depression at

12–13 years of age (Karevold, Roysamb, Ystrom, & Mathiesen, 2009). The authors hypothesized that family adversities increase the level of maternal stress, which, in turn, impacts on the child's mental health, including anxiety levels (Essex et al, 2006; Rutter, Moffit, & Caspi, 2006). These adversities are especially aggravated if the family lacks social support (Leech, Larkby, Day, & Day, 2006). Increased level of maternal distress can make mothers less responsive and less emotionally available for their children and thereby increase their children's negative emotionality and anxiety. On the other hand, the child's excessive levels of emotionality may contribute to increased levels of maternal distress. Two developmental pathways to poor adolescent mental health were identified. The first was through child temperament (emotionality and shyness), as nearly all risk factors (maternal distress, family adversities, and lack of social support) were partly mediated through child emotionality in mid-childhood. Another pathway was through early contextual risk factors, with all direct and indirect contextual impacts observed from before 5 years of age.

Demonstrations from longitudinal studies that childhood temperament predicts adult personality do not in themselves tell us anything about the causal influences on the development of anxiety. Continuity in personality might reflect either the stable genetic influence on the brain centers controlling personality, or stable environmental influences. In the sections that follow, we will argue that genes and environment (as well as their interaction) play key roles in the development of anxiety.

Generational Effects

As we have suggested, the best way to examine personality development is to conduct longitudinal studies, tracking participants over extended time intervals. It is also possible (and easier) to examine age differences in anxiety "cross-sectionally," that is, within a single sample containing persons differing in age. Although data are somewhat mixed, these studies broadly suggest that negative emotionality (and related traits) hit a peak in the difficult adolescent years and then slowly decline during most of the adult years (Donnellan, Trzesniewski, &

Robins, 2009). However, there is a well-known problem with cross-sectional studies of age differences—they may reflect differences between generations (cohorts) rather than true developmental changes. Thus, if we find that "baby boomers" have lower anxiety than today's teens, perhaps the explanation is that baby boomers, on average, grew up with a greater sense of familial and cultural security than today's adolescents feel.

Generational (or "cohort") effects may be investigated by examining archival data on mean levels of anxiety in groups of equivalent age tested in different calendar years. Twenge (2000) tracked down 170 college student samples and 99 samples of children who had completed standard anxiety measures during the period 1952–1993. Meta-analysis of the data showed a surprisingly strong association between the person's date of birth and the person's trait anxiety. Indeed, if the data are reliable, the average American child in the 1980s obtained higher anxiety scores than 1950s child psychiatric patients. A later study (Twenge et al., 2010) confirmed a similar generational effect on clinical symptoms of mood and anxiety disorders, measured with a standard instrument, the Minnesota Multiphasic Personality Inventory. Changes of this kind must reflect changing environmental influences on anxiety; Twenge especially implicates the loss of social connectedness that has taken place in the United States and other nations in the postwar years.

On a cautionary note, analyses of the kind reported by Twenge (2000) can be criticized because they make use of convenience samples; data were not collected originally with the aim of studying personality change. Another generational change reported by Twenge (e.g., Twenge & Campbell, 2008) is increased self-esteem in later generations. Trzesniewski, Donnellan, and Robins (2008) have suggested the apparent effect is an artifact of the way in which the data are sampled. The jury is still out on this important issue, and further research is needed on possible generational changes in anxiety.

HEREDITY AND ENVIRONMENT

As noted in earlier chapters, anxiety is viewed, from a biological perspective, as being functional to survival and adaptation, facilitating the detection of threat or danger in a potentially hazardous environment. Thus, anxiety has considerable survival value in that the rapid and early detection of warning signs of danger in the immediate surroundings enables the individual to avoid, prepare for, and cope more effectively with future threatening encounters (Eysenck, 1982). However, there may be individual differences in the genes that influence the areas of the brain responsive to threat and punishment, which may, in turn, control trait anxiety.

Researchers have used two main approaches in investigating the heritability of anxiety. The first is *behavior genetics*. The idea is to collect data on individuals differing in kinship, and investigate how similarity in trait anxiety varies with similarity in genes. For example, a common design is to compare monozygotic (MZ) twins with dizygotic (DZ) twins. MZ twins come from a single ovum and have identical DNA, whereas DZ twins, like ordinary siblings, come from two eggs, and share half their DNA, on average. If anxiety is heritable, we would expect the MZ twin pairs to be more similar in their anxiety levels—that is, a higher intratwin correlation—than DZ twins. Research may focus on other familial relationships, or on adopted children, who, based on a genetic hypothesis, should resemble their biological parents in anxiety more than they resemble the adopting parents. A second, more recent approach is *molecular genetics* (Arnold, Zai, & Richter, 2004). The aim is to find specific genes that vary across individuals ("polymorphisms") that relate to anxiety. Isolating such genes may increase understanding of brain mechanisms in anxiety. For example, as we shall see, research has focused on genes that may influence the functioning of the serotonin neurotransmitter in the brain.

A Family Affair: Behavior Genetics Studies

We will begin by looking at the rather more extensive evidence from behavior genetics. There is a longstanding controversy concerning the relative importance of genetic versus environmental factors in the development of individual differences in anxiety. Earlier evidence reviewed by Eysenck and Eysenck (1985), based on studies of twins, suggests that genetic factors are of pivotal importance in the development of trait anxiety. MZ twins are indeed more similar in trait anxiety than are DZ twins or ordinary siblings. "Heritability" refers to the proportion of variance in the trait that can be attributed to genetic influences within a given population, although it is a somewhat crude index that must be interpreted cautiously.

Eysenck and Eysenck's review found that heritability indices converged at about .50. Comparably, two more recent studies (Eley et al, 2003; van Beijsterveldt,Verhulst, Molenaar, & Boomsma, 2004), using large twin registry samples (n = 4,564 and 7,600), report heritability estimates around .50 for anxiety problems in children. Taken together, these studies suggest that about 50% of the observed variance in trait anxiety can be accounted for by genetic factors. At the same time, heredity is much less than 100%, demonstrating the important role of the environment in anxiety development. Further, studies show that the nonshared environment (biological and social environmental influences that affect one sibling but not another) might account for a substantial proportion of additional variance in trait anxiety (van Beijsterveldt et al, 2004). At the same time, most behavioral genetic studies suggest that there is at least some role of the "shared environment" in children's anxiety, which can include parenting influences, such as attachment, modeling, and child-rearing practices (McLeod, Wood, & Weisz, 2007).

In addition, anxiety may be influenced by the *interaction* of genes and environment. Genes may influence how the brain develops in response to environmental threats during childhood. As noted by Caspi, Moffitt, Newman, and Silva (1998), genes do not directly cause anxiety or anxiety disorders but rather serve as a form of vulnerability to environmental stress and pathology. The "diathesis × stress model" posits an interaction between stressful conditions and personal vulnerability (diathesis) in precipitating maladaptive outcomes. In keeping with this model, trait anxiety may be expressed, across different threatening situations, as a function of traumatic or stressful life experiences in interaction with genetic vulnerability. The most direct evidence comes from animal studies, in which rats bred for different levels of fearfulness show differing sensitivity to environmental stressors (Gross & Hen, 2004). A comparable approach in humans is to use behavior genetic methods to investigate the extent to which anxiety depends on genetic influence in children and adults that have been exposed to different levels of life events. Lau, Gregory, Goldwin, Pine, and Eley (2007) found that symptoms of both separation anxiety and panic become increasingly dependent on genetic factors with higher levels of life event, consistent with gene-environment interaction. Genes may especially affect personality development when the child is brought up in stressful circumstances.

Another complication is that genes may correlate or covary with environment. The temperamentally anxious child may have qualitatively different environmental exposures than does the dispositionally calm child. Certain parental child-rearing behaviors, often claimed to be important antecedents of anxiety (see the discussion below), may largely be an adaptation, on the part of parents, to biologically determined temperament dispositions or innate pathological characteristics of the child (Hock, 1992). For example, a child's excitable and highly emotional temperament, part and parcel of the child's biological equipment, may maximally try parents' patience and consequently evoke excessive control techniques or punitive child-rearing behaviors on their part. This, in turn, may further strengthen the child's tendency to react with heightened excitability and emotionality to stressful social-evaluative situations (i.e., anxiety). Thus, biological factors may also indirectly impact upon anxiety development in children.

Molecular Genetics: DNA for Anxiety?

Turning to *molecular genetics*, psychophysiological studies have implicated the neurotransmitter serotonin (or *5-HT*) in anxiety and depression (Zuckerman, 2005). For example, some drug treatments for anxiety interfere with reuptake of serotonin at the synapses between neurons, thus increasing its concentration at the synapse. It follows that genes that influence individual differences in serotonin may relate to anxiety. There is indeed a gene that regulates serotonin reuptake at the synapse (the 5-HT transporter, or 5-HTT). There are two versions, or "alleles," of the gene, one long (l) and one short (s), differing by the number of tandem repeats of strings of base pairs of nucleic acid on the DNA molecule. People with the short version (ss or ls) tend to be more anxious and show greater amygdalar response, although the association with personality seems not to be very strong (Munafò, Durrant, Lewis, & Flint, 2009;

Stelmack & Rammsayer, 2008). Fox et al. (2005) have suggested that the gene interacts with maternal levels of social support in its effects on behavioral inhibition, shedding further light on gene-environment interaction.

The reader should keep in mind that at best, the gene coding for 5-HTT only accounts for a small part of the genetic variation in anxiety, so other genes must also be involved. A recent study (Smoller et al., 2008) focused on polymorphisms (i.e., two or more alleles) of the RGS2 gene, which may modulate neurotransmitter activity associated with the cardiovascular element of the physiological "fight-or-flight" response. The gene is known to relate to anxiety in mice. Smoller et al. showed that it relates also to the behavioral inhibition aspect of temperament we discussed earlier. Furthermore, the polymorphism predicted increased activation of the amygdala during processing of emotion. In such ways, researchers are slowly beginning to piece together the jigsaw of how many genes influencing a variety of different brain pathways work together to influence the level of anxiety we can observe in individuals.

Environmental Influences

What then can we say about environmental influences on anxiety? In fact, although people often think of behavior genetics as focusing on the search for hereditary influences on personality, the studies we have reviewed also tell us something about the role of environmental factors. Behavior genetics models divided the influence of environment into two sources, the shared family environment and the unshared environment unique to each child. The family environment is shared by all the children within a given family. We might imagine that there are some families in which parents are uniformly supportive to all their children and go to great lengths to provide physical and emotional security. In this case, we would expect all the children to be low in trait anxiety. By contrast, each child also has experiences that are unique to him or her alone. Such experiences might be beneficial, such as gaining self-efficacy in threatening situations by taking up rock-climbing as a hobby, or being a victim of a traumatizing car crash.

Separating these two forms of environmental influence provides a surprising result—for anxiety, as for most other personality traits, unshared environmental influences explain more of the variance in anxiety than the family environment (Rowe, 1990). That is, once we have accounted for genetic factors, the children within a family are not as similar in personality as we might otherwise suppose. What seems to matter more is the child's unique interactions with parents and significant others in the child's surroundings.

Another extrafamilial source of anxiety is the surrounding culture. Twenge (2000) points out that cultural change may underpin the changes in mean anxiety she identified across generations. She found that two key types of social indicators were linked to childhood anxiety in her data sets from 1954 to 1988: social threat (e.g., crime and suicide rates) and low social interconnectedness (e.g., divorce rate, percentage of people living alone). Interestingly, when these factors were statistically controlled for, there was no significant association between anxiety and economic conditions. At least within a generally affluent Western society, there was no direct association between poverty and anxiety.

Twenge (2000; Twenge et al., 2010) suggests that loss of social connection is the key factor driving the increased anxiety of later-born generations. Other work (e.g., Lazarus, 1999) has also suggested that social support is critical for effective coping with stress. Consistent with Hillary Clinton's principle that "it takes a village" to raise a child, growing up without an extended network of familial and other social support may foster anxiety. Twenge et al. (2010) also identify a somewhat narcissistic trend among contemporary youth to value personal status and appearance over community and close relationships as a factor in rising rates of emotional disorder in American children and college-age children. We might also put an evolutionary spin on these findings. As social animals, we may have evolved to live within extended family groups rather than in the isolation of the nuclear or single-parent family.

Anxiety as a Product of Genes and Environment

In sum, anxiety reflects a multitude of factors. We can crudely separate genes and environment as separate influences. Genetic variation produces individual differences in the sensitivity to threat of the brain systems that control anxiety, for example, by influencing neurotransmitters, including serotonin (5-HT; Lesch & Canli, 2006). The environment functions via the learning mechanisms discussed in the previous chapter (see Chapter 3, Learning Models of Anxiety), including basic conditioning to threat and social modeling. A parent or older sibling who is overly upset, preoccupied, tense, and worried in the face of a stressful encounter would serve as poor role model for the child to imitate (Zeidner, 1998). Learning may be guided by various external influences, including the broad sociocultural environment, the family environment, and the child's unique experiences with family members and others.

At the same time, genes and environment typically covary and interact, so that development reflects their joint influence, even at the level of brain development. Indeed, although life events are typically seen as external environmental influences, twin studies have shown that life-event frequency itself may be partly inherited (Bemmels, Burt, Legrand, Iacono, & McGue, 2008). The child whose temperament encourages him or her to explore the mysteries of electrical outlets, biting insects, and boxes of matches can expect to experience frequent negative life events. The developmental process thus remains largely an enigma, but we can tease out some of the influences and processes that are important for development.

Next, we will look at the rather extensive research on the family environment and child-rearing processes, keeping in mind two important caveats. First, as shown by behavior genetics, family environment has a modest impact at most (its interaction with the temperamental qualities of the child may be more important). Second, in line with the blurry distinction between genes and environment, family environment is itself partly inherited (Krueger, Markon, & Bouchard, 2003). Fancifully, one might imagine that a family whose members are all genetically "wired" for anxiety would create a fortress-like environment, with stocks of canned goods, medicines for every imaginable illness, and regular survival drills. Sensitivity to threat would be passed from parents to children via both genes and exposure to an environment in which threat was a focal point.

Family Environment: How to Raise an Anxious Child

There is a body of research suggesting that anxiety and anxiety disorders aggregate in families (see Moore, Whaley, & Sigman, 2004). Although genetics may play a pivotal role in this aggregation, there is clearly also a role of psychosocial factors in determining how anxiety is transmitted from parents to their offspring, often across generations. One of these psychosocial factors is almost certainly parenting, with theorists in the field of anxiety and anxiety disorder positing an important role for certain parenting styles in the development and maintenance of anxiety.

Researchers have emphasized the importance of family influences, in interaction with temperament, in understanding the developmental background of children's disposition to experience anxiety (Degnan, Almas, & Fox, 2010). It is now readily apparent that early childhood experiences play a major role in determining individual differences in trait anxiety. Potentially important environmental factors contributing to the development of anxiety include maternal uterine environment, family climate, child-rearing patterns, modeling, specific conditioning episodes, and acute and chronic stressors (Krohne, 1992; Rapee, 1997).

In the following section, we aim at unpacking some of the early family experiences critical to the development of anxiety. First, we discuss work on the effects of prenatal maternal environment and child anxiety, and then we move on to summarize work on attachment theory—one of the most important theoretical perspectives that may be used to make sense of many of the empirical findings in this area.

Prenatal Maternal Environment

A body of research suggests that antenatal maternal stress and anxiety are meaningfully related to the child's anxiety. For example, a study by O'Connor, Heron, Golding, Beveridge, and Glover (2002) demonstrated that there is a significant relationship between antenatal and postnatal maternal anxiety and the child's anxiety level at age 4. Clearly, the relationship may be accounted for by genetic as well as environmental factors. A more recent review by Van den Bergh, Mulder, Mennes, and Glover (2005), of 14 prospective studies, has shown a substantial link between antenatal maternal anxiety and cognitive, behavioral, and emotional problems in the child. The authors propose an intriguing, but tentative, causal mechanism accounting for the observed link. Accordingly, in the anxious or stressed mother, cortisol, an important stress hormone, crosses the placenta and affects the fetus by disturbing ongoing development processes. Antenatal maternal stress and anxiety may affect the development of important fetal brain structures that are involved in arousal and emotion regulation, such as the hypothalamic-pituitary-adrenal axis, the limbic system, and the prefrontal cortex. The authors propose that it is warranted to implement programs to reduce material stress in pregnancy in order to avoid these complications.

Attachment Processes

While acknowledging the contribution of innate vulnerabilities in the anxiety experience, current research emphasizes the importance of early caretaking experience in the developmental trajectory of anxiety. Studies of child rearing have focused on a wide array of behaviors and attitudes that may impact on the development of anxiety, including overprotection, lack of warmth, parent-centeredness, intrusiveness, possessiveness, hostile detachment, strictness, and neglect, to name a few. Current research emphasizes the importance of early caretaking experience, particularly as it shapes a child's sense of unpredictability and uncontrollability, in the development and progression of vulnerabilities.

The pioneer of attachment theory was John Bowlby (1960, 1969, 1979) who ingeniously integrated ideas from psychoanalysis, observations of animal behavior, and cybernetic control theory in the 1950s and 1960s. Bowlby's key idea was that the child's mental health depended on forming a secure and stable attachment to the primary caregiver (normally, the mother) in infancy. The "secure attachment" is characterized by warmth, intimacy, and stability, to the satisfaction of both mother and child. Bowlby observed the harmful effects of lack of attachment in hospitals and orphanages, in which children were physically well cared for, but lacked the intimate attachment to a caring parental figure. He was also influenced by Harry Harlow's influential but notorious study of rhesus monkeys, in which he showed that infant monkeys preferred a cloth surrogate mother to which they could cling, in preference to a wire surrogate that provided food but not tactile comfort. Both young children and monkeys sometimes show intense "separation anxiety" when forcibly removed from the mother (see Figure 4.1.)

Ainsworth et al. (1978) developed a formal observational paradigm for assessing the attachment style of young children. The child is placed in a "strange situation," in which the child is separated from the mother and exposed to the presence of a stranger. The child's behaviors are coded and form the basis for classifying attachment style. The majority of children are treated as secure, in that they remain calm during the separation but seek proximity to the mother when she returns. "Anxious-avoidant" children, by contrast, distance themselves from the mother when she returns, and "anxious-resistant" children react more expressively to separation with negative emotions including anxiety and anger. Attachment style appears to be influenced by parenting; secure attachment seems to reflect maternal sensitivity to the infant's needs and emotions (Ijzendoorn & Bakermans-Kranenburg, 2004).

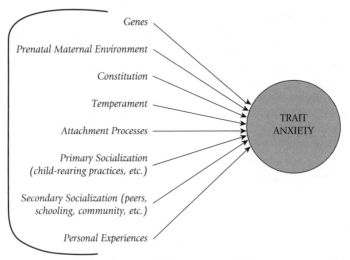

FIGURE 4.1 Distal and proximal determinants of anxiety.

Measurements of attachment style provide a further basis for exploring the childhood antecedents of trait anxiety. It is assumed that the child's attachment style carries forward as a kind of template for the intimate relationships of adulthood; insecure children may be vulnerable to insecurity and ambivalence in adult partnerships. Attachment style does indeed show some continuity from childhood to adulthood in longitudinal studies (Fraley, 2002). It is believed that early attachment experiences are internalized as cognitive schemas that help the adult make sense of close relationships. However, in place of Ainsworth's separate categories of attachment, contemporary research most often uses dimensional models. The leading model (Shaver & Mikulincer, 2009) discriminates level of anxiety and level of avoidance as independent dimensions. The securely attached child (or adult) is then someone who experiences little anxiety in intimate relationships and seeks closeness with the parent or the partner.

Research has confirmed that attachment relates to standard personality dimensions. In a study based on the five-factor model, Noftle and Shaver (2006) found that attachment anxiety correlated most strongly with neuroticism ($r = .42$), whereas avoidance was negatively associated with agreeableness ($r = -.22$) and with extraversion ($r = -.21$). However, it is claimed that even with standard personality dimensions controlled, attachment style remains predictive of relationship quality and emotional responses, including anxiety (Shaver & Mikulincer, 2009). From a developmental perspective, there are two slightly different issues to be considered. First, the infant's attachment style may be a causal influence on broad temperamental and personality qualities, including anxiety. We should note, equally, that infant temperament may impact attachment style—a mother may find it hard to bond with a whiny, distress-prone infant—so that there is likely a reciprocal relationship between temperament and attachment. Indeed, like temperament, attachment style has a substantial inherited component (Donnellan et al., 2009). Second, the learning associated with attachment experiences may internalize cognitive structures that have a rather more specific effect in shaping the adult's beliefs, expectancies, and values in the context of intimate relationships.

Child-Rearing Practices

It follows from attachment theory that the parents' practices and behaviors in raising their child may influence its dispositional anxiety, and considerable research effort has been devoted to studies in this area. It has been found that two distinct dimensions of parenting may impact the development of anxiety: (a) acceptance and support versus rejection and (b) psychological granting of autonomy versus excessive psychological control. Both represent bipolar dimensions, with positive parenting practices (acceptance, autonomy) at one end of the continuum and negative parenting practices (rejection, control) on the other end. Parental *rejection* connotes low levels of parental warmth, approval, and responsiveness (i.e., coldness, disapproval, and unresponsiveness). Low warmth or high criticism levels may convey the message to the child that the world is not safe and that she or he will not be supported in facing challenges. Parental rejection is hypothesized to undermine children's emotion regulation by increasing sensitivity to anxiety.

By contrast, parental *control* involves excessive parental regulation of children's activities and routine, encouragement of children's dependence on parents, and instructions to children on how to think (Moore, Whaley, & Sigman, 2004). Overcontrol may convey the message to the child that he or she is incapable of handling novel or challenging situations and may reduce learning by restricting exposure to these situations (Hudson & Rapee, 2004). Furthermore, children may get to an age where it is developmentally appropriate for them to act independently, but experiencing excessive parental control will instill decreased self-efficacy and increased anxiety. When parents are highly controlling in contexts when it is developmentally appropriate for children to act independently, they may experience decreased self-efficacy and thus increased anxiety (McLeod et al., 2007; Rapee, 2001). Parental encouragement of children's autonomy and independence may augment children's perceptions of mastery over the environment, leading to anxiety reduction. Based on retrospective reports, anxious adults generally remember their parents as being rejecting and controlling.

A number of studies have shown that children's anxiety is significantly related to specific facets of parental rearing attitudes and practices, including (a) acceptance versus rejection and (b) overprotection versus encouragement of autonomy (e.g., Hudson & Rapee, 2004; Whaley, Pinto, & Sigman, 1999). Subdimensions of parental rejection (withdrawal, aversiveness, and lack of warmth) and control (overinvolvement and a lack of autonomy granting) have been shown to be differentially associated with childhood anxiety (Mcleod et al., 2007). For example, research by Bögels and Melick (2004) suggests that parental (primarily paternal) autonomy/overprotection is predominately related to child anxiety, with other dimensions less so.

Recent research (e.g., Dubi, Rapee, Emerton, & Schniering, 2008; Fisak & Grills-Taquechel, 2007) has identified parental modeling of anxious behaviors as another potential parenting factor contributing to child anxiety. This factor refers to parents' tendency to describe day-to-day problems to children as being threatening, dangerous, or irresolvable, or encouraging children to view problems in a catastrophic manner, and punishing children's expressions of positive coping behaviors. Indeed, anxious parents may inadvertently model anxious behavior or poor coping strategies for children, either because of their own negative interpretation biases of environmental events, or in response to their children's anxious behaviors (Degnan et al., 2010). These biases and behaviors, in addition to genetic influences, contribute to a cyclical process, which results in the development and maintenance of anxiety in children. However, this category has yet to be thoroughly studied and vindicated (Degman et al., 2010).

Both overcontrol and rejection may serve to limit the child's ability to use information independently, autonomously, and creatively (Krohne, 1980). Parents who fail to encourage their children to solve problems independently, who are overcritical or ridicule their children's problem-solving efforts, who restrict their children's actions, or who fail to provide suitable coping models, hinder the development of their child's competency expectations. Because dependency on the parents' behavior is maintained, the ability to use information and create new problem-related thoughts and actions is impaired. Parents who provide frequent positive reward (praise, favorable feedback) tend to instill positive consequence expectancies in their children, whereas parents who provide frequent or intense negative punishment (physical punishment, verbal rebukes, and criticism) instill negative consequence expectancies. As a result of the high degree of parental restriction and negative feedback that anxious children often experience in their own socialization, they develop a dispositional expectancy that others in their social environment will respond to their behavior with negative feedback. Anxious children come to expect criticism and failure following problem-solving efforts, thus leading to a strong expectancy of aversive consequences in ego-threatening situations.

Empirical studies have supported the view that parents of anxious children are overrestricting, more rejecting, and less intimate. Rapee's (1997) review of the childbearing literature in relation to anxiety (and depression) concludes that there is consistent evidence to support the conclusion that current feelings of anxiety are associated with perceived parental control and perceived parental rejection. For example, Messer and Beidel (1994) showed that high levels of family control were associated with high levels of trait anxiety as well as lower perceived self-competence.

Other factors may also be important. Victor, Bernat, Bernstein, and Layne (2007) studied 61 children, aged 7–11, suffering from anxiety disorder. The data showed that higher family cohesion at baseline is associated with significant decreases in child anxiety at posttreatment. Specifically, parents from families low in cohesion reported significantly higher levels of parenting stress and psychopathology as compared with parents from families high in cohesion. Also, Peleg-Popko and Dar (2001) suggested that each extreme of family cohesion—that is, overprotection versus disengagement—may lead to anxious behavior in children and adolescents. Furthermore, parenting may take on multiple roles depending upon the context in which it occurs, such as stage of development or presence or absence of other risk or protective factors.

Chorpita and Barlow (1998) summarize a body of evidence and suggest that early experience with uncontrollable events may serve as a primary pathway to the development of anxiety. An immediate sense of diminished control during childhood is commonly associated with the immediate expression of anxiety. A history of a lack of control may put the individual at eventual risk to experience chronic anxiety through learning to process events as not within one's control. By contrast, parental encouragement of children's autonomy and independence may augment children's perceptions of mastery over the environment, leading to anxiety reduction. A review of current studies in nonclinical populations show correlations between the magnitude of control and rejection and anxiety ranging between .2 and .3 (Rapee, 1997). The combination of high parental protection and low care, what Parker (1983) calls *affectionless control*, is likely to have the most consistent negative influence on the development of children. That is, the child may be at increased risk for anxiety as well as other affective disorders when both pathways of control are extremely limited, leaving the child very few degrees of freedom for autonomous behavior. Specifically, the effect of low responsibility of parents, who in turn constrain and narrow behavioral options for their child, has visible implications for the child's development of a sense that events are not under his or her personal control, thus impacting his or her anxiety disposition. We might imagine that children raised in institutions such as orphanages are also at risk of experiencing affectionless control.

Inconsistency of parental behavior is yet another risk factor for anxiety development in parental socialization practice (Krohne, 1980). Parental behavioral inconsistency involves praising a child for a given behavior (e.g., volunteering for social activities after school hours) on one occasion, while punishing the child for the exact same behavior on another. Inconsistent parental behavior evokes feelings of self-helplessness in children, who come to believe that they are not in control of the consequences of their own reactions. Furthermore, inconsistency in parental behaviors contributes to increased ambiguity of the environment, which, in itself, is a particularly important risk factor for anxiety development (Krohne, 1980). Under ambiguous or confusing threat conditions, the child cannot readily identify or implement adaptive behaviors that are potentially available to cope with the danger. Empirical findings on parental consistency are themselves somewhat inconsistent. Krohne (1992) found that inconsistent child-rearing, along with negative parental feedback and controlling tendencies, related to anxiety. Rosenthal (1990), by contrast, failed to find a significant relation between maternal inconsistency and anxiety in the child in a clinical sample of 450 disturbed children and their mothers.

Fine-grained examination of how parents and children interact may also be informative. Herman, ter Laak, and Maes (1972) observed parent-child interactions in a group of children aged 9–10, while the children were performing several cognitive tasks. Parents of high-anxious children offered their children little constructive help, rejected their children's bid for attention, tended to withhold reinforcement after correct solutions, and produced more negative and fewer positive tension releases. By contrast, parents of low-anxious children were observed to help their offspring learn task-oriented responses and effective problem-solving strategies, teach their children to rely on their own resources rather than adult support, and release tension in a more positive way. Hock (1992) confirmed these findings by observing the exchange of aversive communicative behavior between 59 mothers and their 8- to 14-year-old children during a 30-minute simulated homework period. Aversive communicative behaviors included the expression of annoyance, disappointment, or anger concerning the child's behavior; ignoring children's seeking of help; blaming the child for task performance; and restriction and control of the child. The mother's aversive acts correlated moderately with the child's anxiety.

Finally, a recent meta-analysis (Mcleod et al., 2007) gives a sense of the importance of parenting style in childhood anxiety. The meta-analysis showed that parenting practices accounted for only 4% of the variance in child anxiety. The weighted mean effect size was .21 for association between parenting and childhood anxiety, reflecting a relation in which more negative parenting was associated with more child anxiety. Parental control was found to be slightly more strongly related to anxiety than parental rejection (effect sizes of .20 and .25, respectively). Higher levels of parental warmth and autonomy granting were associated with less child anxiety, and higher levels of parental withdrawal, aversiveness, and overinvolvement were associated with childhood anxiety. The data suggest that the presence of aversiveness and/or withdrawal may have a greater impact on anxiety than the absence of positive parenting (i.e., warmth). Also, some parenting subdimensions (e.g., autonomy granting, accounting for 18% of childhood anxiety) demonstrated a stronger association with childhood anxiety than others (e.g., warmth, accounting for less than 1% of the variance). The authors conclude that given the modest association between parenting and child anxiety, the understanding of the origins of children's anxiety will require identifying factors other than parenting that account for the bulk of the variance. As a rule, high levels of family dysfunction are associated with childhood anxiety (Drake & Kearney, 2008).

We can now answer the question we frivolously posed previously. Research suggests a number of strategies parents may employ to raise anxiety, such as:

- Be cold toward the child.
- Model anxious behaviors.
- Find fault with the child often.
- Give him or her no help in finding solutions to challenging problems.

Such behaviors will interfere with secure attachment. A more advanced strategy (inconsistency) is to give negative feedback unpredictably. The child's activities must be limited to those required by the parent; if it fails to accomplish its set tasks, all the better. Family members should also aim to behave as though they are disconnected individuals. Of course, if parents wish their child to be low in anxiety, the opposite practices should be encouraged. In either case, though, parental strategies will have only a limited impact; anxiety will remain influenced by the genes, by the child's own unique exploration of its environment, by moderating effects such as experiences with peers, and by the manifold interactions of genes and environment.

ANXIETY IN CONTEXT: THE SCHOOL ENVIRONMENT

There are only two places in the world where time takes precedence over the job to be done. School and prison.

William Glasser

Thus far, we have discussed anxiety as a general personality attribute. However, as we discussed in earlier chapters, understanding anxiety often requires us to look within particular contexts, such as the rather different threats posed by tests and examinations, social pressures, and terrorism. We do not have space to examine how all these different forms of anxiety develop, so we will focus on one context that has been extensively studied—the school environment. Social evaluative situations are more frequently encountered in school contexts and with higher stakes than practically anywhere during childhood and early adolescence. Consequently, the school and classroom climate would be expected to be an important factor in evoking and maintaining students' anxiety in evaluative settings (Zeidner, 1998).

Most theoretical accounts of student anxiety link the emotional response to the students' motivations. The most obvious source of anxiety is failure—or anticipated failure—in academic work, as we discussed in our initial review of various forms of evaluative anxiety in chapter 1 (see Major Forms of Anxiety...). However, school poses additional threats and challenges. The student may also be anxious about social relationships with others, reflecting motivations to make friends, to be popular, and to avoid being bullied. Yet another potential source of anxiety is parental expectations, if progress is perceived as falling short of parental aspirations.

Early work in the field was linked to the influential theory of achievement motivation proposed in the 1960s by Atkinson and Feather (1966). They distinguished approaching success and avoiding failure as two key motivational tendencies in children. Anxiety may broadly be seen as a product of fear of failure. Children with these motivations tend to avoid moderately challenging tasks, preferring easy ones or difficult assignments (on which failure can be attributed to task difficulty rather than personal failings).

Modern research is often shaped by a more elaborated account of the different motivations that may guide student learning. Elliot (2005) has proposed a "2 × 2" model that crosses two key motivational dimensions. The first (similar to Atkinson & Feather, 1966) distinguishes approach and avoidance as key motivational orientations. The idea also corresponds to the psychobiological theories, discussed in chapter 3 (Biological Perspectives: Functional Neurobiological Perspectives), that differentiate brain systems for approach (reward) and avoidance (punishment). The second distinction is between *mastery* and *performance* goals. The child may be motivated either by the intrinsic interest of the task and the challenge of mastering its demands, or by the need to meet some performance standard or obtain some extrinsic reward (e.g., an A grade). The 2 × 2 model thus differentiates four types of achievement goals:

- Mastery approach (e.g., "I want to learn as much as I can from this class")
- Mastery avoidance ("I am concerned that I am not smart enough to understand this class")
- Performance approach ("I want to get the top grade in this class")
- Performance avoidance ("I don't want to flunk this class")

Several studies (e.g., McGregor & Elliot, 2002; Pekrun, Elliot, & Maier, 2009) have shown that both trait and state test anxiety are linked to performance-avoidance goals. Furthermore, anxiety was shown to mediate between performance-avoidance goals and student performance (Pekrun et al., 2009). Focusing on avoiding failure may undermine the child's confidence by focusing attention on the possibility of failure, as opposed to the intrinsic challenge of learning and the external rewards of success.

Other theorists have drawn attention to motivations beyond immediate academic goals. Sarason, Davidson, Lighthall, Waite, and Ruebush (1960) saw the child as motivated to avoid potential parental rejection due to underperformance, within a psychodynamic theory. The child's overdependence on parents for approval and support leads to a strong fear of failure, together with unconscious hostility. Similar emotions may be transferred to teachers. Hill (1972) also emphasized the role in anxiety of the child's sensitivity to being evaluated and criticized by adults. The evaluations of their peers also become increasingly important in older children. Anxious children tend to avoid situations in which the likelihood of criticism is high and they tend to leave such situations as soon as possible. By contrast, low-anxious children are responsive to the informational component of an adult's reactions rather than to the social cues or contexts in which the reactions are made.

In the following section, we discuss a number of critical dimensions of the school environment, which may help shape and maintain anxious behaviors in students.

Competitive Climate

A highly competitive and evaluative classroom environment may foster an unhealthy orientation among students, in which trying to outperform other students becomes more important than mastery of the school material (Church, Elliot, & Gable, 2001). Since anxious children are already apprehensive about failure, an emphasis on outperforming others should make the consequences of failure even more devastating (Pekrun et al., 2009). Students who do not perform well in such competitive environments often come to see themselves as failures and ruminate about their performance deficits rather than focusing on the task at hand. A study by Harter, Whitesell, and Kowalski (1987) in grades 6–8 showed that students who perceived their school environment as increasingly evaluative and competitive in nature also tended to be more anxious. Another study among college students (Church et al., 2001) indicated that the presence of an evaluation focus coupled with harsh evaluations lead to performance avoidance goal orientations.

Expectancy formulations of anxiety (Pekrun, 2009a, 2009b) predict that the strength of students' anxious reactions to evaluative classroom contexts is a complex function of the perceptions and appraisals of both the objective features of the classroom environment as well as cognitive factors, such as outcome expectancies. Accordingly, the classroom climate may enhance students' anxiety by reducing success expectations for specific academic tasks, by rendering failure outcomes as extremely negative, or by decreasing perceived control over outcomes.

Pekrun (1985) investigated the nexus of relations between failure-related cognitive schemas, classroom atmosphere, and anxiety in a sizable sample ($n = 798$) of sixth-grade German students. Students who view the classroom environment as a competitive and chaotic one, who report receiving more punishment than support from their teachers, and who perceive they are being pressed beyond reasonable limits to do well in school by their teachers, tend to show elevated levels of anxiety.

Teachers were reported to foster a competitive environment by frequently contrasting students' performance with that of others, by granting privileges to smart children, or awarding prizes for best performance. These behaviors, in turn, increased the importance of ability as a factor in classroom life and heightened the negative affect associated with failure. Similarly, data from longitudinal studies showed that classroom climate is predictive of both concurrent and future test anxiety at various grade levels (Schwarzer & Lange, 1983). Specific predictors of anxiety in these studies included students' perceptions of achievement pressure and competition in the classroom (as well as "classroom chaos").

Evaluative Orientation and Practice

A body of research evidence suggests that the teacher's predominant mode of evaluating children's performance in the classroom impacts upon children's motivation and self-perception. Thus, children evaluated in terms of individual reference norms (i.e., their own previous performance) showed less fear of failure, more realistic goal setting, and less low-ability attribution compared to those evaluated in terms of classroom group reference norms (Boggiano & Ruble, 1986). Also, teachers, like parents, who set overly high standards, or criticize their students too harshly, should be more likely to foster anxiety in their students than other teachers (Wigfield & Eccles, 1990). Evaluation practices, such as emphasizing letter grades, can promote a focus on ability perceptions, competition, social comparisons, and negative self-evaluations, which may elicit anxiety in students (Wigfield & Eccles, 1990). Such concerns are especially salient in modern educational practice, which increasingly stresses the importance of standardized testing through initiatives such as "No Child Left Behind" in the United States. We will leave it to readers to judge whether anxiety is an unfortunate but necessary concomitant of raising educational standards, or whether student anxiety is a sign that standardized testing is overemphasized in contemporary education.

Social Comparisons

The social comparison process, in which one's achievements are compared with the norms of a meaningful reference group, allows a quick review of one's relative standing with respect to other target individuals (Suls & Wheeler, 2000). Social comparison helps shape an individual's self-perceptions of ability and achievement, which, in turn, may influence emotions such as anxiety (Regner, Escribe, & Dupeyrat, 2007; Suls, Martin, & Wheeler, 2002). Social comparison theory would suggest that children who believe they are competent relative to their peers should feel more positive about themselves and less anxious compared to those who believe they are less competent than their peers. Peers may influence anxiety by setting minimal expected norms of academic performance, by actually passing judgment on peers' performance, or by deriding and humiliating fellow students when these fail to meet set standards. Because a student's classroom typically serves as the most salient reference group for social comparison processes it stands to reason that students who rank below the norm of the reference group should suffer from low self-concept and higher anxiety (Zeidner & Schleyer, 1999). By contrast, students achieving above the norms would be expected to see themselves as competent and therefore more likely to appraise academic demands as challenging rather than threatening.

However, there may be some exceptions to the noted generalization. For instance, the above-average performance of students in low-status contexts, such as low-track inner-city school classes, may not serve to particularly enhance their academic self-concept. Conversely, mediocre or even below-average performance in some very demanding contexts (e.g., elitistic schools or programs) may be associated with positive self-evaluation and low levels of anxiety. Furthermore, it is not implausible that some relatively bright students may experience anxiety because they compare themselves with the inordinately high norms of an elitistic group (e.g., gifted students), while some below-average students may feel little anxiety and quite comfortable when comparing themselves with poor achievers.

Research evidence suggests that social or scholastic experiences that make social comparisons more salient, particularly when lowering one's relative standing in his or her reference group, raise anxiety (Suls & Wheeler, 2000; Wigfield & Eccles, 1990). Accordingly, the transition between elementary and junior high school itself is often an important source of evaluative threat for students (Wigfield & Eccles, 1989). This is so because school experiences often change at this juncture—students often move from smaller to larger schools, experience ability grouping, and have different teachers and more heterogeneous classmates for each subject, and are graded more strictly. These changes tend to make the school environment more impersonal, threatening, and unpleasant for many students at a time when students themselves are going through major psychobiological changes. By the same token, students who enter a high-level track in school may have a hard time and experience greater test anxiety as they will no longer be favored by social comparison processes.

In a series of studies, Moshe Zeidner and coworkers (Goetz, Praekel, Zeidner, & Schleyer, 2008; Praekel, Zeidner, Goetz, & Schleyer, 2008; Zeidner & Schleyer, 1999) examined the effects of contextual and situational variables on anxiety. One line of research tested the effect of reference or comparison group, often called the "big-fish-little-pond-effect" (Marsh et al., 2008; cf. Pekrun, Frenzel, Goetz, & Perry, 2007; Seaton, Marsh, & Craven, 2009), with respect to anxiety and academic self-concept. Reference group theory posits that self-perceptions in educational settings, such as self-concept and evaluative self-cognitions, are shaped by the process of social comparison. Thus, students compare their own attributes and attainments with their reference groups and use this relativistic impression as one basis for forming their self-perceptions and reaching conclusions about academic and social status. The central hypothesis, deduced from social comparison and reference group theory, was that gifted students enrolled in special gifted classes, will perceive their academic ability and chances for success less favorably compared with students in regular mixed ability classes. Those negative self-perceptions, in turn, will serve to deflate students' self-concept and elevate their levels of evaluative anxiety and result in depressed school grades.

The hypothesis was tested on a sample of 982 gifted students partaking in two types of classes: (a) special homogeneous gifted classes (n = 321) and (b) mixed-ability heterogeneous classes (n = 661), with a one-day pull-out program. Overall, our findings supported the "big-fish-little-pond" effect for anxiety and academic self-concept. Both anxiety and academic self-concept are shown to be of a dynamic character and shaped in part by social comparison processes. Both the worry and emotionality components of test anxiety were lower for gifted children in heterogeneous classes than homogeneous gifted classes. Academic self-concept was observed to be higher for gifted children in homogeneous than in heterogeneous classes. The elevated test anxiety in special homogeneous gifted classes may be accounted for by a combination of factors, including higher teacher and student performance expectations, fierce competition, and a strong fear of failure. Overall, the data are consistent with prior research showing that anxiety varies with changes in students' social reference group.

History of Failure Experiences

Current thinking and research point to a person's continued and accumulated failure experiences in evaluative contexts as a key determinant of individual differences in anxiety (Zeidner, 1998). Accordingly, anxiety is viewed as the product of certain achievement events, such as failure, that sooner or later befall most learners. Anxiety in children is most likely developed through both direct experiences of failure, in which unreasonable demands, negative feedback, and punishments are imposed on students, as well as through observation of other people's experiences with failures (e.g., parents, siblings, peers, etc.). Through direct or vicarious experience, individuals learn to associate the idea of evaluation with lowering of self-esteem and expectation of failure.

Both the *accumulation* and *timing* of failure experiences are key concepts to consider in our efforts to understand failure-induced anxiety (Wigfield & Eccles, 1989). Although one may theoretically develop a generalized anxiety reaction to physically dangerous, evaluative, or social situations because of some shattering "one-time" experience, anxiety is generally shaped by *repeated* failure during critical developmental periods, eventually producing a generalizable apprehension of all achievement activities. Whereas a single failure experience represents a challenge to overcome, continued subsequent failures elicit anxiety caused by the implicit implications of low ability. Continual poor performance over time typically evokes self-directed negative affect, causing a person who repeatedly fails in academic settings to experience aversive emotional states such as anxiety, shame, and humiliation (Covington & Omelich, 1979).

Research (Hill & Eaton, 1977) suggests that children who succeed in cognitive tasks learn to approach new problem-solving tasks as challenging and generally cope effectively with evaluative situations. By contrast, children who have experienced continued failure in academic tasks will approach new tasks with considerable anxiety, develop maladaptive coping strategies, and may be more motivated to avoid failure than to approach success—especially when they believe that the task they are engaged in assesses their ability. As previously mentioned, these two styles of coping may correspond to mastery-approach and performance-avoidance goals (Elliot, 2005).

The timing of failure experiences is also currently held to be of crucial importance. The effects of failure experiences on anxiety appear to be moderated by age. Whereas early failures generally do not have a major effect on children's expectancies for future success and anxiety, as children grow older, failure appears to have a stronger impact on their future expectancies and anxiety experiences (Wigfield & Eccles, 1989). Thus, during elementary school years children with failure experiences and low ability perceptions would not necessarily be anxious because they remain optimistic even after failure. This is presumably so because their ability perceptions are relatively undifferentiated and they basically see ability as an unstable rather than enduring underlying characteristic (Nicholls, Patashnick, & Mettetal, 1986). However, by middle elementary school years, when ability perceptions are more differentiated and more closely related to school performance, children who continually fail may think that their poor performance is due to a lack of academic ability, thus lowering their ability perceptions and enhancing their anxiety in test situations (Covington, 1992).

IN SUM

This chapter surveyed theory and research relating to the developmental origins of anxiety. We focused mainly on the role of *distal* factors, mainly biological constitution, primary socialization practices, and school experiences, in the development of anxiety as a relatively stable trait. Anxiety development may be best understood as shaped by a unique configuration of constitutional, familial, social, educational, and experiential factors. These factors interact and mutually impinge upon each other to shape the course of anxiety development. Research has shown that although personality remains pliable throughout the life course, there is an appreciable degree of continuity between features of childhood temperament, such as negative emotionality and inhibition, and adult personality.

Most broadly, we can see anxiety as the outcome of the interaction of genetic and environmental factors during the course of child development (and beyond). Beyond this rather general statement, research has identified some more specific influences on anxiety. Molecular genetics is beginning to identify specific genes, such as the serotonin transporter gene, that may build threat-sensitive brains. Most of the research on environmental influences in this area has focused on parental behaviors that may support or damage secure attachment, as well as possible sociocultural influences. Parental caring, together with willingness to cede some autonomy to the child, appears to be critical for lowering anxiety.

At an even more fine-grained level, we can study the development of anxiety within particular contexts. We chose vulnerability to anxiety at school as an example. Teaching practices that promote failure, excessive competition, and harsh evaluation may all elevate student anxiety. A personal history of failure in cognitive tasks, combined with a lack of supportive feedbacks from parents and teachers, may constitute a particularly potent influence. The child's style of social interaction with adults and peers is also important, as evidenced by studies of social anxiety. As pointed out by Sarason and his coworkers (Sarason, Sarason, & Pierce, 1990), it usually takes more than simply a history of failure experiences before a full-blown propensity to anxiety develops in an individual. In fact, both research and clinical practice attest to a good number of anxious persons who are quite competent and rarely experience objective failure. Current phenomenological models of stress and anxiety (Lazarus & Folkman, 1984) would suggest it is not failure per se that causes anxiety. Rather, what counts is how people process their objective successes and failures and how they view the test-taking experience.

While stress and anxiety researchers have traditionally emphasized the pivotal role of personal and subjective determinants of anxiety in threatening situations, it is noted that a wide array of *objective* factors in the context need to be considered in any effort to understand the sources and determinants of anxiety. Thus, a useful starting point for the analysis of the determinants of anxiety should probably begin with the objective properties of threatening situations, as well as the meaning attributed to the situation, with particular concern for the congruence between a person's vulnerabilities and the specific nature of the threat (physical danger, social evaluation, etc.) in a particular context.

How Does Anxiety Affect Cognitive Outcomes?

Anxiety is the interest paid on troubles—before it is due.
Martin Covington

Sue Bernard entered the exam hall, situated on the third floor of the Thurstone Psychology Building, with a great deal of apprehension and trepidation. Although she had studied long and hard for her final exam in Biological Psychology, she struggled with the material during the course of the semester and found it exceedingly difficult and hard to assimilate. Her efforts to cope with the bewildering array of new biological terms, concepts, processes, and methods in the textbook and lectures seemed like an impossible task. Having majored in art in high school, with a very limited background in the life sciences, she felt that the bulk of the course material was above her head. She was extremely concerned and worried about the possibility of failing the exam, realizing that this would mean having to drop out of the psychology department and switch majors.

The minute the proctor handed Sue the final exam, her heart began racing and pounding wildly. As she filled out her personal details and read the exam instructions, she began perspiring more than usual, and her body felt tense all over. When she began answering the multiple-choice items on the exam, she found it difficult to concentrate because she found herself preoccupied with thoughts about possible failure. Irrelevant thoughts popped into her head every few seconds, distracting her even further. As the exam progressed, she felt less and less in control and found it difficult to come to grips with her arousal and worry. She invested considerable energy in coping with her emotions and cognitive interferences and tried, without much success, to control her disturbing thoughts. In particular, she found it difficult to retrieve important facts and concepts that she had studied and had firmly committed to memory. Toward the middle of the exam period, her mind went blank and she felt totally paralyzed. Her hands began shaking, her stomach ached, and she sweated profusely. Sue became excessively worried about the possible implications of failure on this exam and felt that despite all the efforts she invested in preparing for the exam, her chances of success were nil. She began pondering whether or not she was really cut out for majoring in psychology and worried about her career options in case of failure. She wanted to get up and escape from the exam hall but was ashamed and afraid to do so. Once she completed the exam, she handed in her booklet without bothering to check her answers. She felt her performance was way below par and that she had bombed on the exam and was doomed to failure.

The foregoing bleak vignette of how anxiety impaired Sue's concentration and cognitive performance is all too representative of the experiences of many anxious individuals. As was the case for Sue, anxious students tend to be easily distracted on cognitive tasks, experience difficulty in comprehending relatively simple instructions and questions, and also have difficulty organizing or recalling relevant information during the task. Like Sue, high-anxious students express concern about the consequences of not performing cognitively at a satisfactory level and embarrassment at probable failure.

It is difficult indeed to communicate the pain, suffering, and misery suffered by high-anxious individuals before, during, and after major ego-threatening or evaluative experiences. Anxiety can play a role in determining a wide array of unfavorable outcomes and contingencies, including poor cognitive performance, scholastic underachievement, and psychological distress and ill health. Indeed, many people have the ability to perform well on cognitive tasks but perform poorly because of their debilitating levels of anxiety. Spielberger (1966), a noted expert in stress and anxiety research, followed up high-anxiety students in college for 3 consecutive years. He found that more than 20% of the high-anxiety students were classified as academic failures, who consequently dropped out of college, as compared with fewer than 6% of the low-anxiety students. Also, high-anxiety college students, relative to their low-anxiety counterparts, report suffering from poor mental health and psychosomatic symptoms. The importance of anxiety as a key construct in understanding sources of impaired cognitive performance and academic underachievement is now readily apparent. This situation demands that we better understand the cognitive processes linked to anxiety, on the one hand, and how anxiety impacts on cognitive performance, on the other.

As pointed out by Rachman (2004), the study of anxiety has been invigorated by the steady infusion into the subject of cognitive concepts and processes. Anxiety lends itself to cognitive analysis as it involves attention, vigilance, memory, reasoning, judgment, and decision making. We begin this chapter by presenting evidence for the impact of anxiety on cognitive performance in a number of specific situations, including academic exams, working with numbers or computers, social interaction, and sports. We then move on to discuss three salient theories attempting to account for the effects of anxiety on cognitive performance. Performance deficits in anxiety may be variously attributed to specific stages of information processing, to deficits in executive control of processing, or to a broader dysfunction in self-regulation. We will focus primarily on the effects of subclinical, "normal" anxiety on attention and performance, referring also to studies of clinical patients where necessary. We will also mainly cover studies that are directed toward anxiety and worry rather than other negative emotions, although negative mood and depression tend to produce a somewhat similar pattern of performance deficits.

ANXIETY AND COGNITIVE PERFORMANCE

Virtually flood of studies has probed the relationship between anxiety and a wide array of cognitive performances. These studies have converged in showing that various types of anxiety interfere with performances and competences in true-to-life situations (see Zeidner & Matthews [2005], for a review). Increased anxiety has been shown to negatively impact performance within domains of functioning that include mathematical ability, academic tests, working memory tasks, reading comprehension, social interactions, sporting behaviors, and musical performance (Eysenck, Derakshan, Santos, & Calvo, 2007). Furthermore, numerous lab-based studies indicate that various processing deficits are related to anxiety, including general impairments of attention and working memory, together with more subtle performance changes, such as failure to organize semantic information effectively (Zeidner, 1998).

With respect to evaluative anxiety, a meta-analytic review by Hembree (1998), based on 562 North American studies, demonstrated that test anxiety correlated negatively, though modestly, with a wide array of conventional measures of school achievement and ability at both the high school and college level. Data collected on students from upper elementary school level through high school showed that anxiety scores were significantly related to grades in various subjects, although the correlation was typically about $-.2$. Cognitive measures (i.e., aptitude and achievement measures combined) correlated more strongly with the Worry component of text anxiety than the Emotionality component ($r = -.31$ vs. $-.15$). Furthermore, anxiety correlated inversely with performance on laboratory cognitive tasks such as problem solving ($r = -.20$) and memory ($r = -.28$). Another meta-analysis (Ackerman & Heggestad, 1997) showed a mean r of $-.33$ between test anxiety and general intelligence test performance. Test anxiety was also correlated in the $-.20$ to $-.30$ range with other broad intellectual abilities including fluid and crystallized intelligence, learning and memory, visual perception, and math ability.

Math anxiety has been reliably related to math performance (Ashcraft & Moore, 2009). One estimate of the strength of the math anxiety–performance relationship is provided by a meta-analytic study (Schwarzer, Seipp, & Schwarzer, 1989), based on 28 studies published from 1975 to 1986 (total N of 9,140). The population estimate, from 47 effect sizes (correlation coefficients), was $r = -.23$. Two later meta-analyses (Hembree, 1990; Ma, 1999) found slightly stronger negative associations of around $-.3$. They also found that math anxiety is distinct from general and test anxieties, although it relates to them. Thus, it is possible to be anxious about math even if one is not generally anxious about being evaluated. Overall, the relationship between math anxiety and performance appears to be very much like the relationship between test anxiety and performance—a low to moderate, but not overwhelmingly strong, one.

The little amount of data currently available suggests that computer anxiety bears a negative impact on competence in using computers. In fact, results of empirical studies are rather mixed, with some showing detrimental effects of anxiety on computer use, and others failing to show any impact of anxiety (Smith & Caputi, 2007). These authors argue that measurement of computer anxiety has been less well developed than that of other aspects of anxiety. They also point out that it may be harder to obtain measures of the user's quality of interaction with computers, which may contribute to null results. Smith and Caputi (2007) suggest that distractibility, worry, and self-denigrating thoughts accompany computer use in users susceptible to anxiety, leading to delays in completion of computerized tasks.

As for test anxiety, the detrimental effects of math and computer anxieties are typically attributed to cognitive interference associated with loss of working memory capacity (Ashcraft & Krause, 2007) or negative self-evaluations and off-task thoughts (Smith & Caputi, 2007). Math anxiety may lower math performance because paying attention to intrusive thoughts during testing acts like a secondary task, distracting attention from the math task (Ashcraft, 2002). However, we cannot assume that a direct causal effect of state anxiety on performance is the only factor contributing to correlations between trait anxiety and performance. Trait anxiety may also signal lack of interest, preparation, and experience.

Anxiety may play an important role in the social realm as in the domain of intellectual performance. For example, social anxiety relates to various difficulties in occupational adjustment

(Bruch, Fallon & Heimberg, 2003). However, a major problem is that the criteria for adequate performance in social settings are less clear than is the case for other forms of evaluative anxiety. Furthermore, socially anxious individuals often perceive themselves as performing poorly when interacting with others, but these perceptions may be misguided, and a product of distorted cognitions of the self, rather than an actual performance deficit. A recent study (Voncken & Bögels, 2008) illustrates two key findings in social anxiety research—(a) the need to measure social performance objectively and (b) anxiety effects may depend on the nature of the "social performance" task. The authors compared patients diagnosed with social anxiety with normal controls. The first task was to give a short speech about the city in which the person grew up or about a vacation destination. The second task was to converse with a confederate of the experimenters, with the purpose of the two people getting to know each other. Video recordings were made so that the person's self-presentation (e.g., fidgeting, laughing nervously) and conversational behaviors (e.g., incoherent speech) could be coded objectively. Voncken and Bögels (2008) found that socially anxious persons believed they delivered the speech poorly, but, in fact, they showed no objective deficit. By contrast, real performance impairments were evident during the conversation. The authors suggested that conversation requires more social skills, in order to maintain the flow of the conversation, than does speech delivery, and so conversation is more vulnerable to social anxiety.

Other studies have confirmed that social anxiety often, but not always, relates to deficits in social behaviors or skills. Scores on social anxiety measures tend to correlate with peer rating of social skills and with observational behavioral measures (Arkowitz, Lichtenstein, McGovern, & Hines, 1975). Bruch (2001) identified various deficits, including inaccurate decoding of nonverbal cues and difficulties in communication, such as lack of fluency and expressiveness in conversational speech. In addition, a longitudinal study by Strahan (2003) found that detrimental effects of social anxiety may predict (self-reported) skill deficits relating to effective verbal discourse, self-presentation, and decoding nonverbal information, but not measures of academic performance such as GPA. There is a sense in which highly socially anxious individuals are doubly disadvantaged. Not only does anxiety impair their social skills, especially in more challenging encounters, but they also have difficulty in evaluating their social performance accurately.

Task-irrelevant thinking appears to play a detrimental role in social behavior, much as it does in test-taking situations (Sarason & Sarason, 1990). As with other forms of evaluative anxiety, social anxiety may impair social performance via diversion of limited attentional resources to self-related processing. Excessive self-focusing may be especially problematic since competence in social settings is linked to attending to other people in the environment.

Turning to sports anxiety, the game of golf is notorious for cases of "choking under pressure." In 1999, Jean van der Velde faced the last hole of the British Open, one of the sport's major championships, with the luxury of being able to take six shots on a par-4 hole to win. After a series of disastrous shots, including one that ended up in a stream, he took seven shots and subsequently lost a playoff for the title. Such performance failures in sports are often attributed to anxiety, disrupting the judgment and fine motor control needed to execute the motor skills involved (Beilock, Kulp, Holt, & Carr, 2004). It is easy to see how sports performance might be vulnerable to anxiety, given that minor changes in performance may be the difference between success and failure, the high stakes of competition, and to the likelihood of evaluation by fans, coaches, and other players.

Traditionally, sports psychologists conceptualized sports anxiety in terms of arousal, which they reported to be related to performance by an inverted-U curve. It was assumed that both under- and over-arousal were detrimental to performance, with a lower optimal level of arousal for more difficult tasks, so that anxiety should be especially damaging to sports requiring complex skills (Tenenbaum & Bar-Eli, 1995). Inverted-U relationships between anxiety and sports performance are occasionally reported, but, in general, studies of psychomotor performance fail to support the validity of the inverted-U hypothesis (Neiss, 1988).

Kleine's (1990) meta-analysis of the anxiety-performance relationship in sports included 50 studies published from 1970 to 1988. On the basis of 77 independent effect sizes (total

N = 589), the population effect size was estimated at $r = -.19$, converging with prior meta-analytic results on test and math anxiety. Separate effect sizes calculated for the Emotionality and Worry components of sports anxiety yielded estimates of $-.08$ and $-.33$, respectively, underscoring the overall importance of the cognitive component. A meta-analysis by Craft, Magyar, Becker, and Feltz (2003) focused on 29 studies (N = 2,905). Mean effect sizes for cognitive anxiety, somatic anxiety, and confidence were .01, $-.03$, and .25, respectively. The failure to find the predicted negative correlation between cognitive anxiety and performance is surprising. It may be a product of psychometric deficiencies in the scales used to measure sports anxiety, discussed by Craft et al.

Although anxiety is predominantly harmful to task performance, it may sometimes have a positive effect: Alpert and Haber (1960) differentiated between *facilitating* and *debilitating* anxiety. Indeed, in sports, some athletes find that moderate anxiety is motivating and helps them to focus on competing (Hanin, 2007). One of the factors that may especially tip the scales toward debilitating effects is the presence of worry, because of its tendency to produce distracting cognitive interference. It is also noted that deficits in cognitive performance or "output" may also be a consequence of poor skill acquisition. For example, socially anxious individuals display objective skills deficits such as difficulties in decoding the meanings of social interaction and in maintaining eye contact (see Bruch, 2001, for a review). However, objective skills deficits may not be directly related to subjective appraisals of competence, as elaborated next. Similarly, deleterious effects of test anxiety may reflect not just cognitive interference but also deficits in study habits and test-taking skills (Naveh-Benjamin, 1991; Zeidner, 1998).

Overall, the anxiety-performance relationship is best viewed as reciprocal in nature (Zeidner, 1998). Thus, high levels of anxiety produce certain aversive patterns of motivation, coping, and task strategies that interfere with learning and performance. The result is that performance suffers, thus leading to further anxiety over time, and generating a vicious circle of increasing anxiety and degrading performance (Wells & Matthews, 1994).

Mediating Versus Moderating Factors

Aside from attempting to establish the nature of the anxiety-test performance relationship, researchers have addressed two important questions related to this relationship, namely: (a) What are the factors that mediate the effects of anxiety on poor performance? (b) What are the personal and contextual factors that may moderate the anxiety-performance relationship? Thus, any discussion of the anxiety-performance relationship needs to distinguish between two often-confused concepts relating to the functions of third variables in this relationship, namely, mediating versus moderating effects (cf. Baron & Kenny, 1986).

Mediating Effects. A mediator variable is one that transmits the influence of an independent variable (a "cause") onto some dependent variable (an "effect"). For example, a simple mediator model for anxiety is that an external threat raises worry, which impairs performance. In this case, worry is the mediator which is the intervening process that is responsible for the effect of threat on performance. Building and testing mediator models is a common research tactic for theory development. In this case, developing the theory of anxiety effects on performance requires that we discover the intervening mediating processes that directly impact performance.

In fact, although worry is a plausible mediator, the whole process by which anxiety serves to debilitate cognitive performance is highly complex, with a variety of factors possibly mediating the effects of anxiety on performance. As will be discussed in the following, deficits related to anxiety have been identified at various stages of information processing (input, cognitive processing, and output), suggesting some general impairment in attention and/or working memory. These various performance deficits are often attributed to high levels of worry and cognitive interference (Cassady & Johnson, 2002; Sarason, Sarason, & Pierce, 1995) or to loss of functional working memory (Ashcraft & Kirk, 2001). As suggested earlier, cognitive interference has also been implicated in detrimental effects of computer anxiety, math anxiety, social anxiety, and sports anxiety (Zeidner & Matthews, 2005).

Note also that correlations between anxiety and performance do not always reflect a causal effect of anxiety. In some test-anxious individuals, it is poor study skills and preparation that cause poor examination performance (Zeidner, 1998), and anxiety is merely a by-product of poor preparation, with no direct effect on performance (and hence there is no mediating process).

Moderator Effects. Although similar-sounding, moderator effects are quite distinct from mediator effects. A moderator variable is an additional variable that influences the effect of an independent variable on a dependent variable. Put differently, the independent variable interacts with a moderator variable in its effects on a dependent variable. For example, in Spielberger's (1966) trait-state model of anxiety (see chapter 1, What Is This Thing Called Anxiety: Trait Versus State Anxiety section; and chapter 3, Cognitive Models: State-Trait and Transactional Models section), trait anxiety moderates the impact of environmental threats on state anxiety. The state-anxiety response is disproportionately high if the person is high in trait anxiety. Researchers tend to focus on moderator hypotheses when the relationship between two variables differs from study to study; a third variable may be moderating the relationship. Figure 5.1 graphically depicts mediating (*A*) and moderating (*B*) effects, respectively.

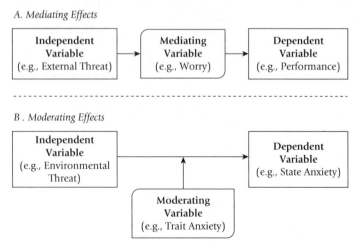

A. Mediating Effects

B . Moderating Effects

FIGURE 5.1 Mediating and moderating effects of anxiety.

Associations between anxiety and performance do indeed vary from study to study, and there seem to be a number of moderator variables that accentuate or reduce deficits in performance. First, the nature of the task may play an important moderating role, with subtle effects related to the qualitative nature of the task. Generally, anxiety is more detrimental to attentionally demanding and complicated tasks, and may even facilitate performance on easy tasks (Zeidner, 1998). In addition, highly evaluative environments and speeded time conditions, compared to neutral and nonspeeded conditions, respectively, may accentuate the depressing effects of anxiety on performance (Zeidner, 1998). Negative feedback appears to be especially detrimental to anxious subjects, whereas providing reassurance and social support may eliminate the deficit.

THEORETICAL PERSPECTIVES

As we noted elsewhere (Zeidner & Matthews, 2005), there are numerous theories accounting for the effects of anxiety on performance. Most of these theories have some demonstrable validity as a basis for predicting correlates of anxiety, including decrements in performance. We present three theoretical perspectives that we believe are informative in explicating the causal process in the anxiety-performance interface.

Information-Processing Models

The classic information-processing models first developed in the 1960s and 1970s suppose that processing is supported by a series of discrete stages. Early sensory processing is followed by selective attention to the most important stimulus in the outside world, which is placed in short-term memory. Higher-order cognitive processes such as reasoning and judgment operate on this conscious memory representation, and may also access long-term memory. If action is needed, a response is selected and then executed by the muscles. Models of this kind imply that rather than thinking in terms of some general effect of anxiety on "information processing," we need to be rather more specific about which stage or stages of processing are most vulnerable to anxiety effects (see Figure 5.2). Does anxiety mainly

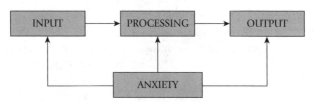

FIGURE 5.2 Effects of anxiety on various stages of information processing.

influence early stages, so that it disrupts selective attention and encoding of stimuli? Or does anxiety affect reasoning and decision-making following initial encoding? Or does anxiety disrupt responding· and motor skills? Researchers have used the experimental methods of cognitive psychology to answer such questions, as we shall describe.

Selective Attention. Early cognitive theories emphasized the influence of anxiety on attention. Broadly, anxious persons appear to be highly distractible, suggesting that they have difficulty maintaining the focus of attention on the task stimuli (Sarason, 1980; Wine, 1980; Zeidner, 1998). According to Wine (1971), highly anxious persons are likely to become extremely self-focused when placed in an evaluative setting. Self-focused attention interferes with their performance by distracting them from focusing on the task—that is, disrupting selective attention (Wine, 1971). A similar theory (Sarason, 1980; Sarason, Sarason, & Pierce, 1990) proposed that trait anxiety and a stressful evaluative context interact to produce worry and heightened self-preoccupation, which interferes with attention (see Figure 5.3 for a graphical depiction of this model). The anxious learners or test taker's are forced to divide their attention between task-relevant activities and self-oriented worries about themselves and the quality of their performance, thereby undermining effective performance. Under ego-threatening conditions, highly anxious individuals do indeed report being preoccupied with how poorly they are doing, how other people are doing, and their overall performance levels (Sarason & Stoops, 1978). Research has also shown that in evaluative conditions, anxious individuals appear to find it difficult to focus attention effectively and spend less time on the task (Deffenbacher & Deitz, 1978).

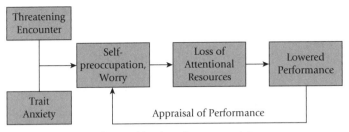

FIGURE 5.3 Sarason's cognitive-interference model.

Memory and Higher-Level Cognition. Anxiety also appears to impair a variety of processes that operate following stimulus recognition, including using working memory, storing and retrieving information in long-term memory, and evaluating and judging stimuli. Research by Ashcraft and Kirk (2001) found that higher math anxiety was associated with lower working memory span when a computation-based assessment of working capacity was administered, whereas no meaningful relationship was found between math anxiety and the language-based assessment of working capacity.

A review of the literature by Eysenck (1992a, 1997) showed that the vast majority of studies report a significant effect of state anxiety on working memory capacity. In particular, the finding that anxiety-linked performance deficits are particularly reliable on tasks that simultaneously require both processing and storage—that is, the combination of cognitive operations for which the working memory is specialized adds support to the centrality of working memory in mediating the effects of anxiety on performance. Similarly, Ashcraft and Kirk (2001) found that higher math anxiety was associated with lower working memory span when a computation-based assessment of working capacity was administered, whereas no meaningful relationship was found between math anxiety and the language-based assessment of working capacity. Recent research links deficits in working memory to similar effects of anxiety on attentional capacity and the executive control systems of the brain that regulate information processing (Ilkowska & Engle, 2010).

Detrimental effects of anxiety on reasoning, problem-solving, and intelligence test performance have also been reported, but they are often of modest size (Austin et al., in press).

Ackerman and Heggestad (1997) reported that a meta-analysis showed a mean r of $-.33$ between test anxiety and general intelligence test performance. The effects of anxiety on reasoning during tests and examinations may be short-lived, consistent with a "stage fright" hypothesis which states that anxious testees may recover from any anxiety effect experienced during the initial stages of a test session (Meijer & Oostdam, 2007). Effects of anxiety on reasoning and intelligence may in part be mediated by its effects on working memory, which is critical for a range of high-level cognitive tasks.

Anxiety may have some more subtle effects on memory also. For example, Tobias (1992) suggested that anxiety may directly interfere in the continual transfer of information between short-term storage and long-term memory, and test anxiety is implicated in difficulties in retrieving information from long-term storage (Zeidner, 1998). At the output stage, anxiety is expected to primarily influence the retrieval of previously acquired information from memory, an effect people probably most closely link to anxiety deficits. In fact, the well-established finding that anxious students perform more poorly in test situations than their less anxious counterparts is usually attributed to interference by anxiety in the retrieval of prior learning from long-term memory.

Cognitive Bias. The research just reviewed makes the assumption that anxiety relates to some general deficits in attention and memory processes. Another possibility is that the effects of anxiety depend on the nature of the stimulus attended to. Specifically, anxiety may actually focus attention on threatening stimuli or potential threats. We can easily imagine that a soldier on patrol would be alert to possible enemy snipers, or a socially anxious individual would be attentive to signs of criticism and rejection from other people.

Mathews and MacLeod (1994) provided an ingenious demonstration of such a *bias* in selective attention, using an emotional Stroop test. The standard Stroop test requires subjects to name out loud the colors in which words are written. If the word is a conflicting color name (e.g., the word *blue*, written in red ink), response is slowed, showing that selective attention is influenced by the content of the word. Mathews and MacLeod showed that anxious individuals were slow to name the ink colors of threatening words such as *failure* and *torture*, suggesting that they involuntarily divert attention to the threat stimulus (which they are meant to ignore). Another technique (the dot-probe task) showed that when words are presented in pairs, anxious subjects tend to attend to the more threatening of the two words. That is, they are faster to respond to a dot stimulus that appears in the position occupied by the threat word.

These effects appear to be quite reliable for general anxiety and a range of more specific conditions such as phobias (Bar-Haim, Lamy, Pergamin, Bakermans-Kranenburg, & van IJzendoorn, 2007). Intriguingly, attentional bias may be found even when the stimulus (e.g., the Stroop word) is masked so heavily that the person cannot consciously identify it (Fox, Russo, & Georgiu, 2005). This finding may suggest that bias operates very early in processing, at an unconscious "preattentive" stage of processing operating prior to conscious recognition. People high and people low in anxiety may thus inhabit different subjective worlds. The anxious people may be anxious in part because their preattentive processing directs their attention toward potential threats, whereas nonanxious people may even neglect threats that are not immediately salient (Williams, Watts, MacLeod, & Mathews, 1997).

Brain-imaging studies reviewed by Canli (2009) suggest that tasks similar to the emotional Stroop tend to activate the amygdala and the anterior cingulate cortex. As discussed in chapter 3, the amygdala is a structure fundamental to emotion generation, and the anterior cingulate may modulate emotional response to cognitive errors and conflicts. Anxious individuals show an enhanced response that may be associated with emotional conflict.

Studies of the various "contextualized" anxieties associated with evaluation concerns have found generally—but not always—similar results. For example, Vasey, El-Hag, and Deleiden (1996) tested for attentional bias in 20 high- and 20 low-test-anxious sixth and eighth graders, using the dot-probe task in which visual attention was indexed by latency for probes presented following neutral and threatening words. High-anxious children tended to allocate attention toward the threat stimuli. Emotional Stroop effects in social anxiety have been replicated several times, although these studies typically use social anxiety patients, rather than nonclinical samples. Typically, social anxiety slows speed of color-naming words such as *boring*, *foolish*, and *inferior* (e.g., Grant & Beck, 2006). By contrast, in a study of math anxiety, Hopko, McNeil, Gleason, and Rabalais (2002) failed to demonstrate any bias associated with a "Stroop" test requiring naming the ink color of math-related words. The study did show that math-anxious undergraduates were impaired on a Stroop-like task requiring counting of numerals printed on cards. Bias in math anxiety may be expressed in attention to the structure of numeric stimuli, rather than to words.

As with selective attention, anxiety may be associated with qualitative biases in later stages of processing as well as with general impairment. Anxious individuals are prone to interpretive biases—that is, exaggerating the threat posed by stimuli or evaluating ambiguous stimuli as being threatening (Ouimet, Gawronski & Dozois, 2009). Negative interpretive biases of emotionally ambiguous stimuli have been reported across a wide array of stimuli—facial expressions, verbal stimuli (threat-neutral homophones such as "die/dye"), and complex social vignettes (Barazzone & Davey, 2009; Bishop, 2007). Indeed, Bishop's (2007) recent review suggests that anxious individuals interpret emotionally ambiguous stimuli more negatively than their less anxious counterparts. Anxious individuals judge future negative life events to be more likely to occur and are more prone to choose negative or less positive interpretations of emotionally ambiguous stimuli than non-anxious controls. As we have already discussed in the context of social skills, anxious individuals tend to underestimate their own performance and competence (Wells & Matthews, 1994).

Similar biases are evident in more complex language-based tasks. In several studies, Calvo (e.g., Calvo, Eysenck & Castillo, 1997) has shown that when subjects read ambiguous sentences, high-anxious persons show a bias toward inferring threatening meanings. The bias in inference seems to operate relatively late in processing. Work on decision-making suggests that anxiety may change how the person "frames" the problem, in relation to defending against threat (Nabi, 2003). Biasing effects of anxiety on memory are generally less robust than for selective attention, but some studies suggest that anxiety makes it easier to retrieve threatening information from memory (Russo et al., 2006).

Attentional Control Theory

A limitation of standard information-processing models based on a series of stages is that they fail to capture the dynamic nature of processing. Three particular dynamics are relevant. First, modern cognitive neuroscience suggests that the brain is a parallel processing device. It executes many "subprograms" simultaneously, in different brain areas, with much communication between programs as they run. Thus, an effect of anxiety on one program can easily propagate to others. Second, the brain includes systems dedicated to regulating and controlling the operation of its specialized subprograms, located in the prefrontal cortex. These are referred to as "executive processes," and it is increasingly believed that anxiety and other emotions affect this cognitive control of lower-level processes (Matthews, Gruszka, & Szymura, 2010). Third, standard models see processing as a linear sequence from stimulus to response. However, as Neisser (1967) pointed out, stimulus intake is itself dependent on the person's plans for actions, which direct an active sampling of the environment. Attentional bias might then reflect an active search for threats requiring defensive action rather than an automatic increase in the priority of threat stimuli (Wells & Matthews, 1994).

Eysenck's (1992) hypervigilance theory accommodates some of these dynamic factors. People predisposed to anxiety engage in high rates of visual scanning in all new or ambiguous situations. If attention processes pick up a potential threat signal, then anxious individuals tend to focus their attention narrowly. This narrowing of attention is accompanied by elevations of arousal and increased effort. Given that attentional processes are of limited capacity (Kahneman & Triesman, 1983), a narrow focus of attention, directed at the perceived source of threat, is accompanied by a relative neglect of other stimuli. The narrowing of attentional focus drains away attention from other tasks, leading affected people to experience problems in concentration and other areas. Thus, the effects of anxiety depend on the person's strategy and motivation—searching for possible danger versus "locking on" attention to an actual threat. Eysenck (1992) also pointed out that anxious people may be aware of the disruption of attention during task performance, and they may apply effort to refocus on the task, thus compensating for being distracted. Thus, performance effectiveness may be maintained even if processing efficiency is compromised.

The attentional control theory of anxiety, proposed by Eysenck et al., (2007), is a further development of this perspective. Eysenck supposes that attention depends on the dynamic balance between a goal-directed (top-down) executive attentional system and a more reflexive, stimulus-driven (bottom-up) system. Attention depends both on the influence of highly salient stimuli that can "capture" the stimulus-driven system and on the executive processes that implement strategic choice of attentional focus. For the typical male college undergraduate, getting some work done on his laptop computer in a Starbucks frequented by attractive female coeds requires the goal-directed system to override the stimulus-driven system.

Anxiety is associated with increased influence of the stimulus-driven attentional system and decreased influence of the goal-directed system. These effects of anxiety are greater when anxiety levels are high (high stress) and when threats activate the stimulus-driven system. In experimental studies of anxiety on attentional bias, the diversion of attention to threat stimuli, such as the emotional Stroop words, reflects the weakness of executive control over attentional capture by threat stimuli.

Overall, anxiety disrupts the functioning of the goal-directed attentional system, producing several effects including the reduced ability to inhibit incorrect prepotent responses, increased susceptibility in distraction, impaired performance on secondary tasks in dual task situations, and impaired switching performance. However, as Eysenck et al. (2007) noted, recent research has shown that several distinct executive processes may be distinguished, including inhibition of distracting stimuli, switching between different task sets, and updating working memory. They argue that anxiety seems to have more robust effects on inhibition and switching than on memory updating. In sum, anxiety impairs processing efficiency because it reduces attentional control, especially in the presence of threat-related distracting stimuli. As a result, the probability that processing resources will be diverted from task-relevant stimuli to task-irrelevant stimuli on tasks involving the inhibition and/or shifting functions is increased.

Attentional control theory also provides a basis for the cognitive neuroscience of attention. A recent unpublished study conducted by M. Eysenck and his coworkers at the University of London (Santos, Wall, & Eysenck, 2010) used functional magnetic resonance imaging to assess the brain activation of 20 students (with high vs. low test anxiety) as a function of varying demands on the attentional control system via a computer-assisted attention-demanding cognitive task (task switching). The data indicated that high-state-anxious subjects, compared to their low-anxious counterparts, showed greater activation in the left and right superior frontal gyrus, which has been implicated in central executive functioning. However, there was no effect of state anxiety on performance. Thus, high state anxiety appears to be associated with impaired processing when high attentional control is necessary.

Self-Regulative Theory of Anxiety

Deficit theories of anxiety and performance are limited by their neglect of the interplay between the person's handling of environmental threats and the person's dispositional vulnerability. Next, we discuss further the dynamic interaction between personal and situational demands, with reference to the S-REF (self-referent executive function) theory of emotional distress (Matthews & Wells, 1999; Wells & Matthews, 1994; Zeidner & Matthews, 2000). The theory builds on earlier work on transactional stress processes (Lazarus, 1999) and cybernetic models of self-regulation (Carver & Scheier, 1989), to specify how anxiety and worry are generated by executive processing of self-referent information. This processing is shaped by declarative and procedural self-knowledge held in long-term memory. Dispositional or trait influences on anxiety are controlled by individual differences in the content of self-knowledge (Matthews, Schwean, Campbell, Saklofske, & Mohamed, 2000), consistent with evidence previously reviewed. The S-REF model also has implications for understanding and treating clinical anxiety, to which we will return in the next chapter.

Self-referent processing is generated initially by intrusions of threatening cognitions or images generated by external stimuli or internal cycles of processing: in the case of evaluative anxiety, thoughts of failure. These intrusions activate executive processing that seeks to initiate appropriate coping (see Figure 5.4). Choice of a coping strategy is influenced by retrieval from long-term memory of self-referent knowledge and schematic plans for action. In the short term, acute distress and worry are generated by accessing negative self-beliefs, that one lacks personal competence, for example, and by choosing counterproductive coping strategies, such as self-blame and avoidance, that focus attention on personal shortcomings. Of special importance are metacognitive beliefs that maintain negative self-referent thinking—for example, it is important to monitor one's worries (Wells, 2000). In the longer term, distress may be maintained by dysfunctional styles of person-situation interaction. The well-adjusted person modifies self-knowledge to accommodate reality and the learning of more effective coping strategies, such as resolving to study harder after a poor examination performance. However, perseverative worry appears to strengthen and elaborate negative self-beliefs, such as being unable to cope with examinations. In addition, avoidant coping strategies lead to lack of exposure to situations that might enhance task-relevant skills. The test-anxious person may be reluctant to study because the study situation focuses attention on the feared event.

The self-regulative model potentially offers the most complete account of the detrimental effects of anxiety on attention. The source of anxiety is dysfunctional self-knowledge (both declarative and procedural), but its expression as maladaptive situational coping, and its perpetuation over time, require the dynamic perspective of the transactional model of stress and emotion (Lazarus, 1999; Matthews et al., 2000). The actions of the anxious person, such as behavioral avoidance and self-denigration to others, lead to environmental exposures that confirm negative cognitive biases, and block adaptive skill learning and restructuring of self-knowledge. Among the various consequences of these processes are the disruptions in information processing seen in acute states of anxiety and worry. Self-referent processing driven by metacognitive goals initiates dysfunctional coping strategies (emotion focus, avoidance, and self-handicapping) that draw attentional resources, working memory, and effort away from the task at hand, leading to impairments if the task is demanding. Vigilant

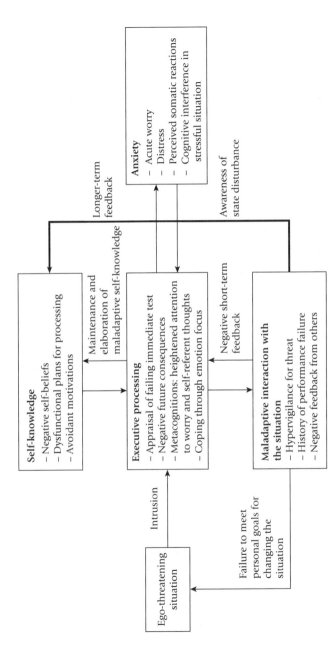

FIGURE 5.4 A prototypical self-regulative model of anxiety.

monitoring for potential threats leads to potentially distracting attentional biases: although such biases are often seen as "automatic," evidence shows that they are typically sensitive to contextual factors, implying strategic influence (Matthews & Wells, 1999). The dynamic perspective also suggests that performance deficits may reflect not just acute cognitive interference but also actual skills deficits resulting from avoidance coping. The self-regulative model also highlights the interplay between motivation, cognition, and emotion in anxiety. Effects of anxiety on behavior are not solely the product of disruptive thoughts and feelings but also of the anxious person's goals for coping with perceived evaluative threats.

Several studies have confirmed the utility of the self-regulative perspective in understanding the detrimental effects of anxiety on performance. A longitudinal study confirmed that there is a reciprocal, dynamic relationship between task stress and performance, consistent with the transactional theory of stress (Matthews & Campbell, 2009). In this study, task demands (high time pressure) elevated anxiety, which in turn impaired working memory. Later studies showed that dysfunctional self-regulation is associated with performance impairment. Matthews, Hillyard, and Campbell (1999) investigated the role of metacognitions in trait and state test anxiety, using the scale developed by Cartwright-Hatton and Wells (1997). They found that trait test anxiety was associated with a dysfunctional pattern of metacognition, such as believing that one's own thoughts are uncontrollable and dangerous. Furthermore, this style of metacognition predicted the level of intrusive "cognitive interference" experienced during an actual university examination, and maladaptive coping. One of the problems faced by test-anxious individuals is managing their own thoughts and concerns. Matthews and Campbell (2009) had subjects perform an attentional task requiring rapid information processing under extreme overload conditions (as high as 150 stimuli/minute in one condition). Participants who appraised task demands as uncontrollable, and coped by using emotion focus and avoidance, showed greater performance impairments and greater task-induced distress.

Table 5.1 summarizes the main effects of anxiety on cognitive performance at various stages of information processing.

TABLE 5.1   INFORMATION-PROCESSING DEFICITS IN
HIGH-ANXIOUS INDIVIDUALS

Deficit Area	Brief Description
I. Information encoding	
1. Encoding difficulties	Experiencing encoding difficulties.
2. Interpretive bias	Exhibiting selective attentional bias favoring threat.
3. Restricted range of cue utilization	Attending to fewer environmental features and having a narrow range of cue utilization.
4. Distractibility	Difficulty in concentrating on cognitive tasks, dividing their attention between the multiple requirements of the complex task and various task-irrelevant activities.
II. Information storage and processing	
5. Short-term storage	Reduction in cognitive capacity devoted to the task, thus reducing resources for short-term memory tasks in test-anxious persons. Working memory is particularly affected.
6. Long-term storage	Impaired retention of information in long-term memory, leading to greater retention loss over time.
7. Depth of processing	Emphasis on processing superficial features of verbal stimuli at the expense of deeper semantic processing and focusing on shallow or physical features rather than deep or semantic features of stimuli.
8. Elaboration and rehearsal	Failure to adequately rehearse or elaborate upon information.
9. Conceptual organization	Shallow encoding and organization of semantic material, by reducing the quality of elaborations and associative paths.
10. Strategic processing	Arousal hinders complex tasks requiring rehearsal or strategic operations, whereas automatic or highly learned operations are relatively unaffected.

(*Continued on next page*)

TABLE 5.1 INFORMATION-PROCESSING DEFICITS IN
HIGH-ANXIOUS INDIVIDUALS (CONTINUED)

Deficit Area	Brief Description
11. Language processing	Vocabulary deficits, deficiencies in comprehension and reading efficiency, selectively detrimental to the efficiency of text-level processes, such as those involving integrating information across sentences.
12. Decision making	Difficulty in absorbing decision-relevant information, difficulty in scanning of alternatives, and adoption of more cautious decisional criteria.
13. Metacognition	Deficient metacognitive knowledge, including knowledge and executive processes used to control learning.
III. Information retrieval	
14. Interference and anxiety blockage	Cognitive interference and self-preoccupations with task-irrelevant information.
15. Information retrieval	Impaired retrieval of material and lowered performance.

SUMMARY AND CONCLUSIONS

The disruptive effects of anxiety on cognitive processes may be felt acutely within our performance-oriented society. People whose anxiety impairs their performance in completing standardized tests, in working with computers, or negotiating challenging social encounters will be seriously disadvantaged in life. Worry and self-preoccupation are the most harmful elements of anxiety. Researchers have made considerable progress in mapping the harmful effects of anxiety on performance in various evaluative contexts, especially in stressful situations. Indeed, it appears that these various forms of anxiety are quite prevalent.

To understand the impacts of anxiety on performance further, we need to build and test cognitive models of anxiety. The simplest such models set out a linear sequence of processing stages between stimulus and response. From this perspective, it appears that anxious subjects may suffer from varying degrees of deficits and interference at three broad stages of information processing—that is, stimulus encoding, central processing, and retrieval from memory. In addition to general processing deficits, anxiety also relates to qualitative biases in cognition, centered on prioritization of threat. These biases include selective attention bias (threats are preferentially attended to) and interpretive bias (stimuli are evaluated as threatening).

Although the application of standard information-processing models has been informative, they fail to capture the dynamic nature of processing, both with regard to internal interactions between different processing systems and to the interplay between processing and the external environment. Attentional control theory describes the executive processes that regulate lower-level stimulus-driven processing. According to the theory, both the distractibility and threat-sensitivity of anxious persons reflect deficits in executive control of the stimulus-driven system. Self-regulative theory sees performance correlates of anxiety as a consequence of self-referent executive processing (persistent worry), which diverts attention toward emotion-focused coping or to an active search for a threat. The theory also emphasizes that excessive self-referent processing interferes with skill acquisition. For example, social anxiety leads to avoidance of social encounters and lack of opportunity for learning social skills and building social confidence.

Thus, research has been quite successful in identifying a range of processes that may contribute to performance deficits in anxiety. Cognitive neuroscientists are also making progress in delineating the brain systems sensitive to anxiety, such as prefrontal areas that support executive processing. More research is needed, detailing how anxiety influences the more complex processing competencies that are often important in real-life settings, including various facets of judgment and decision making, inductive and deductive processes, ideation, and creative behavior. Perhaps the greatest challenge for research is to develop an understanding of dynamic processes in anxiety, especially in real-life settings. Broadly, it seems that anxiety relates to multiple internal processes, and to ways of coping with external threat that may exacerbate performance difficulties. However, it remains somewhat mysterious how the influence of anxiety on cognition plays out over extended time periods, such as taking a demanding semester-long course or completing a critical project at work. Research is also needed in the area of remediation of the cognitive deficits associated with anxiety.

Does Intervention Help?

How a man rallies to life's challenges and weathers its storms tells us everything of who he is and all that he is likely to become.

St. Augustine

n chapter 1, as you may recall, we presented the scenario of Linda, who suffered from a disturbing social anxiety disorder. At the core of Linda's problem was her excessive sensitivity and reactivity to social scrutiny, evaluation, and criticism. When interacting with others at work or in social circles, she felt uncertain and uncomfortable, being convinced she was awkward and socially inept and would be socially rejected by her coworkers and peers. When she did talk to people, she was acutely aware of how anxious she felt and how her social anxiety prevented her from comfortably interacting with others and expressing herself effectively. She seemed to readily access negative personal experiences, especially those involving rejection. Consequently, she tended to keep to herself, interacting only minimally with others on a social basis. However, as noted, Linda's negative perception of herself as socially inept was far from being an objective picture, as she did have decent social skills but lacked the wherewithal and

177

confidence to employ these skills effectively in social contexts. Her tendencies to avoid others, because she felt rejected, made her problems worse.

Most of us can readily empathize with the pain and suffering someone like Linda must feel in daily life, and the dire social consequences of her condition. How do people like Linda, who suffer from an anxiety disorder, differ from others who experience more normal levels of anxiety? How do anxious individuals cope with anxiety? How can they be helped? This chapter sets out to answer these questions. We begin by attempting to differentiate between normal and abnormal forms of anxiety. Next, we examine how people cope with stress and anxiety and then we move on to discuss a broad arsenal of intervention techniques found effective in ameliorating anxiety, including emotion-oriented, cognitive-oriented, and pharmacological interventions. We conclude by presenting a number of considerations in the clinical treatment of anxiety.

NORMATIVE VERSUS PATHOLOGICAL ANXIETY

There has been a steep increase in research and public interest in anxiety and its disorders. Anxiety disorders are among the most common types of psychopathology (Achenbach, Howell, McConnaughy, & Stanger, 1995), and they generally maintain a chronic course when untreated, resulting in substantial impairment across the life span (Feldner, Zvolensky, & Schmidt, 2004). A large-scale survey conducted in the United States has concluded that anxiety disorders constitute the single largest mental health problem in the United States (Barlow, 2002) and the most common category of diagnoses in the *Diagnostic and Statistical Manual of Mental Disorders* (DSM-IV, 1994). More people visit doctors for anxiety than for colds, and anxiety is now more common in the population than depression (Barlow, 1973). Indeed, anxiety is a predisposing factor to major depression (Bagby, Joffe, Parker, Kalemba, & Harkness, 1995) and to suicide attempts (Coryell, Noyes, & House, 1986). Researchers have also linked self-reports of anxiety to a variety of physical ailments, including asthma, coronary heart disease, irritable bowel syndrome, ulcers, and inflammatory bowel disease (for a review, see Edelmann, 1992). Out of the big-five traits, N, closely akin to trait anxiety, was the strongest predictor of life satisfaction, happiness, and negative affect in a meta-analytic study (DeNeve & Cooper, 1998). Also, high levels of anxiety predispose people to marital problems (O'Leary & Smith, 1991) and sometimes lead to alcohol and drug abuse (Chambless, Cherney, Caputo, & Rheinstein, 1987).

According to a recent review by Mineka and Zinbarg (2006), approximately 29% of the U.S. population is estimated to have, or to have had, one or more diagnosable anxiety disorders at some point in their lives. Furthermore, it is estimated that about 50% of the visits Americans make to mental health professionals are anxiety related. Approximately 20 million Americans suffering from various anxiety disorders that lead to an estimated economic cost of more than $50 billion per year in loss of work productivity, health care, and hospital care (LeDoux, 2006).

How can we know if the anxiety suffered by someone like Linda is normative or should be diagnosed as an anxiety disorder? Clearly, it is perfectly normal to experience some degree of anxiety when faced with stressful or threatening situations; most people experience anxiety in their lives at one time or another in reaction to threatening or dangerous events. As previously discussed, normal anxiety has considerable utility and adaptive value in that the rapid and early detection of warning signs of danger in the immediate surroundings enables the individual to avoid, prepare for, and cope more effectively with future threatening encounters (Eysenck, 1982; Ohman, 2008). Specifically, anxiety prepares the organism's body for quick and vigorous actions by energizing and activating the sympathetic and somatic nervous system for immediate reactions to threatening or dangerous stimuli. Thus, when a person is faced with danger or threat or an aversive situation, an adaptive anxiety response is elicited and this subsides when the aversive situation diminishes.

There is currently a debate between two conceptions of anxiety as they relate to normal versus pathological levels of anxiety—the *continuity* versus *qualitative difference* conceptions.

The continuity conception posits that anxiety is best conceptu-alized as lying on a continuum, with a low amount of anxiety at the lower end; higher levels of anxiety at the middle; and a severe amount of anxiety at the upper end of the contin-uum. That is, anxiety disorders are at the upper extreme end of the continuum, representing a severe level of uneasiness and intense feelings of alarm, apprehension, dread, and panic, that interferes with daily functioning. By contrast, the qual-itative difference conception posits that anxiety disorders are best viewed as being qualitatively different from normal levels of anxiety. It is useful to clinical psychologists to work with discrete diagnostic categories, and they have a simplifying quality (i.e., a person either has or does not have an anxiety disorder). However, the dimensional approach is more infor-mative and accurate. Indeed, excessive anxiety can be seen as one of several abnormal dimensions that can be used to build up a comprehensive account of pathology in personality (Widiger & Lowe, 2007). Other dimensions include antisocial personality, social inhibition, and compulsivity (Matthews et al., 2009).

The writers of this book broadly espouse the dimensional conception of anxiety. However, there may be a discontinuity between normality and abnormality in relation to significant problems in living, at which point the person is likely to be steered toward professional help. Anxiety may be no more than a source of discomfort to the person up until the point that he or she has to stop working or encounters marital problems because of its severity. As we will discuss later, this is a transac-tional perspective, which sees problematic anxiety as reflecting the person's pattern of interaction with the social environment around them.

It would be fair to say that anxiety, like most things in life, may be good in small to moderate amounts but becomes bad and maladaptive in extremely excessive amounts. Overall, the major anxiety disorders are characterized by grossly exagger-ated versions of normal anxiety and distress that we all have experienced. At the same time, researchers have attempted to distinguish normal from abnormal anxiety using a multitude of differentiating criteria. These include intensity of affective reac-tion; appropriateness of anxiety level to the threat; rationality of response; duration and recurrence of emotional state; degree of suffering from the anxiety; perceived controllability; severity of cognitions; coping styles; and effects of anxiety on coping and functioning. Thus, in the face of a threatening event, normal anxiety reactions are more or less proportional to the threat, entail reasonable worry about the consequences, moderate arousal, and a minimal disruption to daily life and coping abilities. In contradistinction, anxiety reactions that are excessive and disproportional to the threat involve extremely high levels of arousal, and seriously disrupt coping and social functioning are labeled as an "anxiety disorder."

Table 6.1 summarizes a number of differences found in the clinical literature in attempting to differentiate between normal and pathological anxiety levels.

Thus, clinical psychology gives us procedures for discriminating normal and abnormal levels of anxiety, which seem to work at least tolerably well in clinical practice. We should note some potential issues in making the discrimination. First, the student should keep in mind that anxiety in real human beings is not as straightforward as a diagnostic manual might suggest. Each anxious person has his or her own individual quirks and life circumstances, which may not be captured by the diagnostic scheme. In addition, two or more emotional disorders often occur together ("comorbidity"). It is not unusual for anxiety patients to also meet criteria for depression or eating disorders, for example, and vice versa.

Second, although we need practical tests for deciding whether people need psychiatric treatment or not, the boundary between normal and abnormal functioning may be decidedly blurred. People with "subclinical" levels of anxiety may be experiencing substantial distress without actually meeting the requisite clinical criteria. An important trend in current abnormal psychology, as suggested above, is to see conditions such as anxiety as reflecting dimensions rather than categories. That is, clinical anxiety is not an all-or-nothing category. Rather, there is a continuum of different levels of anxiety that shade into increasing degrees of abnormality at the top end of the spectrum. Thus, there is no sharp cutoff between normality and abnormality (although clinicians still have to make distinctions about whether the anxiety requires treatment).

TABLE 6.1 COMPARISON OF NORMAL VERSUS PATHOLOGICAL (ABNORMAL) FORMS OF ANXIETY, BY KEY DIMENSIONS

Criteria	Normal	Abnormal
Nature	Normal cognitive, affective, and somatic reactions to impending threat or danger.	Abnormal, excessive, erratic, or extremely exaggerated cognitive, affective, and somatic reactions to impending threat or danger.
Intensity	Experiencing appropriate levels of anxiety, given impending threat.	Being overwhelmed by inappropriate and excessive levels of anxiety, given impending stress or threat.
Persistence and duration	Relatively transient, short bouts of anxiety.	Persistent and relatively longer periods of severe anxiety.
Recurrence	Relatively infrequent anxiety reactions that usually do not repeat themselves without specific threat.	Relatively frequent anxiety reactions, which tend to be recurrent even in absence of objective threat.
Appropriateness of response to situation or context	Generally proportional to severity of aversive event.	Generally in disproportion to severity of event.
Intensity of personal distress and suffering	Feelings of varying degrees of tension, worry, uneasiness.	Being overwhelmed by feelings of elevated levels of dread and unbearable panic and suffering.
Perceptions of reality and rationality	Relatively realistic perceptions, given existing threat, with anxiety having meaning in light of situation, though exaggerated at times.	Often exaggerated or warped perceptions, with little rational meaning (e.g., sudden panic attack), with catastrophic interpretations of past events.

Cognitions	Unwanted cognitions (e.g., worry, cognitive interference), particularly related to future events going on in one's life, emanating largely from an outside event.	Chronic, unwanted worry, intrusive thoughts, and ruminations, having automatic quality and emanating largely from within the person. Persistent thoughts often interfere with cognitive functioning.
Competence and self-regard	Somewhat reduced.	Greatly reduced.
Perceived control	Mild to moderate.	Low.
Defenses and coping strategy	Normal use of defense mechanisms and both problem-focused and emotion-focused strategies.	Frequent use of avoidance, ritual acts, or thoughts regarding means of protecting individual from society. Extreme resistance to thinking of impending threats.
Coping capacity	Intact.	Seriously diminished.
Ego resiliency	Ego functioning remains intact and person is generally successful in coping with the anxiety.	Anxiety tends to paralyze the individual and person finds it difficult to cope with the anxiety.
Effects on behavior	Minimal to moderate effects on social and behavioral functioning; person is able to resume normal pattern of life.	Seriously impedes psychosocial and behavioral/somatic functioning, with frequent breakdown in social functioning. Long-term problems in ability to work and maintain relationships. Tends to paralyze the individual, and unable to cope, and results in impeded psychosocial functions.
Adaptiveness of behavior	Adaptive—signals that threat is imminent and calls for action. Person is able to resume normal pattern of life.	Nonadaptive—interferes with achieving personal goals. Long-term problems in ability to work and maintain relationships.

In any case, when anxiety goes awry and becomes excessive, irrational, or leads to a dread of daily routine situations or events, it can cause untold psychic pain and discomfort and develop into a host of disabling and costly anxiety disorders (panic attacks, generalized anxiety disorders, obsessive behaviors, social phobia, and posttraumatic stress disorder [PTSD]). The *DSM-IV* (1994) lists over a dozen disorders in which the main symptom is excessive fear or anxiety (see Table 6.2 for a summary of major anxiety disorders).

TABLE 6.2 SUMMARY OF MAJOR ANXIETY DISORDERS

Specific Anxiety Disorder	Brief Description
General anxiety disorder	Marked by chronic, excessive, unrealistic anxiety about possible future misfortune (e.g., ill health, financial disaster, welfare of loved ones, or some combination of misfortunes) and almost constant nervousness and wide range of worries extending over long periods of time (several months).
Disorder	Characterized by rapid onset of repeated episodes of intense fear and sudden attacks of anxiety in which person experiences intense terror and dread; symptoms include sharply increased heart rate, rapid breathing, noticeable sweating, trembling, chest pain; often unexpected and comes out of the blue.
Phobia	Intense fear and extreme anxiety evoked in the presence of particular stimuli (open spaces, closed spaces, heights, animals, etc.), generally interfering with everyday life. The central feature is the extreme, persistent, circumscribed fear of a specific event, object, or place.
Obsessive-compulsive disorder	Repetitive efforts to prevent and protect oneself and prevent undesirable outcomes. Person plagued with stereotypic acts and repetitive thoughts and behaviors, some of unacceptable or repugnant nature. Need to ward off disaster by performing certain compulsive acts (washing hands) or thinking of certain ideas (ritual repetition of material learned during particular time period).

(Continued)

TABLE 6.2 SUMMARY OF MAJOR ANXIETY DISORDERS
(CONTINUED)

Specific Anxiety Disorder	Brief Description
Posttraumatic stress disorder	Syndrome following a life-threatening horrific experience. The syndrome includes prolonged bouts of intrusive thoughts and reliving events, frequent distressing recollections (flashbacks, nightmares) of traumatic events, attempts at avoiding events, arousal, exaggerated startle reflex, etc. Involuntary tendency to recall or reexperience events in flashbacks or dreams; strong tendencies to avoid people or places associated with original stress.

It is noted that it is really difficult to pinpoint how much anxiety is within the normal range and how intense anxiety has to be before being considered abnormal. Also, the current system used by the *DSM-IV* for diagnosing anxiety disorders is categorical, despite the fact that many of the diagnostic items are continuous and quantifiable. It is also important to remember that what is considered to be "excessive anxiety" is a function of a person's life circumstances; we tend to define what is excessive in terms of what seems appropriate under someone's circumstances. For example, if one lives in a war-ridden country, such as Afghanistan, Sudan, or Colombia, then it makes sense for people to be exceptionally anxious, aroused, and worried about future dangers, as the world really is a dangerous place (Rosen & Schulkin, 2004). Given the multifaceted nature of these disorders, a multifaceted approach that recognizes the interplay of personal and environmental factors is needed to effectively address the mental health problem of anxiety-related psychopathologies.

Theoretical Conceptions of Pathological Anxiety

A number of interesting hypotheses have been proposed to account for pathological anxiety. As in the case of "normal," subclinical anxiety, both biological and cognitive models have been suggested. Indeed, it is probable that biological and cognitive risk factors interact to produce clinical anxiety. One influential model of panic disorder (Barlow, 2002) supposes that some individuals are neurobiologically overreactive to stress. At a cognitive level, the panicker comes to associate elevated bodily arousal with a sense that emotions are uncontrollable, generating apprehension about future panic attacks, and increased vulnerability to panic.

Rachman (2004) theorizes that anxiety disorders may be a price paid for the "wired-in" evolutionary bias toward minimizing maximum losses and avoiding type II errors (Rachman, 2004; see our chapter 1, Anxiety: What Is it Good for?). Accordingly, the human organism is wired to prefer a "mini-max" decision strategy (i.e., choosing a strategy that minimizes maximum loss) when under potential threat, by playing it safe and evoking defenses and avoidance behavior even in situations that turn out to be nonthreatening ones. This built-in bias may predispose humans toward anxiety disorders by guaranteeing effective defense systems when a person's life is at stake. Anxious persons, waiting for the least favorable outcome to happen, may prevent themselves from experiencing positive outcomes in life and often are unable to gain gratification. Thus, anxiety disorders are the failure of evolutionary-designed mechanisms to perform their inherent function.

Beck and Emery (1985) theorize that those individuals who develop an anxiety disorder continue to remain in a "danger mode" and are geared to defensive action patterns linked to anxiety long after the actual danger has passed (Beck & Emery, 1985). The symptoms of an anxiety disorder are inappropriate responses based on excessive estimates of danger in a given situation, on one hand, and underestimation of the person's ability to perform or cope adequately, on the other. The *cognitive* reaction in maladaptive anxiety focuses attention on danger and may produce "tunnel vision," which blocks out extraneous ideation. The cognitive capacity may be so taxed by coping with danger that little capacity remains to satisfy other demands on processing. The affective reaction reflects several built-in mechanisms to cope with threat. The *behavioral* symptoms reflect hyperactivity of the behavioral system (restlessness) or its inhibition (tonic immobility—freeze reaction). Thus, according to Beck and Emery (1985), anxiety disorders stem from a malfunction of the system for activating and terminating a defensive response to a threat.

At a cognitive level, the content of people's beliefs about themselves—or self-schema—may shape vulnerability (Clark, Beck, & Alford, 1999). Anxiety disorders are generally associated with beliefs in personal vulnerability and inability to cope with threats. However, patients experiencing the different disorders shown in Table 6.2 appear to have internalized somewhat different sets of self-beliefs (Wells & Matthews, 2006). Generalized anxiety relates to a sense of one's own worries spinning out of control (Wells, 2000) and to looming danger that is appraised as rapidly escalating (Riskind, Williams, & Joiner, 2006). Cognitions in panic disorder relate more to beliefs that bodily sensations signal some disaster, such as a heart attack. PTSD centers on beliefs that the trauma experienced is common and beyond personal control and obsessive-compulsive disorder to exaggerated personal responsibility for disturbing thoughts and images. Distortions in thinking drive both anxiety and efforts at coping that are misdirected and ineffective.

Rosen et al. (1998) offered a neurobiological explanation that is congenial with the two hypotheses presented earlier, helping to explicate the biological underpinnings of anxiety disorders. Rosen and coworkers hypothesized that pathological anxiety evolves directly from normal fear responses, with psychosocial stressors initiating changes in the brain's fear circuits that lead to enhanced perception and response to subsequent threat and danger. Thus, during normal fear states, activity in the brain's fear circuits increases but subsides when the danger diminishes. However, during and following severe or persistent stressful episodes, the fear circuits may become over-activated. Lower firing thresholds for activation and connectivity in these circuits may evolve and fear-related responses may become independent of the triggering stimuli. Repetitive activation of the amygdala, through repeated negative experiences and consequent repeated episodes of excessive anxiety, may produce chronic hyperexcitability in the amygdala. Eventually, the activation of the fear circuits becomes independent and autonomous from the triggering stimuli, thus being out of the conscious control of the individual and becoming "functionally autonomous."

Dynamics of Cognitive Vulnerability

Both biological and cognitive accounts of anxiety disorders have been elaborated further, but we do not have space to do justice to the various theories of vulnerability. As an example, we will outline the perspective on vulnerability to disorder provided by the self-referent executive function (S-REF) model (Wells & Matthews, 1994) that we described in the previous chapter (see chapter 5, Theoretical Perspectives: Self-Regulative Theory of Anxiety). The model is of interest because it attempts to describe the changes in cognitive processing that may generate and perpetuate anxiety disorders.

As we saw in the last chapter (see chapter 5, Theoretical Perspectives: Self-Regulative Theory of Anxiety), the S-REF model attributes anxiety (and other negative emotions) to a maladaptive style of self-regulation that is driven by negative self-beliefs held in long-term memory. What, then, makes anxiety pathological? In common with other cognitive theories of anxiety (e.g., Riskind & Alloy, 2006), the S-REF model in part attributes abnormality to faulty self-knowledge, such as gross overexaggeration of threat and underestimation of personal coping abilities. However, the model goes further in three respects. First, it emphasizes the importance of "procedural" knowledge as well as explicit or "declarative" knowledge. The anxious person develops damaging cognitive routines for handling potential threats, like shunning invitations to social events, which may not be consciously accessible. Second, the S-REF model highlights the role of metacognitions in pathology, such as meta-worry—that is, worrying about one's own worry (Wells, 2000). Excessive monitoring of worry may intensify it to the point where it cannot readily be "switched off" when the person needs to focus on some external activity. Third, prolonged worry blocks modification of dysfunctional beliefs and may encourage behavioral avoidance strategies that prevent effective coping. For example, the socially anxious person who becomes a hermit loses the opportunity to enhance social skills and to receive positive feedback from interactions with others. Thus, the S-REF model sees pathology as reflecting not just intense anxiety but, more fundamentally, styles of processing threat and maintaining negative self-beliefs that promote harmful interactions with the outside world.

Figure 6.1 shows an outline of the vulnerability factors recognized by the S-REF model (Wells & Matthews, 1994, 2006). A key element is "dysfunctional self-knowledge," broadly defined to include negative self-beliefs, harmful metacognitive beliefs, and processing routines or "procedures" that lead to counterproductive coping efforts. Dysfunctional self-knowledge is built up by developmental processes (see chapter 4, Heredity and Environment). A comprehensive review suggests that early learning and socialization, when considered together with temperamental vulnerabilities, can serve as diatheses that make certain individuals more susceptive to adverse and stressful experiences, sometimes leading to the development of anxiety disorders (Mineka & Zinbarg, 2006). Consideration of the diatheses, as well as of various contextual variables during and following traumatic learning events, can lead to a rich and nuanced understanding of the etiology and course of anxiety disorders.

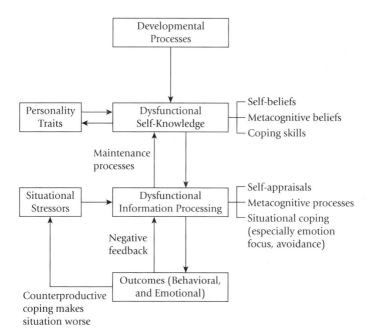

FIGURE 6.1 An outline of cognitive vulnerability factors in the S-REF model of anxiety.

Once dysfunctional self-knowledge is established, contributing to the individual's personality, it increases the likelihood that situational stressors will elicit various maladaptive styles of information processing that lock the person into a vicious cycle of continuing worry and exaggerated awareness of threat. This style of processing in turn maintains dysfunctional self-knowledge. It also elicits the harmful patterns of interaction with the outside world we have already discussed, such as excessive avoidance of feared situations.

Having sketched some of the psychological factors that shape excessive and pathological anxiety, we turn next to interventions. We will focus initially on how best to cope with the normal anxieties of everyday life. We will briefly review the impact of coping on anxiety and practical techniques for enhancing coping. We will then turn to therapies for treating clinical anxiety.

COPING WITH ANXIETY

Whether 'tis nobler in the mind to suffer, the slings and arrows of outrageous fortune or to take up arms against a sea of troubles, and by opposing, end them.

William Shakespeare, *Hamlet*

Everyday anxiety requires us to *cope*—that is, to deal directly with the source of threat, or manage our feelings about it constructively. We naturally develop a repertoire of coping strategies for dealing with the difficulties that arise at work, in relationships, and in financial matters. Most people attain reasonable competence in coping through learning and experience. However, where people face significant—but still nonclinical—anxiety, they may benefit from interventions that enhance their powers of coping. In this section, we present a brief survey of what is known about coping strategies and their effectiveness, and outline some practical techniques directed to improving coping skills. Coping is a cognitive-psychological construct (although it does have psychobiological correlates), and so our discussion will be based on the cognitive theories of emotion discussed in chapter 3 (see Cognitive Models). Coping is especially prominent in Lazarus's (1991, 1999) theory of emotion, which emphasizes the dependence of emotions on the person's active attempts to manage the demands and challenges of life.

Coping, broadly speaking, involves a person's constantly changing cognitive and behavioral efforts to manage (i.e., reduce, minimize, master, and tolerate) the internal and external demands of a transaction that is appraised as stressful (Lazarus, 1999; Lazarus & Folkman, 1984). Accordingly, when the demands of a threatening situation, such as an important job interview or a hot date with a promising romantic partner, are perceived as stressful and taxing one's personal resources, efforts are directed at regulating emotional stress and/or dealing with the problem at hand (Folkman & Lazarus, 1986) in order to manage the troubled person—environment transaction (Lazarus, 1990). Coping processes are of prime importance in that they affect adaptational outcomes (Lazarus & Folkman, 1984). Effective coping will help an individual adapt to a stressful situation by reducing distress and anxiety, but misplaced, counterproductive coping attempts may make the situation worse and eventually lead to elevated anxiety.

Coping efforts are centered and structured around certain goals, issues, and patterns of challenges referred to as *coping tasks* (Cohen & Lazarus, 1979). Successful coping depends on the successful resolution of the particular situation-specific coping tasks. With respect to coping with failure on an important job assignment, adaptive coping would involve the employee's need to enhance his or her prospects for success in the future (e.g., by improving specific skills, seeking help, and working longer hours), learning to tolerate or adjust to the reality of failure, maintaining a positive self-image, maintaining emotional equilibrium and decreasing emotional stress, and maintaining a satisfying relationship with the environment (e.g., not taking out one's frustration, on account of occupational failure, on others in the immediate environment).

The coping process is typically described as a linear sequence consisting of three subprocesses—that is, primary appraisal, secondary appraisal, and specific coping responses (Lazarus, 1999). *Primary appraisal* is the process of perceiving and evaluating a situation as involving threat, challenge, harm, or benefit to oneself. *Secondary appraisal* is the process of bringing to mind a variety of potential responses to situations appraised to be threatening or challenging. Primary and secondary appraisals converge to determine whether the person-environment transaction is regarded as significant for well-being and, if so, whether it is primarily *threatening* (containing the possibility for harm or loss) or *challenging* (holding the possibility of mastery/benefit). Appraisals shape subsequent coping; for example, if a situation is appraised as being beyond personal control, there is little point in trying to cope through direct action. Although the subprocesses may operate in sequence, they also typically interact. For example, a secondary appraisal of personal helplessness may feed back to primary appraisal and ramp up the perceived level of threat.

Although researchers have employed various classification schemes in categorizing general coping strategies, there is some consensus surrounding the major categories of coping strategies (for a critical view see Skinner et al., 2003), which include:

1. *Problem-focused coping* is designed to manage or solve the problem by removing or mitigating the anxiety-evoking situation (e.g., preparing a complex PowerPoint presentation for the annual board meeting). Because problem-focused coping would be expected to alter the actual terms of the individual's stressful relationship with the environment, this should lead, in turn, to more favorable cognitive appraisals and a more positive response to the ego-threatening situation. However, problem-oriented coping can also have adverse effects, including elevated situational anxiety, in that dealing with the stressor can arouse thoughts about the impending threat (Pekrun, in press). Over the long run, however, the beneficial effects of problem-focused behaviors, such as improving one's competencies to deal with the stressful circumstances, are believed to outweigh any negative situational effects.

2. *Emotion-focused coping* is designed to regulate, reduce, or eliminate the anxiety symptoms and negative affect associated with the anxiety-evoking situation (e.g., use of relaxation techniques, seeking emotional support from friends, denying the importance of an impending public speech,

distancing oneself from the physical threat, smoking or alcohol consumption). Sometimes, emotion-focused coping involves the reduction of emotional tension by simply accepting anxiety and the possibility of failure (i.e., "secondary control"; Morling & Evered, 2006; Rothbaum, Weisz, & Snyder, 1982). Emotion-focused techniques also involve induction of positive anxiety-incompatible emotions, such as using humor, listening to relaxing music, or cognitively reappraising the threatening situation as being more controllable or less subjectively important. Many of these strategies may in fact be effective in reducing negative emotions.

3. *Avoidance-oriented* coping refers to the use of either person-oriented strategies (e.g., avoidance or seeking of others) or task-oriented strategies (e.g., zapping TV channels and engaging in nonrelevant tasks) designed to mentally or behaviorally avoid or escape an anxiety-evoking situation. Examples of such strategies include effort withdrawal, physical escape, denial, procrastination, and focusing attention on task-irrelevant issues (Pekrun, in press). Although avoidance strategies can lead to a reduction in immediate state anxiety, the long-term effects of avoidance can also be severe. First, consciously avoiding the experience of anxiety can lead to a detrimental increase of less conscious emotional arousal on a physiological level (Spangler et al., 2002). Moreover, although these strategies may temporarily reduce anxiety, the underlying factors contributing to the experience of anxiety (e.g., low perceived control) remain untreated.

Coping strategies may protect us by eliminating or modifying the conditions that produce stress or by keeping the emotional consequences within manageable bounds (Zeidner & Hammer, 1990). Coping may also affect outcomes through its impact on the frequency, intensity, duration, and patterning of physiological stress reactions, and the resultant affective and somatic outcomes. Often, coping strategies may impede—rather than promote—health-related behaviors. For example, a person's health may be negatively affected when coping involves risk taking (high-speed car racing) or substance abuse.

Effectiveness of Coping Strategies

The psychology of stress gives us a rich descriptive account of different types of coping. The practical question, though, is, "What works?" If we want to help people cope better, we need to determine which coping strategies are most effective in reducing anxiety. Unfortunately, the simple question of what works has no simple answer. A basic difficulty is that it is difficult to assess coping effectiveness—which may further vary across research paradigms, contexts, and even sociocultural settings; a coping response might be judged successful relative to one outcome criterion but not another. Indeed, the resolution of one coping task might even come at the expense of another—for example, working long hours to succeed on the job but at the same time contributing to problems at work or a marriage breakdown (Zeidner & Saklofske, 1996).

Coping effectiveness must be examined in the context in which problems occur; "without information about the social context we would have half the story" (Lazarus & Folkman, 1984, p. 299). Also, evaluations of coping effectiveness must be sensitive to broader social (Weidner & Collins, 1993) and cultural factors (Marsella, DeVos, & Hsu, 1985), including social values. Preferred coping methods and perceived effectiveness must be appraised relative to a social or cultural group values, norms, world view, symbols, and orientation. Consider the case of a female student who devotes herself to her children or ailing parents at the expense of her academic studies or personal achievement goals at work. The evaluation of this coping approach is not merely a scientific but a moral matter and may differ in traditional versus achievement-oriented societies. Evaluating coping effectiveness must be further addressed relative to people's normative response to a stressor.

Thus, any statement about coping effectiveness is at best a broad generalization. With this caution in mind, there are a number of specific techniques that have been typically judged by researchers as adaptive, and others that have been judged as maladaptive, whereas other techniques present dilemmas to researchers (Carver, Scheier, & Weintraub, 1989). Theorists have frequently emphasized the positive effects of problem-focused coping on psychological outcomes (Lazarus & Folkman, 1984). In fact, active coping is preferred by most persons and is generally more effective in stress reduction (Gal & Lazarus, 1975). Active coping provides a sense of mastery over the stressor, diverts attention from the problem, and discharges energy following exposure to threat. Non-problem-solving strategies are increasingly used when the source of stress is unclear, when there is a lack of knowledge about stress modification, or there is little one can do to eliminate stress (Pearlin & Schooler, 1978). Logical analysis, purposeful planning, positive reappraisal, suppression of competing activities, acceptance, and use of humor may also be adaptive in a variety of situations (Carver et al., 1989).

By contrast, theorists have frequently emphasized the *negative* effects of avoidance and emotion-focused coping on psychological outcomes, especially when the threatening situation can be ameliorated by the subject's responses (Lazarus & Folkman, 1984). The clinical literature points toward prolonged but unproductive brooding over problems (rumination or perseverative worry) as being likely to exacerbate anxiety (Wells, 2000). Behavioral or mental disengagement, ventilation of emotions, and tension reduction strategies (e.g., use of alcohol and drugs) are generally candidates for dysfunctional coping tactics for the amelioration of anxiety, while moderate use of some tactics in coping with anxiety, such as cigarette smoking and overeating, may serve as effective short-term affect-regulation mechanisms, thus reducing negative affect. However, if practiced in excess and over time, these tactics may be injurious to health (Wills, 1986). On the other hand, there may be psychological benefits to more constructive forms of emotion-focused coping such as gaining understanding of one's emotional reactions to an uncontrollable event, such as bereavement. Overall, emotion-focused coping or avoidance may help in maintaining emotional balance, but an adaptive response to remediable situations still requires problem-solving activities to manage and remove the threat.

Researchers often face something of a dilemma in considering how to treat strategies that have multiple functions such as relaxation, exercise, or turning to prayer/religion (Carver et al., 1989). For example, from the perspective of stress reduction, relaxation techniques or exercising in the gym would imply emotion-oriented coping. However, to the extent that alleviation of emotional tension and anxiety improves self-agency and problem-focused behavior, these specific techniques can also subserve problem-oriented objectives. Another case in point: a student might turn to religion in coping with exams as a source of emotional support to relieve anxiety, as a vehicle for positive reinforcement and growth, or even as a form of active coping. In the face of failure on an important exam, feelings of helplessness and depression may be moderated by the belief that one's fate is in the hands of God, much like in the case of loss or bereavement (cf. a review of the literature by Stone, Helder, & Schneider, 1988). Thus, use of discrete coping categories runs the danger of assessing behavioral "surface structures" of coping while perhaps missing deeper structures of functional equivalence.

Similarly, avoidance coping has both its adaptive and maladaptive aspects. On one hand, there is a wealth of data to indicate that avoidance coping, reflecting a temporary disengagement from active or instrumental coping, is positively tied to concurrent distress (Aldwin & Revenson, 1987; Holahan & Moos, 1985). On the other hand, avoidance has been argued to be a useful tactic at times because it gives the person a psychological breather and an opportunity to escape from the constant pressures of the stressful situation (Carver, Scheier, & Pozo, 1992). For example, in the "waiting phase" after an exam or a medical operation, it may be quite functional to simply avoid any action at all. Thus, caution needs to be exercised when a priori defining avoidance strategies as being maladaptive.

Overall, the transactional model of stress and coping (Lazarus, 1999; Lazarus & Folkman, 1984) offers several basic working assumptions impacting on current conceptualizations about adaptive coping. First, coping strategies should not be pre-judged as adaptive or maladaptive. Rather, the concern must be for whom, and under what circumstances, a particular coping mode has adaptive consequences, rather than the wholesale categorization of coping as adaptive versus maladaptive. For example, active coping might be adaptive during the earlier phases of an illness, when something can still be done about the situation, whereas wishful thinking or emotional social support might be more adaptive after an operation, when the person is immobile in the hospital bed. Further, coping is a process embedded in context. Therefore, responses may vary not only across contexts but also change over time in response to external conditions, and as a function of the skill with which it is applied. Thus, coping strategies found to be effective in the context of family disputes may not be effective in coping with occupational stress or grave traumatic stressors. Another assumption is that coping effectiveness must be empirically demonstrated, with coping strategies not classifiable as being adaptive versus maladaptive on an a priori basis (cf. Zeidner & Saklofske, 1996). Finally, coping efforts should not be confounded with coping outcomes (Lennon, Dohrenwend, Zautra, & Marbach, 1990).

Stress Management and the Training of Coping Skills

The transactional model of stress provides a useful framework for thinking about alternative paths to managing stress. Its basic position that external stressors influence cognitive processes which, in turn, drive stress response, suggests three alternate strategies for intervention, discussed as follows.

Environmental Interventions. In some settings, such as the workplace, it may be possible to change the external, objective environment so as to reduce demands on the person that are excessively threatening. For example, physical stressors like loud noise may be mitigated, and jobs may be redesigned to prevent excessive workload and to give workers more control over their work activities. It is also important to address social demands such as poor supervision, lack of social support within the workplace, and ambiguity over the worker's precise role. Giga, Cooper, and Faragher (2003) point out that organizational interventions are often effective in mitigating stress and anxiety but tend to be underused. Employers may be inclined to shift responsibility for mental well-being to the individual, rather than encouraging organizational change. Another context where the environment is relevant is in education. Test anxiety may be reduced by making the test environment more pleasant to work in, and structuring test questions and procedures to support the examinee (Zeidner, 1998).

Cognitive Modification. One of the implications of the transactional model is that anxiety management is not simply a matter of cognitive restructuring. If a person works in a genuinely horrible workplace, or if he or she lives in a country beset by war or terrorism, no amount of cognitive intervention will remove anxieties that are based on reality. Nevertheless, there may be circumstances where the person can be supported in appraising his or her situation more constructively and in developing more effective coping skills. In the former case, the overanxious person may be helped to evaluate the situation more realistically, without exaggerating danger, or to be more aware of his or her own coping skills and strengths. In the latter case, the emphasis is typically on training for specific behavioral skills, such as social skills, that will allow the person to deploy problem-focused coping successfully. Emotion-focused coping may also be trained, for example, by helping the person learn to regulate his or her emotions adaptively, for example, in anger management. In the organizational context, stress management can be trained through group classes, although it is important for the organization to maintain an ongoing commitment (Giga, Cooper, & Faragher, 2003). Many of the techniques here are derived from clinical psychology—even when suitable for nonclinical populations—and we will return to them in detail in the next section.

Alleviating Stress Response. Drugs or relaxation techniques may be used to reduce stress and anxiety responses. Indeed, anxiolytic drugs are among those most commonly prescribed by physicians. Various psychological techniques are also shown by research to be effective. These include deep muscle relaxation, biofeedback (learning to control bodily responses via a feedback signal), meditation, and yoga. Such interventions may be criticized as attacking the symptom rather than the cause of anxiety. Certainly, it is often true that more fundamental issues should be addressed, whether environmental or personal. However, there are several points in favor of a symptom-based approach. First, it may be effective in dealing with short-term stressors, which will resolve themselves naturally. Second, it provides the stressed individual with a "breathing space" from the problems in which he or she can explore alternative therapies. Third, anxiety management programs may seek to provide the person with control over symptom relief, so that it can be used as a coping strategy. Several programs seek to train the person to recognize symptoms of impending anxiety and apply response management techniques such as deep muscle relaxation on their own initiative (Barrios & Shigetomi, 1979).

CLINICAL INTERVENTIONS

A bewildering array of anxiety treatment programs have been developed and evaluated over the past three decades for normative, subclinical, as well as clinical forms of anxiety. Treatment fashions and orientations have swayed sharply from the psychoanalytic to the behavioral and more recently to the cognitive perspective—essentially mirroring the evolution of the behavior therapies.

There is no simple organizing principle with which to categorize the plethora of therapeutic techniques and approaches that have proliferated over the past few decades. Current attempts have typically focused on treatments directed toward either the emotional, cognitive, or behavioral facets of anxiety. Thus, treatment programs typically include "emotion-focused" treatments, designed largely to alleviate negative emotional affect experienced by anxious persons; "cognitive-focused" treatments, designed to help the anxious client cope with worry and task-irrelevant thinking; and skills training, designed to improve various skills (social, athletic, motor, study, and test-taking skills) and enhance their performance. In addition, the past few decades have evidenced the development and usage of a wide array of anti-anxiety drugs that serve as important adjuncts to psychological treatments and interventions. In the next section, we briefly survey key intervention techniques and methods offered for the entire spectrum of anxiety states, from mild through severe and pathological.

Emotion-Focused Interventions

The emotion-oriented therapies aim primarily at reducing the heightened emotional responses of anxious persons when faced with stressful situations. Based on the assumption that anxiety comprises a physiological component, attempts to alleviate anxiety symptoms should prove successful, in part, if they focus on reducing levels of arousal or on altering ways in which people appraise their arousal in threatening situations. The basic strategy in these treatments is directed to teach the anxious client certain skills (mainly relaxational) so that when confronted by anxiety-inducing situations in the future, he will be able to handle them adequately. The therapies also provide opportunities for application of training either within the therapy setting or in real-life situations (the dentist's office, workplace, school, etc.).

These emotion-focused procedures typically include a number of common components, such as theoretical explanations of anxiety as a conditioned response and the "deconditioning" rationale for treatment; instructions in specific methods for reducing anxiety, such as relaxation and guided imagery; guided practice in therapeutic methods; and practice (homework, in vivo practice). By and large, these emotion-focused treatments rely on key behavioral learning principles (counterconditioning, reciprocal inhibition, extinction, observational and coping skills learning, etc.) and also draw from an arsenal of behavioral techniques, such as deep muscle relaxation, guided imagery, and graduated hierarchies. For example, relaxation and guided imagery is not unique to a particular anxiety behavioral intervention method but is employed in several methods, including relaxation as self-control, systematic desensitization, and anxiety management training.

Systematic desensitization, originally designed to inhibit excessive physiological responding and anxiety-evoking imagery in the face of aversive stimuli (Wolpe, 1958), is generally considered to be the most popular procedure for the treatment of anxiety. The "classical" behavior therapy tradition (Wolpe, 1958) views anxiety as a classically conditioned emotional reaction resulting from a person's aversive experiences in ego-threatening situations. Systematic desensitization proposes that anxiety reactions to threatening situations may also be unlearned through specific counterconditioning procedures (Sieber, O'Neil, & Tobias, 1977).

The anxious client is typically trained in a deep muscle relaxation procedure and, while relaxed, instructed to visualize an ordered series of increasingly stressful scenes (an "anxiety hierarchy"). The anxious client proceeds up the imagined hierarchy until he or she is able to visualize the most anxiety-evoking scenes on the list without experiencing anxiety (Emery & Krumboltz, 1967). Through repeated pairings of imaginal representations of threatening situations with deep relaxation, the bond between the threatening evaluative scenes and anxiety is expected to be weakened. In this manner, the anxiety is said to be "counterconditioned" and inhibited by the incompatible relaxation response. Following successful treatment, the client is usually able to approach the previously anxiety-evoking situation with little or no anxiety (Sieber et al., 1977). Following are a number of key principles of this salient anxiety-alleviation procedure:

1. *Providing clients with a rationale for treatment.* The rationale aims at providing clients with the concept of anxiety as a learned emotional-cognitive-behavioral complex. In addition, desensitization is presented as a process that can be used to unlearn anxiety reactions by replacing the anxiety response with a calm relaxed state (Deffenbacher & Suinn, 1988). Relaxation training is explained as blocking the anxiety psychologically and physiologically, as one cannot be tensed up, and calm and relaxed at the same time.

2. *Relaxation training.* Although there are many different relaxation training procedures (e.g., biofeedback, meditation, etc.), progressive relaxation is the one most frequently used (Deffenbacher & Suinn, 1988). Prior to beginning progressive relaxation training, a relaxation image is often constructed to be used later in the relaxation process. The relaxation image consists of a specific moment in the person's life that was very relaxing and calming (e.g., hearing some birds chirping gently in the trees, strolling along the beach, feeling a gentle breeze across your face, fishing under the blue skies, reading a favorite novel in the late hours of the night, listening to a favorite piece of classical, jazz, or pop music; Deffenbacher & Suinn, 1988).

3. *Hierarchy construction.* The goal of hierarchy construction is to develop a list of stressful evaluative situations that can be clearly visualized and that elicit increasing amounts of anxiety. Typically, a hierarchy will include anywhere from

8 to 20 items, with an attempt to have the items equally spaced in anxiety-arousing capacity. Generally, the hierarchy begins with nonthreatening or only slightly threatening items (e.g., announcement of an upcoming exam), and proceeds through more and more personally threatening items (e.g., receiving a poor grade on a major exam). When deeply relaxed, the evaluative stimuli are presented in hierarchical order so that the subject imagines the least anxiety-provoking scene first and then progresses to increasingly powerful scenes as rapidly as possible, without disturbing the level of relaxation. As the client moves gradually up the hierarchy, anxiety is deconditioned as relaxation is counterconditioned to the anxiety arousing stimuli from the hierarchy.

Barrios and Shigetomi (1979) reviewed studies of the effectiveness of several techniques of this kind. They concluded that, typically, such interventions for anxiety are more effective than doing nothing at all. However, mixed results have been obtained in comparisons of anxiety management programs with conventional behavior therapies and with "attentional placebo" conditions. These latter are control conditions that require participants to attend to the therapists, for example, in a group discussion, but have no content relating to anxiety management. Barrios and Shigetomi also point out that many evaluation studies are methodologically flawed so that it is difficult to determine how well the intervention actually worked.

Emotion-focused treatments may be more effective if combined with therapy modes focusing specifically on cognitive change. An example is Meichenbaum's (1985, 2009) stress inoculation training. It comprises three phases. First, the trainee is educated about sources of stress, within a given context. Next, the person is trained in both emotion-directed and cognitive techniques for managing stress. Finally, the trainee practices his or her newly acquired coping skills in real or simulated situations. Stress inoculation captures one of the key aspects of stress within the transactional model (Lazarus, 1999)—that it is experienced and managed within a particular context. The technique has been applied successfully in a variety of contexts including occupational stress, test anxiety, and pain management. An interesting extension is the use of virtual reality environments to provide immersive simulations of stressors. For example, military veterans with PTSD may be helped through carefully managed exposures to simulated combat environments (Stetz, Wildzunas, Wiederhold, Stetz, & Hunt, 2006).

With clinical patients it becomes increasingly important to treat underlying cognitive causes of anxiety, as well as providing symptom relief. Next, we discuss the cognitive-oriented interventions developed and validated by cognitive-behavior therapists.

Cognitively Oriented Interventions

Recent years have witnessed a proliferation of cognitively oriented intervention programs that emphasize the mediating role of cognitive processes in sustaining or eliminating anxiety. "Cognitive therapy" is a generic term that refers to a wide array of therapeutic approaches directed toward modifying the worry and irrational thought patterns of anxious clients. Broadly speaking, cognitively oriented approaches to anxiety intervention are quite similar in assuming that cognitive processes are determining factors in anxiety, although they differ in terms of actual intervention procedures. A fundamental assumption, shared by contemporary cognitive models of anxiety, is that cognitive processes mediate the person's emotional and behavioral responses to stressful situations. It follows that in order to modify the negative emotional reactions of anxious clients to anxiety-evoking situations, therapy needs to be directed at reshaping the faulty premises, assumptions, and negative attitudes underlying maladaptive cognitions of anxious subjects. Given their multiple emphasis on modifying emotional processes, irrational thoughts and cognitions, and behavioral deficits, this results in a powerful approach that merges emotionally oriented, cognitively oriented, and behaviorally oriented techniques to alleviate clients' anxiety.

According to Beck and Emery (1985), leaders in the field of cognitive therapy, an effective way of reducing a person's anxiety is to create a warm therapeutic relationship and encourage the client to face frightening relationships and talk about them realistically. The therapist needs to be sincere and empathetic and correctly understand what the patient is saying and convey this understanding to him. Also, the therapy is viewed as a collaborative effort between therapist and patient. The patient supplies raw data and the therapist provides structure and expertise in how to solve the problem. In cognitive therapy, the therapist often uses the Socratic Method and uses questions as leads, as often as possible. This induces clients to become aware of their thoughts and examine them for distortions. The therapist helps the client substitute more balanced thinking and to make plans to develop new cognitive patterns. The therapist models cognitive strategies and ways of rational thinking for the client (What do I have to lose or gain? What would be the worst thing to happen? How can I learn from experience?). Because the client's thinking is in a state of disorder, anxious, overwhelmed by fearful thoughts, and the person feels loss of control, cognitive theory gives the anxiety-ridden person a highly structured format for approaching a problem, thus providing reassurance to the client. The therapist trains the client how to respond to his or her distorted thoughts with logic and systematic testing of assumptions. The client then learns to identify and modify long-held assumptions and sometimes faulty underlying conclusions.

Beck and coworkers view cognitive therapy as being "problem oriented." The therapy is based on an educational model; with its basic premise being that with practice one can learn more effective ways of leading one's life. Therapy focuses on helping the client learn how to learn and on removing obstacles and blocks that prevent the client from learning. The emphasis of treatment is on forming of hypotheses, gathering of facts, and testing of hypotheses. Specifically, therapy focuses on identifying and solving current problems by implementing four basic steps. First, it helps the client conceptualize his or her problems ("Do you fear your supervisor because you fear rejection from an adult figure?"). Second, cognitive therapy helps choose an effective therapeutic strategy to reduce anxiety (e.g., relaxation, accepting anxiety, coming to terms with who we are and others as they are). Third, during the course of cognitive therapy the client is helped in choosing a technique to implement this strategy. Fourth, during the course of cognitive therapy the effectiveness of the chosen strategy is assessed.

Metacognitive Interventions

Conventional cognitive therapy focuses primarily on the *content* of cognition, such as the negative self-schemas highlighted by Beck and Emery (1985). In a development of the cognitive approach, Wells (2000, 2008) has argued that it may also be beneficial to change the ways in which troubling thoughts are controlled and regulated (i.e., a more process-based approach). Regulation of thinking depends on metacognitions, as described by the S-REF model (Wells & Matthews, 1994) we outlined above. Thus, "metacognitive therapy" may be necessary for anxiety patients. Standard cognitive therapy addresses irrational beliefs such as believing one is likely to have an accident, whereas metacognitive therapy focuses on processes that might lead a person to worry continually over being in an accident.

Wells (2000, 2008) has developed metacognitive therapies that are based on the S-REF model. In particular, therapy seeks to give the client the power to gain control over the cycles of maladaptive self-regulation that generate perseverative worry and maintain dysfunctional self-knowledge. One such technique is *attention training.* The client is trained in various forms of attention, including dividing and switching attention, using a variety of sounds as stimuli. Increased skills in attentional deployment help the person to direct attention away from personal concerns when desired and promote detachment from potentially disturbing thoughts. Although attention training is not directed toward the *contents* of thought, it has been shown to be effective in treating a range of anxiety disorders including panic disorder and social phobias, as well as major depression, and hypochondriasis. Interestingly, Siegle, Ghinassi, and Thase (2007) found that, in depressed patients, attention training influenced the amygdala response to emotional stimuli, highlighting the interconnections of cognitive and neural processes in psychotherapy.

Another form of metacognitive therapy targets harmful metacognitions directly. In this case, the treatment may be tailored toward the particular metacognitions characteristic of the different anxiety disorders. In GAD, the key metacognitions include beliefs that worries are uncontrollable, and that lack of control is dangerous (Wells, 2000). Metacognitive therapy seeks to change these beliefs through verbal strategies and behavioral experiments that allow the client to explore the consequences of worrying in a safe environment. Wells (2010) report a pilot treatment trial that showed metacognitive therapy was considerably more successful than a standard relaxation technique in treating GAD, with benefits persisting over a 12-month period.

A brief summary of key emotion-oriented and cognitive-oriented treatments for anxiety and their reported effectiveness are presented in Table 6.3. It is noted that the distinction between the various treatment orientations is quite fuzzy, and the multitude of current approaches are becoming increasingly difficult to distinguish. Although there may be highly specific interventions, which have an affective (e.g., relaxation therapy) or cognitive (e.g., rational emotive therapy) orientation, most methods are normally embedded in a multidimensional context. At present, a combination of procedures (whether combined in a truly integrative manner or in the stance of technical eclecticism) seems to best represent the true nature of the anxiety intervention process.

Pharmacotherapy

Biological psychiatry has repeatedly demonstrated the effectiveness of a number of different drug groups in alleviating anxiety. Drug treatment is viewed as a useful adjunct to psychotherapeutic treatment, rather than as a stand-alone treatment method (Tyrer, 1999). Until the development of modern anti-anxiety drugs, the only drugs that could successfully quell anxiety were such drugs as barbiturates, opioids, and alcohol—all which had many negative side effects. Quite fortunately for victims of anxiety, modern drugs (e.g., valium) seem to produce no serious physical side effects.

The most effective of commonly prescribed anti-anxiety drugs include *benzodiazepines* (e.g., valium), producing calmness by promoting GABA-mediated inhibition of the fear system (Panksepp, 1998). The treatment was revolutionized by discovery of the drug chlordiazepoxide, known by the brand name Librium. Then, valium, a potent benzodiazepine, became available and conquered the market. Drugs such as Librium and valium have greater specificity (i.e., targeting anxiety specifically) and better "safety margins" than other drugs on the

TABLE 6.3 SELECTED ANXIETY INTERVENTIONS

Treatment	Description	Effectiveness
I. Emotion-oriented intervention techniques		
Relaxation training	Recommended on the premise that maintaining a relaxed state, via deep breathing and muscle relaxation exercises, would counteract a person's aroused state. Presumably, if a person knows when and how to apply relaxation, it will be applied directly as a counterresponse to anxiety.	Meta-analytic research tends to support the effectiveness of relaxation therapy in decreasing somatic manifestations of anxiety.
Systematic desensitization	Situation-specific anxiety is viewed as a classically conditioned emotional reaction resulting from a person's experiences in aversive situations. Systematic desensitization proposes that anxiety reactions to threatening situations may also be unlearned through specific counterconditioning procedures. The anxious client is typically trained in a deep muscle relaxation procedure and, while relaxed, instructed to visualize an ordered series of increasingly stressful scenes (an "anxiety hierarchy"). The client imaginally proceeds up the hierarchy until he or she is able to visualize the most stressful scenes on the list without experiencing anxiety. Through repeated pairings of imaginal representations of threatening evaluative situations with deep relaxation, the bond between the threatening evaluative scenes and anxiety is expected to be weakened.	Meta-analytic data lend support to the effectiveness of systematic desensitization in reducing anxiety, particularly test anxiety, in school-children and college students.

(Continued on next page)

TABLE 6.3 SELECTED ANXIETY INTERVENTIONS (CONTINUED)

Treatment	Description	Effectiveness
Anxiety management	Teaches highly anxious subjects to recognize their situation-specific-related arousal responses as they are building, and then to use them as cues for initiating the coping response of relaxation in threatening situations.	A body of research supports the effectiveness of this technique in reducing anxiety. Thus, anxiety management training appears to be as robust and effective as, if not more so than, related interventions. Reductions in debilitating anxiety were maintained for follow-up periods ranging from several week to several months.
Modeling	Involves the live or symbolic (e.g., through videotape) demonstration of desired coping behaviors in a stressful situation, such that they can be subsequently imitated by the anxious person. It is assumed that exposure to models displaying adaptive behavior may play a positive role in facilitating performance. Clients are instructed to vividly imagine the stressful evaluative scene and to focus on the anxiety and associated response-produced cues (e.g., racing heart, neck and shoulder tensing, dryness of the mouth, and catastrophic thoughts). Clients are then trained to use these cues to prompt adaptive coping skills to actively relax away tension, and reduce anxiety before it mounts too severely.	A body of research lends support to the effectiveness of modeling in treating anxiety. In particular, exposure to models who are task-oriented and provide attention-directing cognitive structuring clues is beneficial to the performance of anxious persons. Of additional benefit is evidence, in the behavior of the model, that he or she is successfully coping with the worry and tension associated with anxiety.

II. Cognitive-oriented techniques

Cognitive-attentional training	Cognitive attentional training provides specific training in the redirection of attention to task-focused thinking and emphasizes the inhibition of task-irrelevant thinking and nonproductive worry. Attentional training programs traditionally provide clients with instructions to attend fully to the task and to inhibit self-relevant thinking while working on a variety of tasks.	The beneficial effects of attentional instruction on the anxiety and cognitive performance of high-anxious persons are supported by some empirical research. Task instructions that provide individuals with information about appropriate problem-solving strategies, and away from self-preoccupied worry, may be particularly helpful to the anxious individual's cognitive functioning.
Cognitive restructuring	The rationale is that anxious persons will be able to master their anxiety by learning to control task-irrelevant cognitions that generate their anxiety and direct attention from their task-directed performance. The two most prominent cognitive therapeutic methods in anxiety intervention are Rational Emotive Therapy and Systematic Rational Restructuring. Both forms of treatments are based on the premise that anxiety or emotional disturbance is a result of illogical or "irrational" thinking. Systematic Rational Restructuring aims at helping anxious clients to discover the worrisome task-irrelevant thoughts they entertain, to eclipse such thoughts, and to substitute positive self-statements that redirect their attention to the task at hand.	A number of studies provide evidence showing that these techniques may be effective in reducing anxiety.

(Continued on next page)

TABLE 6.3 SELECTED ANXIETY INTERVENTIONS (CONTINUED)

Treatment	Description	Effectiveness
Cognitive-behavioral modification	A multifaceted program merging both cognitively-focused and emotionally-focused techniques (as well as skill training in many cases), thus offering the anxious client the best of many worlds. This multimodal treatment attempts to deal with the multiple manifestations of anxiety, including negative motivational or affective tendencies, irrational thought patterns, and skills deficits, and emphasizes the application and transferring of acquired coping skills to in vivo anxiety-evoking situations.	"Multimodal" treatment packages, such as cognitive-behavior modification, are most likely to be effective via their support for the inclusion of multiple domains related to anxiety. These procedures are relatively effective in reducing self-reported levels of debilitating anxiety, and are equally effective, more or less, in reducing both cognitive and affective components of anxiety.

market. The major problem with this class of drugs is the dependency developed by some clients during long-term use.

Additional anti-anxiety drugs that have proven effective include *β-blocking drugs* (β-noradrenergic blockers) and *monoamine oxidase inhibitors* (MAOs). MAO inhibitors (e.g., phenelzine) have been proven to be highly effective for control of social phobias and other neurotic personality disorders. However, for common symptoms of anxiety, β-blockers (e.g., propranalol) still appear to be the drug of choice. β-blockers are particularly effective for control of anxiety that accompanies certain activities, such as public presentations (e.g., reducing anxiety of the first violinist performing before an international audience). Whereas propranolol has been shown to be particularly congenial for treating panic attacks and physical symptoms of anxiety, MAO inhibitors (e.g., phenalzine) have shown effective control of the symptoms of social phobias.

A number of additional anti-anxiety drugs on the market include *azaspirodecanediones* (e.g., buspirone), antihistamines (e.g., promethazine), *tricyclic antidepressants* (e.g., chlomipramine), and *serotonin reuptake inhibitors* (SSRIs; e.g., paroxetine). Tricyclics are effective in reducing panic attacks and childhood anxiety disorders. Buspirone, a very popular non-benzodiazepine drug, has anxiety modulation effects through the 5-HT (serotonin) system. Buspirone has few side effects and does not cause dependency sedation or other effects. However, this drug has limited use because it is not as effective as benzodiazepine drugs, and new agents—e.g., those that inhibit *cholecystokinin* (CCK) and other *neuropeptide receptor systems,* as well as those that stimulate *neuropeptide Y oxytocin systems*—show promise.

CLINICAL CONSIDERATIONS

Successful psychotherapy is much more than a "cookbook" approach of mechanical application of a predetermined treatment. Clinicians must deploy a variety of therapeutic skills in order for therapy to be effective in reducing anxiety. Because of this, we advise readers to be wary of "self-help" books and Web sites—psychotherapy is one of those activities not to be tried at home. If you do think you experience excessive anxiety, consult a qualified professional. The following considerations should be held in mind by both researchers and practitioners when developing, implementing, or evaluating anxiety intervention programs.

1. *Performing careful diagnosis of client's problem.* To tailor treatment programs to meet the specific needs and problems of the client, a logical first step is a careful diagnostic assessment and analysis of the nature of the anxious person's affective and cognitive problem(s). For some anxious subjects, provision of skills training may be the treatment of choice, whereas for others it would involve teaching relaxation skills, building up of self-confidence in a particular area (e.g., computer skills), or addressing metacognitive dysfunction. Information about the following aspects of the client's problem might be particularly useful:

   ● Nature of the problem as experienced and defined by the anxious client
   ● Perceived severity and generality of the problem
   ● Duration and extent of anxiety
   ● Perceived origins of anxiety
   ● Situation-specific factors which intensify or alleviate anxiety reactions
   ● Specific consequences of anxiety for the client
   ● Suggested changes the client views as potentially helpful.

A careful diagnostic assessment may suggest factors other than anxiety proper that underlie one's heightened emotional reactions in evaluative situations.

2. *Meeting preconditions for therapeutic effectiveness.* In order for an anxiety intervention program to work, a number of preconditions need to be met. First, anxious individuals ought to possess certain relevant skills in their behavioral repertoire (e.g., problem-solving, relaxation, study/test taking skills, metacognitive strategies) to apply under appropriate ego-threatening circumstances. Second, anxious clients must be sufficiently motivated to deal directly with stressful situations and have the wherewithal and self-efficacy to efficiently implement the coping skills they have at their disposal. Third, anxious persons must be provided with an

adequate amount of practice and experience in applying various coping skills in true-to-life anxiety-evoking situations in order to ensure transfer of therapy from the treatment environment to the real world.

3. *Adjusting treatment to the needs of particular "types" of anxious individuals.* Interventions and therapeutic techniques would be most effective if they could be adjusted to suit the needs of different types of anxious persons. Because there are different types of high-anxious individuals, each characterized by different problems and concerns (e.g., failure in meeting personal or social expectations, low feelings of self-efficacy and failure acceptance, poor job or social skills, etc.), no single treatment program would be expected to be equally effective across the board. Thus, for some highly perfectionist test-anxious students, therapy may focus on lowering socially prescribed performance expectations, whereas for other "failure accepting" students, therapy may consist of raising performance expectancies and enhancing perceived self-efficacy. Comparably, persons high in social anxiety with sound social skills should profit from behavioral treatment focusing on anxiety reduction. By contrast, those with defective social skills and high anxiety in social situations would profit from a combined intervention program to improve their social skills as well as decrease anxiety.

4. *Basing treatment on the broader diagnostic picture and specific goals of therapy.* The choice of which therapy to use will be influenced not only by the diagnosis of the specific nature of the client's problem and type of anxiety, but by the broader diagnostic picture, the immediate and long-term goals of treatment, and the therapeutic orientation adopted. For example, although relaxation may not increase the performance of anxious students with study-skill deficits, it may be prescribed by the therapist to help the student achieve the immediate goal of achieving control over evaluation anxiety as a first step toward academic problem-solving. Thus, once the anxiety that interferes with learning new study skills is removed, the next step would then be training the student in efficient study skills. Furthermore, there are different ways that a therapist may view his or her anxious clients' problems (distorted thinking styles, poor problem-solving skills,

etc.). And each of these views may give rise to different treatment procedures.

5. *Consideration of individual differences.* Before implementing a particular treatment, one needs to determine to what extent the treatment may interact with particular client characteristics. For example, some interventions may reduce anxiety or successfully increase the performance of high-anxious individuals, only to have a negative effect on the anxiety performance of others who are low in anxiety. Another case in point: Whereas some people might considerably benefit from relaxation training, experiencing a substantial decrease in anxiety, some have difficulty in acquiring relaxation skills and benefit little from relaxation training. Some clients may even experience relaxation-induced anxiety during relaxation training!

6. *Addressing multiple modalities and loci of therapeutic impact.* One important consideration is that the various components of anxiety must be dealt with if the anxiety experienced in anxiety-evoking situations is to be reduced and improved performance is to occur as a result of treatment. It is important to have interventions sufficiently complex to deal with the major facets (cognitive, affective, and behavioral) of the anxiety experience. Indeed, a treatment would be expected to be most effective if it impacts upon the entire range of components and chain of events leading to anxious manifestations in ego-threatening situations (arousal, worry, meaning system, internal dialogue, behavioral acts, etc.), rather than focusing on only one aspect of the process.

7. *Interaction among components of anxiety.* A basic consideration is that anxiety is more than a combination of physiological arousal, negative self-preoccupation, and a deficit in stress-related coping skills, and poor social skills. It is the complex interaction among these diverse components that seems to define anxiety. Because the cognitive, affective, and behavioral components of anxiety interweave in contributing to the problem of anxiety and its treatment, it is predicted that an induced change in one system would generally be followed by a change in the other. Thus, therapeutic approaches, which emphasize cognition, often extend to the emotional life, too, and vice versa. For example, it is likely

that emotion-focused training (e.g., progressive relaxation) may make the client less anxious and result in a decrease in anxiety-focused, task-irrelevant ideation. By the same token, some forms of cognitive therapy may provide anxious subjects with an increased sense of perceived control, which might spill over into the emotional domain and result in lower emotional arousal in a stressful situation.

SUMMARY AND CONCLUSIONS

As discussed, it is extremely difficult to precisely differentiate and define the nature of normal versus abnormal forms of anxiety. Indeed, the cutoff point for distinguishing normal from abnormal levels of anxiety tends to be rather ill defined and somewhat arbitrary. Furthermore, because excessive anxiety may reflect abnormality in both biological and cognitive-psychological processes, there are a variety of treatment approaches.

At present, there is no consensus about which coping strategies for relieving anxiety are most effective and adaptive. It is not yet entirely clear whether coping influences adjustment, whether coping tactics covary with adjustment, or whether coping and distress are mutually intertwined reflections of yet some other human condition or characteristic. Further research is needed to clarify how the various coping strategies may resolve problems, relieve emotional distress, and reduce the likelihood of future difficulties. Future research should shed light on what outcome measures should serve to validate coping as being adaptive or maladaptive in an ego-threatening situation; how long a time lag there should be between assessment of coping and outcomes; how coping in anxiety-evoking situations differs from coping in other situations; whether it makes sense to talk about coping when individuals are really responding to challenges as opposed to threats; and what is the ordinary balance of helpful coping to harmful coping with stressful situations. Future research will hopefully clarify the kind and extent of the effect of coping on adaptational outcomes.

Because anxiety has many facets, including arousal, subjective feeling of dread, worry cognitions, and escape tendencies, there is frequently a loose coupling among the components in intervention. Thus, the components of anxiety may show some asynchrony or different rates of change in response to treatment. For example, cognitive-behavioral therapy aims first at the client's maladaptive cognitions, whereas behavioral therapy regularly aims at the client's behavior, with the first possibly occurring earlier in the chain.

It is now readily apparent that anxiety intervention should be based on a careful theoretical analysis of the nature of anxiety and its key components and manifestations. Traditionally, however, anxiety treatment studies have mainly evolved from interest in specific behavioral treatment techniques, rather than from an analysis of the nature and effects of anxiety (Spielberger, Anton, & Bedell, 1976). Indeed, most investigators who have applied behavioral methodology to the reduction of anxiety have generally given little attention to relating the treatment process to important theoretical conceptions. Recent advances in therapy, such as metacognitive theory, are increasingly concerned with the dynamic processes that may initiate and maintain excessive worry and anxious emotion. The current diversity of cognitive-oriented, emotion-oriented, and pharmacological treatments for anxiety treatments, while supplying the clinician with a rich variety of treatment options to choose from in rendering services, also reflects a state of uncertainty marked by the lack of consensus regarding the most effective method for treating anxiety.

Looking Ahead to a Cognitive Science of Anxiety

Anxiety might have goaded some of our prelinguistic, pre-deliberative-reasoning ancestors into action, but that doesn't make it the right system for creatures like us, who do have the capacity to reason.

Gary Marcus (2008), *Kluge*, p. 154

I n this final chapter, we offer a perspective on the journey taken by anxiety research and where its future destinations are. In our view, the dominant paradigm for the psychology of anxiety has been cognitive-psychological. The view that anxiety is essentially a bias in thinking has been established by key pioneers in the field, including Charles Spielberger, Richard Lazarus, Aaron Beck, and Norman Endler. Lines of research supporting the cognitive hypothesis include the effects of appraisal on anxiety, the role of worry in mediating anxiety effects on behavior, and the correspondences between anxiety and clinically oriented phenomena such as attentional bias and dysfunctional self-beliefs. Cognitive models have provided effective bases for interventions, both for managing everyday anxiety and in cognitive-behavioral therapies for clinical patients.

As a conclusion to *Anxiety 101*, we will cover three key topics. First, we will summarize the case in favor of cognitive psychology as the dominant paradigm for future anxiety research. We will look at the cognitive perspective on the origins of anxiety, on its consequences for behavior, and at its therapeutic implications.

Second, we will see how cognitive anxiety research may be elaborated within a broader "cognitive science" framework. We will highlight the prospects for integrating cognitive and biological perspectives within cognitive neuroscience and the role of self-regulation in anxiety.

Third, we will consider some possible challenges to the cognitive paradigm. Does the focus on cognition and information processing lead to neglect of unconscious facets of anxiety? Could we indeed develop a pure neuroscience-based account of anxiety, to which cognitive models are peripheral? A different kind of critique comes from recent social psychology. Are broadly defined constructs like *appraisal* appropriate for understanding anxiety within the individual person?

We will conclude with some brief reflections on the multi-leveled nature of anxiety and the challenges it poses for psychological theory.

COGNITIVE MODELS OF ANXIETY AS STANDARD THEORY

As we discussed in chapter 3 (see Cognitive Models), the cognitive paradigm marked a decisive break with previous concepts of anxiety, focusing initially on psychoanalysis, and then on learning and drive theory. Spielberger's (1966) groundbreaking theory expressed the central tenets of the cognitive theory that remain influential today. State anxiety is generated by cognitive appraisals that external events are threatening. Thus, processing threat appraisals produces both anxious emotion (including physiological symptoms) and intrusive thoughts (worries) that can disrupt attention and behavior. Trait anxiety corresponds to a more long-lasting bias in appraisal processes that accentuates potential threats. Spielberger also recognized the self-regulative aspect of anxiety, pointing out that the person's appraisals and management of his or her own anxiety responses can serve to exacerbate anxiety.

Spielberger's (1966) cognitive theory of anxiety also gained traction through the widespread adoption of his State-Trait Anxiety Inventory (STAI) questionnaire as the gold standard for measurement of trait and state anxiety (see chapter 2, Subjective Scales for Measuring Anxiety). Although the STAI does not differentiate the various facets of anxiety, other scales (notably those of Sarason [1984]) separate anxious emotion, bodily symptoms, and worry. As discussed in chapter 5 (see Anxiety and Cognitive Performance), studies using these more fine-grained scales have confirmed Spielberger's central hypothesis that it is the cognitive elements of anxiety (worry) that are the primary source of performance impairment.

Much of the contemporary cognitive psychology of anxiety can be seen as elaborating on Spielberger's basic position. The appeal of cognitive models is that, seemingly, they can explain the full spectrum of findings on the psychology of anxiety, including its origins, consequences, and pathology.

Origins of Anxiety

It is useful to distinguish "distal" and "proximal" sources of anxiety (see chapter 4, Some Basic Issues)—that is, the long-term development of vulnerability to anxiety versus the immediate factors that provoke anxiety in a given, stressful situation. Cognitive models provide a coherent account of anxiety vulnerability that builds on Beck's work on various emotional disorders (e.g., Beck & Emery, 1985). Central to Beck's approach is the idea that faulty thinking makes us mentally sick. That is, it is the *content* of thoughts about oneself that causes anxiety and mood disorders. In the case of anxiety, the person holds harmful beliefs that exaggerate personal vulnerability to threat. Such beliefs are not always easily accessed consciously but they shape how the person processes information in potentially threatening situations.

Other cognitive theorists have emphasized process rather than content in cognition. The highly anxious person is like a vehicle with a faulty alarm that sounds an internal horn even when no intruder is actually trying to break in. This perspective connects with one of the major cognitive theories of emotion, appraisal theory (Scherer, 2009). Anxious emotion is a by-product of evaluating the personal significance of events. Its purpose is to make the person sit up and pay attention to the possible danger (signal function) and to communicate danger to other people who may be able to assist (Oatley & Johnson-Laird, 1996).

Appraisal theory is most directly concerned with short-term, proximal emotion processes, but there may also be stable biases in appraisal. Some individuals may develop appraisal processes that are prone to exaggerate threats quite early in childhood (see chapter 4, Some Basic Issues: Temperament in Children), leading to lifelong vulnerability to anxiety. In the case of clinical anxieties, the person may go through life habitually reacting to threats that are minor or entirely illusory.

Cognitive accounts of the sources of anxiety have gained credibility from fine-grained investigation of the information-processing structures and routines involved. Beck et al.'s (1985) schema theory implies that negative self-beliefs are held in a special-purpose memory structure, the self-schema. Experimental studies have confirmed that memories of the self have a special status (Klein, Sherman, & Loftus, 1996). As discussed in chapter 4 (Heredity and Environment: Attachment Processes), the child's attachment to the mother may shape the schema-like cognitive structures which subsequently provide an internal model for later intimate relationships.

Similarly, the idea of a bias in appraisal has a counterpart in the experimental studies of interpretive bias that we reviewed in chapter 5 (Information-Processing Models, Cognitive Bias). A bias in language processing in anxious individuals leads them to access threatening interpretations of ambiguous stimuli. Most intriguingly, recent studies (e.g., Wilson, McLeod, Mathews & Rutherford, 2006) suggest that training people to attend to threats or interpret ambiguous stimuli as threatening increases vulnerability to stressful emotion. Training studies provide some of the most direct evidence that changes in information processing lead to changes in emotional functioning. Wells and Matthews (1994) suggest that threat detection in anxious patients operates as a perverse skill. The socially anxious person may have routines for processing interpersonal behavior that extract a personal criticism from some innocuous remark.

Consequences of Anxiety

As we discussed in chapter 1 (Major Forms of Anxiety in Modern Society), there is a rich tradition of research on "anxiety in the field," which has explored how anxiety is expressed in contexts including formal evaluations and the objective dangers posed by terrorist attacks. As with causes of anxiety, consequences may unfold over shorter and longer time spans (Lazarus, 1999). In the short term, anxiety is distracting; it becomes hard to focus effectively on an exam question or a job interview. In the longer term, depending on personal resilience, chronic anxiety can wear the person down and lead to various mental and physical health problems. In the extreme case, traumatic events may cause long-lasting posttraumatic stress disorder (PTSD).

Cognitive theory has proved to be helpful in understanding both short- and long-term consequences of anxiety. In the case of chronic anxiety, the landmark theory is Lazarus and Folkman's (1984) transactional theory of stress. As well as emphasizing appraisal as a cause of negative emotions, the theory states that consequences of emotion depend on coping. This emphasis on active attempts at managing stressful encounters— successful or otherwise—sets cognitive stress theory apart from earlier theories that tend to see the anxious person as a victim of unconscious conflicts, overactive brain punishment systems, or unfortunate learning histories (see chapter 3).

Coping is a deceptively simple but powerful idea. Coping—in the sense of choosing a course of external action or internal emotion regulation—implies sophisticated cognitive activity. The person requires an internal "mental model" of the stressful situation, as well as beliefs about how best to intervene in the situation. Coping is typically extended in time so that the person must also process feedback relating to the success of coping efforts and adjust coping accordingly. As with anxiety, coping research is supported by the availability of valid assessment tools, and a plethora of empirical studies based on measuring coping in a variety of stressful contexts (see Zeidner & Saklofske, 1995).

Cognitive theory has been vindicated in studies of the acute effects of anxiety on task performance. Spielberger's (1966) original theory was rather vague in its statement that anxiety interferes with processing activities. Experimental studies, including those reviewed in chapter 5 (Theoretical Perspectives: Information-Processing Models) now give us a rather more detailed understanding of the nature of "cognitive interference." We have moved from the general statement that anxiety interferes with attention to theories that refer to focal constructs in cognitive psychology, including working memory and attentional resources (Sarason et al., 1995; Zeidner, 1998). The most recent work in this area (Eysenck et al., 2007) has identified specific executive control processes, such as inhibiting distracting stimuli, and shifting task set, that may be critical to anxiety impairments.

Recent experimental studies also confirm that anxiety relates to bias in selective attention (Bar-Haim, Lamy, Pergamin, Bakermans-Kranenburg, & van IJzendoorn, 2007). In the anxious person, attention is "sticky"; it tends to fasten onto sources of threat even when the task requires that it is directed elsewhere. There has been some lively debate over information-processing models that may explain these data in detail. There may be both an unconscious bias toward threat operating early in processing, as well as a voluntary influence as the anxious person searches strategically for possible threats (Mathews, 2004; Matthews & Wells, 2000). While controversies remain, research has done quite well in describing how anxious persons process information, in relation to the standard architectures for cognition established by mainstream cognitive psychology.

Interventions

On the basis that "nothing is as practical as a good theory," cognitive theories also pass the test of providing effective treatments for anxiety. As discussed in chapter 6 (see section on Clinical Interventions), cognitive interventions appear to be of value in treating both distressing but relatively minor "subclinical" anxiety, and more serious psychiatric disorders.

If we start with the simple idea that anxiety is faulty thinking, then interventions that correct the fault should work to alleviate the condition. The pioneering cognitive therapies introduced by Albert Ellis and Aaron Beck seek to do just this. Some progress can be made simply through conversation with the patient. The cognitive therapist seeks to expose and challenge the person's mistaken beliefs. Frequently, therapists integrate this pure form of cognitive therapy with behavioral techniques ("cognitive-behavior therapies"), such as "experiments" that expose the person to feared situations to help them learn the error of their thoughts. Importantly, this family of techniques is not just a fireside chat with the patient about their troubles; interventions are derived from an explicit cognitive-psychological theory of the specific disorders (Wells, 2000). In addition, different sets of dysfunctional beliefs and processes can be identified for each major disorder (e.g., generalized anxiety, panic, and PTSD), so that treatment can be tailored to the patient's specific condition.

There have been numerous reviews of the effectiveness of cognitive and cognitive-behavior therapies. A recent review of studies of actual clinical practice (Stewart & Chambless, 2009) concluded that such therapies produce improvements that are "large" in a strict, statistical sense. For most anxiety disorders, treatment improved symptoms by about 1 standard deviation (SD), as opposed to about a quarter of an SD reported for placebo treatments. Improvements for PTSD patients verged on the spectacular (over 2.5 SD). The benefits of cognitive therapies also seem to hold up over time (Butler, Chapman, Forman, & Beck, 2006), although few studies have investigated periods longer than 12 months. Cognitive therapy works, much of the time.

As we also saw in the previous chapter (see chapter 6, Clinical Interventions: Cognitively Oriented Interventions), cognitive interventions for relatively mild, subclinical anxiety are also effective. Sometimes, we just need to regain perspective on our problems, and find effective strategies for coping. We also saw that "emotion-oriented" techniques that are directed toward relief of anxiety symptoms may also be of value. There is not really any conflict here with the cognitive perspective, though. Anxiety management and other stress relief procedures aim to train people to regulate their own anxiety in real life. That is, the specific procedure (e.g., muscle relaxation, positive imagery) is brought under the cognitive control of the processes that regulate coping.

TOWARD A COGNITIVE SCIENCE OF ANXIETY

We have just argued that cognitive theories of anxiety provide a "standard theory" that informs all branches of anxiety research. "Standard" does not mean "universal"—we will discuss dissenting voices in the next section. We can also go beyond standard information-processing models by developing a farther-reaching cognitive science of anxiety, an enterprise that suggests a number of promising directions for future research. In this section, we discuss what is meant by "cognitive science," and how researchers may be able to extend standard anxiety models.

"Cognitive science" is the interdisciplinary study of how intelligent systems, broadly defined, process information so as to accomplish purposeful actions. It covers not just cognitive psychology but other fields including computer science, linguistics, philosophy, and neuroscience. Cognitive scientists may study artificial systems and nonhuman animals as well as people. Perhaps we can get a deeper understanding of human anxiety if we look more generally at principles for processing and responding to threat.

Cognitive science recognizes that "cognition" requires different levels of explanation. The tri-level hypothesis (Dawson, 1998; Pylyshyn, 1999) proposes that there are three complementary ways in which we can understand the operation of an information-processing device, be it artificial or natural. The lowest level refers to the physical hardware, which might be silicon microcircuits or neurons. The biological theories that relate anxiety to specific brain systems we discussed in chapter 3 (see Biological Perspectives: Functional Neurobiological Perspectives) are expressed at this level. The next level is one of "programming." Explanations refer to "virtual" computations, like the lines of codes in a computer program. Most of the cognitive psychology of anxiety (e.g., chapter 5, Theoretical Perspectives: Information-Processing Models) assumes that anxiety relates to steps in the mental "programs" for encoding and analyzing stimulus input—for example, the subroutines that evaluate how threatening a stimulus as. At the top level is the "knowledge" level, which refers to the person's high-level goals and beliefs about how to attain those goals. For example, an anxious person might place a high priority on avoiding perceived threats, as well as beliefs that they are highly vulnerable. This level of analysis often features in clinical accounts of anxiety, as well as in social-cognitive models.

As we have said, standard cognitive theories are expressed at the intermediate, programming level, based on information-processing models of attention, memory, and so on. An explicit cognitive science approach will help to elaborate models of this kind. Much of the early work on processing models refers to anxiety effects on rather broadly defined constructs such as attentional resources. Greater precision may be attained by developing detailed simulations of processing that can be represented as computer programs and support models of increasing fidelity. For example, the appraisal process can be simulated as multiple interacting levels of processing from which the subjective experience of anxiety emerges (Scherer, 2009). Scherer's componential patterning model distinguishes separate processing levels related to (a) low-level pattern matching (e.g., detecting spiders), (b) unconscious schematic processing (e.g., of well-learned social cues, (c) cognitively mediated associative processing (e.g., of contextual cues), and (d) conscious, effortful deliberation (e.g., thoughtful analysis of a threat).

There is also scope for developing the "artificial intelligence" of anxiety. Imagine the autonomous robots of the future that may be designed to carry out somewhat challenging tasks such as exploring the surface of Mars, traffic control, and security operations. Such a robot needs "anxiety" in the functional sense of being able to anticipate threats to its physical integrity or competence to perform its assigned tasks. (We are not saying that the robot experiences emotions or has any conscious experience!) Robot designers will need to include programming that detects and analyzes threats and modifies its behavior accordingly. One of the design challenges will be to balance self-preservation goals against those relating to the robot's primary purpose. What level of risk, if any, is acceptable for a robot prospecting for minerals on Mars? Too little "anxiety" and the robot may drive itself off a cliff; too much and it may be paralyzed into inaction. As with humans, the robots of the future will need to balance their "anxieties" against other motivations.

Robot designers may be able to learn from the neurobiological circuitry of human anxiety in finding the optimal resolution to motivational conflicts. Conversely, the tests of artificial devices may provide a stringent test of theories of human anxiety. Perhaps we will find that some of our psychological models fail to work very well when built into a physical device or an autonomous agent.

A broader cognitive science perspective may also look beyond information-processing models in expanding our horizons for looking at anxiety. The tri-level framework suggests that neural-level and knowledge-level explanations will both add to the conventional cognitive psychological understanding of anxiety. First, we can explore the neurological underpinnings of the information-processing routines that relate to anxiety, such as selective attention. Second, we can develop theories at the knowledge level that elaborate on the motivational and self-regulative aspects of anxiety.

Cognitive Neuroscience

Psychobiological theories of anxiety have played a central role in the field (see chapter 3, Biological Perspectives). The most direct indication is the association between state anxiety and autonomic arousal that gives rise to the familiar physical symptoms of anxiety, such as a racing heart and sweaty palms. The psychobiological approach has also proved its worth through demonstrations of effects of the genes on the development of anxiety (chapter 4, Heredity and Environment: Molecular Genetics: DNA for Anxiety?) and the effectiveness of drug treatments for anxiety (chapter 6, Clinical Interventions: Pharmacotherapy). However, as we also saw, untangling the causal relationship between physiological arousal and anxious emotion is tricky—indeed, it is a classical problem for the psychology of emotion. One view, to which we will return in a later section, is that the physiology is of primary importance and cognition secondary. Alternatively, it may be more productive to focus on the functioning of specific brain areas in threatening environments than on more general arousal states.

Anxiety relates to activation of both subcortical limbic system circuits, sites traditionally associated with emotion and motivation, and with cortical circuits (traditionally, higher-order cognition). Thus, the brain has no single "anxiety center"; instead, anxiety is a property that emerges out of the interaction of multiple circuits. As we have seen (chapter 3, Biological Perspectives: Functional Neurobiological Perspectives), modern brain-imaging techniques such as functional magnetic resonance imaging (fMRI) allow us to establish correlations between anxiety and activation of specific brain areas, while the person performs some relevant task such as viewing threatening images.

A classical cognitive psychologist might point out that such evidence localizes the information-processing circuitry of interest to specific brain areas, but does not tell us *how* the information is processed so as to build a mental representation and guide response. Cognitive neuroscience counters this objection by seeking to build detailed models that simulate how brain circuits function so as to support "virtual" information processing. This approach has already informed understanding of attentional bias in anxiety.

For example, one of the major cognitive neuroscience theories of attention was proposed by Michael Posner (e.g., Posner & DiGirolamo, 1998). In brief, he delineates three different neural networks that support orientation toward stimuli in space, executive control of attention, and maintenance of alertness. Each can be mapped out within the brain, using fMRI and other techniques. Each network can also be decomposed further into subsystems. For example, shifting the focus of attention between different places in the visual field requires disengaging attention from the location attended to initially, moving to a new spatial location, and then engaging the new location. Experimental studies (e.g., Derryberry & Reed, 2002) show that anxiety relates especially to disengagement from locations associated with threat. Attention locks onto threat, and is difficult to "unstick" or disengage subsequently. As discussed in chapter 5 (Theoretical Perspectives: Attentional Control Theory), anxiety also relates to executive control, and we can also narrow down the relationship to specific executive functions such as inhibition (Eysenck et al., 2007). Thus, the models provided by cognitive neuroscience give us a more detailed understanding of both the specific information-processing routines and the brain systems that are infused by anxiety.

We can take the models one step further by developing *connectionist* or *neural network* models of anxiety and information processing. These are models that more closely resemble actual neural functioning than traditional cognitive psychological models. Processing is controlled by activation, which may spread between associated *units* or *nodes* in the network. Each unit calculates an activation output from the various activation inputs it receives, according to a fixed set of rules, or algorithms, rather as the integration of inputs to a neuron determines its rate of firing. Processing is controlled implicitly, rather than explicitly, as a consequence of the interactions between the different units, governed by simple mathematical algorithms that control activation levels. More sophisticated models may impose a modular structure comprising different subnetworks, consistent with neuropsychological evidence. Models may also demonstrate learning from performance feedback, through the application of a simple algorithm to an initial network, in which units are randomly interassociated. As well as being explicit, capable of learning, and neuropsychologically plausible, connectionist models possess some more subtle advantages. They can work with "graded" representations—that is, those that are incomplete or ambiguous, as people often seem to do. In addition, they can demonstrate emergent properties that arise spontaneously out of the dynamic properties of the network.

Matthews and Harley (1996) provided an early demonstration of how these models may be applied to anxiety and attentional bias, in a simulation study of the emotional Stroop. As described in chapter 5 (Theoretical Perspectives: Information-Processing Models), anxious individuals are slow to name the ink colors of threatening words, suggesting a bias in selective attention toward threat. Matthews and Harley borrowed an existing network model of the standard Stroop test, and adapted it to simulate the emotional Stroop. They were able to use the model to compare different mechanisms for bias in anxiety. The first version simulated frequent exposure to threat (as might happen during a trauma-ridden childhood), the second version represented an innate sensitivity to threat (as might be set by the genes), and the third version simulated a strategic preference for attending to threat. Consistent with the S-REF model of anxiety described in chapter 5 (Theoretical Perspectives: Self-Regulative Theory of Anxiety) and chapter 6 (Clinical Interventions: Metacognitive Interventions), the strategic mechanism provided the closest correspondence to real empirical data on the emotional Stroop and related tasks.

The findings of Matthews and Harley (1996) are intriguing but not decisive. The network they used does not resemble real neural networks closely, and so the study functioned more as a demonstration of the approach than as a detailed simulation. However, future research will develop more accurate simulations of attentional bias, using models that are directly informed by our increasing understanding of the underlying neurology. For example, Siegle and Hasselmo (2002) developed a simulation of depressive rumination (similar to worry) which was based on knowledge of how neural activation may be "recycled" between areas in the limbic system and cortex so as to maintain awareness of negative thoughts over a prolonged period.

As connectionism becomes increasingly informed by neuroscience, we can increasingly anticipate a productive merging of neurological and information-processing models so that we can pinpoint rather precisely how anxiety biases possessing. At least in relation to attention and decision making, such models will likely emphasize cortical rather than subcortical circuits. In addition, there are good prospects for modeling cortical regulation of the anxiety generated by subcortical circuits (e.g., amygadala circuits), as discussed in chapter 3 (Biological Perspectives: Functional Neurobiological Perspectives).

Anxiety and Self-Knowledge

The classic information-processing theories of anxiety describe a linear process. Events trigger appraisals of threats, which in turn elicit anxiety, which then influences attentional and other processes controlling behavior. Anxiety appears as a mechanistic by-product of information processing. Alternatively, perhaps we could see anxiety as almost a kind of choice, or at least influenced by the person's intentions. There are occasions where a voluntary aspect to anxiety seems plausible. Imagine you have been bothered by a nagging headache for some time. You may find yourself reflecting on whether just to wait for it to go away or whether to treat it as a potentially serious medical symptom and seek medical help. Your decision on "whether to get anxious" seems partly under your control. If you have a particularly busy week and no time to get to the doctor, you might choose to ignore the symptoms. Conversely, if one of your friends died of a brain tumor, you would be more inclined to talk yourself into seeing the doctor.

Such scope for taking control of anxiety can be straightforwardly seen as a question of coping—avoidance versus task-focus in the example. The point here is that voluntary control over coping gives us some degree of control over anxiety. Because anxiety is associated with uncertainty and, often, with future events, it may be especially controllable. Fear, by contrast, is typically elicited by an immediate, physical danger and so is less malleable. The capacity to regulate anxiety contrasts with the mechanistic view of anxiety generation proposed by a simple appraisal theory. In chapter 6 (Coping with Anxiety) we said that it may be difficult to decide which coping strategies are most effective. Similarly, we cannot say in any general sense that it is better to avoid or to experience anxiety. Sometimes, feelings of anxiety are simply a distraction to our purposes; on other occasions, anxiety may be a motivator. People probably should go to the doctor if they experience persistent medical symptoms, before it is too late.

Investigating such emotion regulation is challenging for two reasons. First, it is difficult to observe or measure the internal processes involved, given that introspection is unreliable as a source of evidence. Second, people show a great deal of flexibility and even inventiveness in their use of emotion-regulation strategies. Studies of emotion regulation (in a general sense) show that strategies include internally focused cognitive strategies ("talking up" one's mood), externally focused recreational and social activities and strategies focused directly on emotional experiences such as drinking alcohol (Thayer, 1996).

Nevertheless, there are promising lines of inquiry that may be further developed. One approach—with a clinical flavor—is to examine metacognitions and thought-control strategies. As we saw in chapter 6 (Normative Versus Pathological Anxiety: Theoretical Conceptions of Anxiety), generalized anxiety patients are simultaneously disturbed by their worries but also motivated by beliefs that worry is effective for problem-solving. Therapies that challenge dysfunctional metacognitions and give the person attentional skills for regulating worry are effective in treating anxiety (Wells et al., 2010).

Metacognitions may regulate not only the experience of anxiety, but also the extent to which the person can make use of anxiety functionally, in support of some personal goal. As discussed in chapter 5 (Anxiety and Cognitive Performance), some athletes find anxiety helpful as a motivating factor in accomplishing peak performance (Hanin, 2007). If the athletes are able to interpret their anxiety as a sign that they are keyed up and ready to perform, this metacognition might actually facilitate performance. Conversely, understanding anxiety as a harbinger of impending performance breakdown may lead to choking under pressure. Other examples of how metacognitions of anxiety may be detrimental come from test anxiety research. For example, some "self-handicapping" test-anxious students use their anxiety as an excuse not to apply themselves to their studies (Zeidner, 1998).

Perhaps we can even see effective voluntary control and regulation of anxiety as a form of emotional intelligence (Zeidner, Matthews, & Roberts, 2009). Emotional intelligence is a broad and sometimes inchoate concept, but one of its facets its effective mood regulation. Recognizing that one is anxious, thinking clearly about the sources of one's anxiety, and being able to regulate the mood state as needed to perform some task may be signs of emotional intelligence (cf., Salovey et al., 1995). Mayer, Salovey, and Caruso (2000) also see assimilating emotion into thought as an aspect of emotional intelligence. Being able to view our anxiety in a constructive light, as a motivator in sports, for example, may fall under this heading.

CHALLENGES TO COGNITIVE THEORY

In the previous section we saw how the broader perspectives of cognitive science may usefully extend the reach of the "standard information-processing theories of anxiety," including those of Spielberger (1966), Sarason et al. (1995), and Eysenck (1997). However, there are some more radical challenges to the cognitive paradigm, which we will look at next. Psychobiologists, researchers on the unconscious, and social psychologists may all have objections, of rather different sorts. Our intention here is simply to provide the flavor of alternative ways of understanding anxiety, and the ways in which cognitive psychologists might respond. We do not aim to explore the arguments in detail in this introductory book, but readers are encouraged to read further themselves.

Challenges in Measurement: What Are Questionnaires Missing?

The acceptance of the Spielberger anxiety questionnaires (e.g., Spielberger & Reheiser, 2004) as the anxiety gold standard may seduce us into accepting the cognitive theory that accompanies it. But what if the Spielberger questionnaire misleads us? As we have already seen, psychobiological theories would see the self-reports that the questionnaire utilizes as only a poor reflection of the more fundamental neural processes. A more direct challenge derives from the new wave of "implicit anxiety" measures that we discussed in chapter 2 (Behavioral Measures of Anxiety). Behavioral tests may detect individual differences in anxiety that are not accessible to consciousness. Furthermore, implicit anxiety measures are only modestly correlated with conventional explicit questionnaire measures, if at all (Stieger, Göritz, & Burger, 2010). Such findings might lead us toward an almost Freudian position that explicit anxiety is only the tip of a much larger iceberg made up primarily of unconscious processes.

Our view is that the issue is more one of measurement than of cognitive theory. It is important to detach cognition and consciousness. The term "cognition" may make us think of deliberate, mindful reflection in conscious awareness, but cognitive processes may equally well be unconscious. Appraisal theories (Scherer, 2009) allow for some appraisal processes operating unconsciously, and so it is not really surprising that we can obtain implicit measures.

What remains to be investigated is the nature of "implicit" anxiety. The power of conventional trait anxiety scales is that they bind together a variety of aspects of the person's experience of anxiety, including the cognitive, emotional/somatic, and behavioral facets described in chapter 1. The anxiety measured by questionnaires seems to cover a wide swath of the personality landscape, and measures of anxiety and related traits for negative emotion do indeed predict a wide range of real-life criteria (Matthews, Deary, & Whiteman, 2009). By contrast, implicit measures are narrower in scope, in some cases perhaps representing little more than a specific attitude. It is unclear whether different implicit measures actually represent some common, broad-based underlying factor (Bosson et al., 2000). The idea that we have unconscious anxiety traits that exist in a parallel universe to conventional personality is certainly intriguing (and consistent with psychoanalytic thinking). However, much more evidence is needed to substantiate such an idea.

The Challenge from Embodiment: Is Anxiety a Somatic State?

As already discussed, neurological and cognitive theories of anxiety do not need to be incompatible. Use of cognitive neuroscience methods, including brain-imaging and connectionist modeling, has promise for integrating these two variants of theory. However, neuroscience may also provide the platform for questioning the basic validity of information-processing models. A growing trend in psychology is to see cognition as "embodied." Thinking depends not on abstract representations but is rather directly linked to perception and action. Emotions may be embodied through being more closely integrated with bodily changes than conventional cognitive theory allows (Ziemke & Lowe, 2009). Imagine that, like a brain in a jar in a cheesy science fiction movie, you receive sensory information but no internal ("interoceptive") signals on the state of your body—could you still feel anxious?

The best-known theory of this kind is Damasio's (1994) somatic marker hypothesis. It is claimed that emotions correspond to "body maps" held in specific brain areas (e.g., somatosensory cortex, ventromedial prefrontal cortex). Somatic markers are generated from both current body state and "as-if" projections of future events. Emotions may be seen as "gut feelings" that are more effective in guiding the complex decision making of real life than is systematic reasoning. Evidence for the theory has come mainly from studies of individuals with damage to the brain areas supporting somatic markers. Such people make poor decisions on gambling tasks, supposedly because they lack the somatic markers that would indicate that a given choice is likely to lead to a negative outcome.

Damasio's theory is not exclusively concerned with anxiety, but the general principles should apply. Anxiety is the subjective experience of the brain's representation of the corresponding somatic state, presumably including the various indices of autonomic arousal such as elevated heart rate. Cognitive appraisal, seen as a separate, evaluative process detached from somatic change, is not relevant. Indeed, we may question whether cognitive "causes" can even be separated from emotional "effects." Cognition and emotion may be common expressions of the same underlying brain networks (Ziemke & Lowe, 2009).

In countering this position, we start by noting there is indeed a long tradition in emotion research of seeing the internal feedback signals generated by the body as playing an important role in emotion. However, there is no evidence to suggest that such somatic signals are the *only* influence on emotion, and much data to suggest that cognitive processes that are not obviously embodied are at least as important. Multileveled appraisal theories such as Scherer's (2009) provide a means of integrating signals from a variety of different sources dynamically. Indeed, the functional value of anxiety may be that it is an integration of signals from qualitatively different sources that could not otherwise be mutually interrelated.

Another issue is that evidence for the somatic marker hypothesis comes primarily from studies of the decision making of brain-damaged patients, using gambling tasks (see Dunn, Dalgleish, & Lawrence, 2006). It is unclear whether the theory could, for example, predict how environmental stressors influence anxiety in normal individuals, or generate predictions that are different from those of contemporary appraisal theory. A methodological weakness is that there is no straightforward, validated measure of somatic markers that could be used in research studies (although indirect evidence may be obtained from fMRI and autonomic arousal measures. Detailed reviews of the theory (Dunn et al., 2006; Rolls, 1999) have also questioned how well it really explains the available evidence.

The Challenge from Animal Models: Is Human Anxiety Nothing Special?

A different kind of neuroscience critique comes from researchers using animal models of anxiety. An intriguing finding is that most of the major human personality traits appear to have counterparts in other mammals (Gosling & Harley, 2009). For example, horses, dogs, and cats may vary in "trait anxiety" as expressed in behavior; indeed, there is a substantial research effort based on breeding rats for genetic fearfulness. (These would not make good house pets; they defecate a lot.) If these animal temperaments correspond to human anxiety, then perhaps the core of what it means to be anxious may not include the higher-order cognitive functions, such as abstract reasoning, that are exclusive to humans. Instead, anxiety may fundamentally reflect subcortical systems such as Panksepp's (1998) fear circuit (see chapter 3., Biological Perspectives: Functional Neurobiological Perspectives). As in classical behaviorism, the cognitions that accompany anxious emotion may just be a kind of surface froth whipped up by these more basic processes.

In chapter 3 (Biological Perspectives: Functional Neurobiological Perspetives), we also discussed Reinforcement Sensitivity Theory (Corr, 2009) which attributes anxiety to a Behavioral Inhibition System, and fear to a separate neural circuit. This theory too sees anxiety as an emotion that is essentially similar in all mammals. Following a modern behaviorist trend, it allows mammals to possess cognitive representations, for example, of goals and expectancies. However, these are not (of course) language based, and so, again, the theory downplays the significance of the verbal processing (worry) that is a feature of human anxiety.

As cognitive psychologists, we can agree that the evolutionary continuity of anxiety between different mammalian species is important. Indeed, the need to survive and reproduce in an often threatening world provides some consistent selection pressures. However, as we stated in chapter 3 (Biological Perspectives: Evolutionary Perspectives), anxiety in humans may constitute a richer brain/mind state than in other mammals because of our greater capacity to build and project mental models that encode the various threats to our physical and psychological well-being. Rolls (1999) suggests that humans have evolved a separate language-based processing system for "multistep syntactic planning" that allows us to build qualitatively more powerful models of present and future events than are available to other animals. We need to understand these cognitive elaborations of the more primitive anxiety state in order to obtain useful predictive models of trait anxiety (Matthews & Gilliland, 1999). As we saw in chapter 5 (Anxiety and Cognitive Performance), worry, rather than autonomic arousal, is often the key element of anxiety for performance impairment. Our capacity for voluntary regulation of anxiety, as discussed above, may also be distinctively human.

The Challenge from Social Psychology: Is Anxiety Personalized?

The final challenge comes from an entirely different source, social psychology. The historical background is that social psychology has traditionally been antagonistic to the idea that individuals possess stable personality characteristics, including anxiety (e.g., Mischel, 1968). Instead, social psychologists have found the learning models reviewed in chapter 3 (Of Historical Interest: Learning Models of Anxiety) more congenial. Individual differences in anxiety are situation-bound, depending on what has been learned in the particular situation. If your family is nice but your boss is horrible, you may exhibit anxious behaviors at work, but not at home. Furthermore, social theorists have tended to emphasize the interpersonal nature of emotions. Anxiety arises out of social interactions, rather than residing "inside the head" of any individual (e.g., Hampson, 1988).

The accumulating weight of evidence in favor of personality trait models (Matthews et al., 2009) has tended to suppress the more radical critiques of traits. Research on social anxiety, for example, has confirmed that some people are indeed generally vulnerable to finding social encounters threatening (Mellings & Alden, 2000), sometimes to a pathological extent. At the same time, the modern interactionist perspective recognizes the importance of situations and learning processes.

Anxiety researchers accept that individuals differ in their susceptibility to anxiety in the different contexts we described in chapter 1 (Major Forms of Anxiety in Modern Society). We can separate test anxiety, math anxiety, sports anxiety, and other context-bound anxieties through both measurement and theory, although an anxious temperament may increase vulnerability to the full spectrum.

More recent social-cognitive research accepts that traits exist, but questions their utility for predicting behavior with any precision. Shoda, Mischel, and Wright (1994) performed detailed analyses of the consistencies in behavior of individuals. Specifically, they intensively observed children's aggressive behaviors at a summer camp over a six-week period. They found that consistency in behavior was evident not so much in overall aggression, but in aggression within specific situations (e.g., being teased by another being warned by an adult). They suggest that personality should not be seen in terms of general traits, but "behavioral signatures"(Zayas, Whitsett, Lee, Wilson, & Shoda, 2008). These take the form of ... statements, for example, IF you are teased by another child, THEN react aggressively. Similarly, for anxiety, the IF parts of the statement would state the circumstances evoking anxiety for the individual, and the THEN parts would specify how that anxiety was expressed (e.g., withdrawing from the situation, seeking reassurance). A measure of trait anxiety would fail to capture how vulnerability to anxiety and the way it was expressed varied from situation to situation for each individual.

The Cognitive-Affective Personality Systems (CAPS) model of Mischel and Shoda (1995, 1998) seeks to relate these situation-bound consistencies to a dynamic processing system. Personality depends on highly interconnected cognitive and emotional subsystems, including various components including affects, goals, expectancies, beliefs, competencies, and self-regulatory plans and strategies. Details of the model are beyond our present scope. Its implication for understanding anxiety is that we cannot get very far with standard anxiety scales. Instead, we need to look at the dynamics of anxious emotion and cognition within individuals.

The issue here corresponds to the long-running debate in personality psychology regarding nomothetic and idiographic approaches. Nomothetic models seek to establish general principles applicable to all individuals. Developing a standard measurement scale for trait anxiety is a typical nomothetic research effort—scores on a standard questionnaire are equally meaningful for all individuals. Idiographic models, of which CAPS is one, seek to identify the personal qualities specific to the individual, qualities which may have no general applicability. Each person may have a unique behavioral signature that describes when and how the person becomes anxious. Clinical psychologists must build up an idiographic "case conceptualization" that describes the triggers for anxiety, the thoughts associated with anxiety, and its behavioral expression for each individual client.

The two approaches have coexisted (however uneasily) throughout the history of personality research and will most likely continue to do so. Certainly, the broad principles of trait anxiety theory will not capture all the differences in anxiety vulnerability between individuals. But perhaps they do not need to do so. The nomothetic cognitive theory of how appraisals generate anxiety, how worry interferes with attention, and so forth, may do a reasonable job of explaining how the constructs concerned are *typically* interrelated, even if analysis of individuals provides a more complex and nuanced picture. Furthermore, working with constructs, such as test anxiety, that are narrower than general anxiety, but are relevant to more than a single individual may provide a useful halfway house. I (Moshe Zeidner) have shown how there are different categories of test-anxious individuals—for example, those lacking study skills, those vulnerable to performance worries, self-handicappers, and several other types (Zeidner, 1998). We may need more coarse- or fine-grained accounts of anxiety, depending on the specific research problem of interest.

CONCLUSIONS

Anxiety is easy to experience but hard to understand, at least for psychologists. The conclusion we feel most confident in advancing is that anxiety must be understood at multiple levels. A comprehensive theory of anxiety would encompass its neurological, cognitive, motivational and experiential aspects. It would specify how genetic and environmental factors work together during development to build the brain structures and cognitive "programs" that provide stability in trait anxiety into adulthood. It would provide predictive models specifying how trait anxiety interacts with environmental stress factors to influence the full range of behavioral variables, as well as physiological responses. Such a model would incorporate the self-regulative processes that give us some control over our anxieties and their impact on behavior. It would describe how anxiety plays out in the different contexts in which we perceive threats ranging from social criticism to physical dangers. At a practical level the general theory would give us techniques for alleviating the bothersome anxiety of everyday life and life-changing clinical anxiety disorders. We are a long way from possessing such a theory, but we hope this book has succeeded in presenting some of the keystones of this future construction.

As a final thought, perhaps the single greatest challenge for any anxiety theory, be it cognitive or social, is to find a means of integrating the different facets or levels of anxiety: brain systems and the DNA and evolutionary processes that shapes them, biases in attention and memory, and high-level social motivations and self-understanding. We have suggested (Matthews & Zeidner, 2004; Zeidner & Matthews, 2000) that the common element may be adaptation. Threats and dangers are woven into the human condition, but we have choices (conscious and unconscious) over how to cope with them. Anxiety, ultimately, may be the representation of that choice—whether to focus on threat so as to anticipate and preempt it, or whether to remain detached from threat until the point where defensive action is imminently required.

References

Abbott, M. J., & Rapee, R. M. (2004). Post-event rumination and negative self-appraisal in social phobia before and after treatment. *Journal of Abnormal Psychology, 113,* 136–144.

Achenbach, T. M., Howell, C. T., McConnaughy, S. H., & Stanger, C. (1995). Six-year predictors of problems in a national sample of children and youth: I. Cross-informant syndromes. *Journal of the American Academy of Child and Adolescent Psychiatry, 34,* 336–347.

Ackerman, P. L., & Heggestad, E. D. (1997) Intelligence, personality and interests: Evidence for overlapping traits. *Psychological Bulletin, 121,* 219–245.

Aggleton, J. P., & Mishkin, M. (1986). The amygdala: Sensory gateway to the emotions. In R. Plutchik & H. Kellerman (Eds.), *Emotion: Theory, research, and experience* (Vol. 3, pp. 281–299). Orlando, FL: Academic Press.

Ainsworth, M. S., Blehar, M. C., Waters, E., & Wall, S. (1978). *Patterns of attachment: A psychological study of the strange situation.* Oxford, England: Lawrence Erlbaum.

Aldwin, C. M., & Revenson, T. T. (1987). Does coping help? A reexamination of the relation between coping and mental health. *Journal of Personality and Social Psychology, 53,* 337–348.

Allen, G. J., Elias, M. J., & Zlotlow, S. F. (1980). Behavioral interventions for alleviating test anxiety: A methodological overview of current therapeutic practices. In I. G. Sarason (Ed.), *Test anxiety: Theory, research and applications* (pp. 155–185). Hillsdale, NJ: Erlbaum.

Alpert, R & Haber, R. N (1960). Anxiety in academic achievement situations. *Journal of Abnormal and Social Psychology, 61,* 207–215.

Alpers, G. W. (2009). Ambulatory assessment in panic disorder and specific phobia. *Psychological Assessment, 21,* 476–485.

American Psychiatric Association. (1994) *Diagnostic and statistical manual of mental disorders* (DSM-IV-R, 4th ed.). Washington, DC: Author.

REFERENCES

Arkowitz, H., Lichtenstein, E., McGovern, K., & Hines, P. (1975). The behavioral assessment of social competence in males. *Behavior Therapy, 6,* 3–13.

Arnold, P. D., Zai, G., & Richter, M. A. (2004) Genetics of anxiety disorders. *Current Psychiatry Reports, 6,* 243–254.

Arrindel, W. A., Pickersgill, M. J., Merkelbach, H., Ardon, M. A., & Cornet, F. C. (1991). Phobic dimension III: Factor analytic approaches to the study of common phobic fears: An updated review of findings obtained with adult subjects. *Advances in Behaviour Research and Therapy, 13,* 17–130.

Asendorpf, J. B. (2008). Developmental perspectives. In G. J. Boyle, G. Matthews, & D. H. Saklofske (Eds.), *The SAGE handbook of personality theory and assessment, Vol. 1. Personality theories and models* (pp. 101–123). Thousand Oaks, CA: Sage Publications.

Ashcraft, M. H. (2002). Math anxiety: Personal, educational, and cognitive consequences. *Current Directions in Psychological Science, 11,* 181–185.

Ashcraft, M. H., Krause, J. A., & Hopko, D. R. (2007). Is math anxiety a mathematical learning disability? In B. B. Daniel & M. M. Michèle (Eds.), *Why is math so hard for some children? The nature and origins of mathematical learning difficulties and disabilities* (pp. 329–348). Baltimore, MD: Paul H. Brookes Publishing.

Ashcraft, M. H., & Krause, A. (2007). Working memory, math performance, and math anxiety. *Psychonomic Bulletin & Review, 14,* 243–248.

Ashcraft, M. H., & Moore, M. (2009). Mathematics anxiety and the affective drop in performance. *Journal of Psychoeducational Assessment, 27,* 197–205.

Ashcraft, M. H., & Kirk, E. P. (2001). The relationships among working memory, math anxiety, and performance. *Journal of Experimental Psychology: General, 130,* 224–237.

Atkinson, J. W., & Feather, N. T. (1966). *A theory of achievement motivation.* New York: Wiley.

Austin, E. J., Boyle, G. J., Groth-Marnat, G. , Matthews, G., Saklofske, D. H., Schwean, V. L., et al. (in press). Integrating intelligence and personality. In G. Groth-Marnat (Ed.), *Integrative assessment of adult personality* (3rd ed.). New York: Guilford.

Averill, J. R. (1980). A constructivist view of emotion. In R. Plutchik & H. Kellerman (Eds.), *Emotion: Theory, research and experience, Vol. 1, Theories of emotion* (pp. 305–339). San Diego: Academic Press.

Averill, J. R. (1997). The emotions: An integrative approach. In R. Hogan, J. A. Johnson, & S. R. Briggs (Eds.), *Handbook of personality psychology* (pp. 513–541). San Diego: Academic Press

Bagby, R. M., Joffe, R. T., Parker, J. D. A., Kalemba, V., & Harkness, K. L. (1995). Major depression and the five-factor model of personality. *Journal of Personality Disorders, 9,* 224–234.

Baloglu, M., Abbasi, A., & Masten, W. G. (2007). A cross-cultural comparison of anxiety among college students. *College Student Journal, 41,* 977–984.

Bandura, A. (1965). Behavioral modification through modeling procedures. In L. Krasner & L. P. Ullmann (Eds.), *Research in behavior modification: New developments and implications* (pp. 310–340). New York: Holt, Rinehart & Winston.

Bandura, A. (1997). *Self-efficacy: The exercise of control.* New York: W. H. Freeman & Co.

Barazzone, N., & Davey, L. (2009). Anger potentiates the reporting of threatening interpretations: An experimental study. *Journal of Anxiety Disorders, 23,* 489–495.

Bar-Haim, Y., Lamy, D., Pergamin, L., Bakermans-Kranenburg, M. J., & van IJzendoorn, M. H. (2007). Threat-related attentional bias in anxious and nonanxious individuals: A meta-analytic study. *Psychological Bulletin, 133,* 1–24.

Barlow, D. H. (2000). Unraveling the mysteries of anxiety and its disorders from the perspective of emotion theory. *American Psychologist, 55,* 1247–1263.

Barlow, D. H. (2002). *Anxiety and its disorders: The nature and treatment of anxiety and panic* (2nd ed.). New York: Guilford Press.

Baron, R. M., & Kenny, D. A. (1986). The moderator-mediator variable distinction in social psychological research: Conceptual, strategic, and statistical considerations. *Journal of Personality and Social Psychology, 51,* 1173–1182.

Barrett, L. F., & Wager, T. D. (2006). The structure of emotion: Evidence from neuroimaging studies. *Current Directions in Psychological Science, 15,* 79–83.

Barrios, B. A., & Shigetomi, C. C. (1979). Coping-skills training for the management of anxiety: A critical review. *Behavior Therapy, 10,* 491–522.

Baum, A., Singer, J. E., & Baum, C. S. (1981). Stress and the environment. *Journal of Social Issues, 37,* 4–35.

Beasley, T. M., Long, J. D., & Natali, M. (2001). A confirmatory factor analysis of the Mathematics Anxiety Scale for children. *Measurement and Evaluation in Counseling and Development, 34,* 14–26.

Beck, A. T., & Emery, G. (1985). *Anxiety disorders and phobias: A cognitive perspective.* New York: Basic Books.

Beck, A. T., Epstein, N., Brown, G., & Steer, R. A. (1988). An inventory for measuring clinical anxiety: Psychometric properties. *Journal of Consulting and Clinical Psychology, 56,* 893–897.

Beckers, J. J., Wicherts, J. M., & Schmidt, H. G. (2007). Computer anxiety: "Trait" or "State"? *Computers in Human Behavior, 23,* 2851–2862.

Beidel, D. C., & Turner, S. M. (1997). At risk for anxiety: I. Psychopathology in the offspring of anxious parents. *Journal of the American Academy of Child and Adolescent Psychiatry, 36,* 918–924.

Beilock, S. L., Kulp, C. A., Holt, L. E., & Carr, T. H. (2004). More on the fragility of performance: Choking under pressure in mathematical problem solving. *Journal of Experimental Psychology: General, 133,* 584–600.

Bemmels, H. R., Burt, S. A., Legrand, L. N., Iacono, W. G., & McGue, M. (2008). The heritability of life events: An adolescent twin and adoption study. *Twin Research and Human Genetics, 11,* 257–265.

Benson, J., & Bandalos, D. (1989). Structural model of statistical test anxiety in adults. In R. Schwarzer, H. M. Van der Ploeg, & C. D. Spielberger (Eds.), *Advances in test anxiety research* (Vol. 6, pp. 137–151). Lisse: Swets & Zeitlinger.

Ben-Zur, H., & Zeidner, M. (1989). Sex differences in anxiety, curiosity and anger: A cross-cultural study. *Sex Roles, 19,* 335–347.

Betz, N. E. (1978). Prevalence, distribution, and correlation of math anxiety in college students. *Journal of Counseling Psychology, 25,* 441–448.

Betz, N. E., & Hackett, G. (1983). The relationship of mathematics self-efficacy expectations to the selection of science-based college majors. *Journal of Vocational Behavior, 23,* 329–345.

Biederman, J., Hirshfeld-Becker, D. R., Rosenbaum, J. F., Hérot, C., Friedman, D., Snidman, N., et al. (2001). Further evidence of association between behavioral inhibition and social anxiety in children. *The American Journal of Psychiatry, 158,* 1673–1679.

Bippus, A. M., & Daly, J. A. (1999). What do people think causes stage fright? Naïve attributions about the reasons for public speaking anxiety. *Communication Education, 48,* 63–72.

Bishop, S. J. (2007). Neurocognitive mechanism of anxiety: An integrative account. *Trends in Cognitive Science, 11,* 307–316.

Blanchette, I., & Richards, A. (2003). Anxiety and the interpretation of ambiguous information: Beyond the emotion-congruent effect. *Journal of Experimental Psychology: General, 132,* 294–309.

Blankstein, K. R., Toner, B. B., & Flett, G. L. (1989). Test anxiety and the contents of consciousness: Thought-listing and endorsement measures. *Journal of Research in Personality, 23,* 269–286.

Bleich, A., Gelkopf, M., & Solomon, Z. (2003). Exposure to terrorism, stress-related mental health symptoms, and coping behaviors among a nationally representative sample in Israel. *Journal of the American Medical Association, 290,* 612–620.

Bögels, S. M., & van Melick, M. (2004). The relationship between child-report, parent self-report, and partner report of perceived parental rearing behaviors and anxiety in children and parents. *Personality and Individual Differences, 37,* 1583–1596.

Boggiano, A. K., & Ruble, D. N. (1986). Children's responses to evaluative feedback. In R. Schwarzer (Ed.), *Self-related cognitions in anxiety and motivation* (pp. 195–227). Hillsdale, NJ: Erlbaum.

Borkovec, T. D., Robinson, E., Pruzinsky, T., & DePree, J. D. (1983). Preliminary exploration of worry: Some characteristics and processes. *Behaviour Research and Therapy, 21,* 9–16.

Bosson, J. K., Swann, W. B., Jr., & Pennebaker, J. W. (2000). Stalking the perfect measure of implicit self-esteem: The blind men and the elephant revisited? *Journal of Personality and Social Psychology, 79,* 631–643.

Bowlby, J. (1960). Grief and mourning in infancy and early childhood. In Eissler (Ed.), *Psychoanalytic study of the child* (Vol. 14, pp. 9–52). New York: International Universities Press.

Bowlby, J. (1969). *Attachment and loss. Vol. 1. Attachment.* New York: Basic Books.

Bowlby, J. (1979). *The making and breaking of affectionate bonds.* London: Tavistock.

Bozionelos, N. (2001). Computer anxiety: Relationship with computer experience and prevalence. *Computers in Human Behavior, 17,* 213–224.

Breuer, J., & Freud, S. (1955/1895). Studies in hysteria. In J. Strachey (Ed.), *The standard edition of the complete psychological works of Sigmund Freud* (Vol. 2). London: Hogarth Press.

Brosnan, M., & Goodison, P. (2010). Anxiety, flow, and boredom: Optimizing computer-based learning in the classroom. In J. C. Cassady (Ed.), *Anxiety in schools: The causes, consequences, and solutions for academic anxieties* (pp. 27–42). New York: Peter Lang.

Brothers, D. (2003). After the towers fell: Terror, uncertainty, and intersubjective regulation. *Journal for the Psychoanalysis of Culture & Society, 8,* 68–76.

Bruch, M. A.(2001). Shyness and social interaction. In C. W. Ray & L. E. Alden (Eds.), *International handbook of social anxiety: Concepts, research and interventions relating to the self and shyness* (pp. 195–215). New York: John Wiley & Sons.

Bruch, M. A., Fallon, M., & Heimberg, R. G. (2003). Social phobia and difficulties in occupational adjustment. *Journal of Counseling Psychology, 50,* 109–117.

Bryant, C., Jackson, H., & Ames, D. (2007). The prevalence of anxiety in older adults: Methodological issues and a review of the literature. *Journal of Affective Disorders, 109,* 233–250.

Burns, M. (1998). *Math: Facing an American phobia.* Sausalito, CA: Math Solutions Publications.

Bursal, M., & Paznokas, L. (2006). Mathematics anxiety and preservice elementary teachers' confidence to teach mathematics and science. *School Science and Mathematics, 106,* 173–180.

Butler, A. C., Chapman, J. E., Forman, E. M., & Beck, A. T. (2006). The empirical status of cognitive-behavioral therapy: A review of meta-analyses. *Clinical Psychology Review, 26,* 17–31.

REFERENCES

Butler, G., & Mathews, A. (1983). Cognitive processes in anxiety. *Advances in Behavior Research and Therapy, 5,* 51–62.

Bynner, J., & Parsons, S. (1997). *Does numeracy matter? Evidence from the national child development study on the impact of poor numeracy on adult life.* London: Basic Skills Agency.

Calvo, M. G., & Miguel-Tobal, J. J. (1998) The anxiety response: Concordance among components. *Motivation and Emotion, 22,* 211–230.

Calvo, M. G., Eysenck, M. W., & Castillo, M. D. (1997). Interpretation bias in test anxiety: The time course of predictive inferences. *Cognition and Emotion, 11,* 43–63.

Canli, T. (2009). Neuroimaging of personality. In P. Corr & G. Matthews (Eds.), *Cambridge handbook of personality* (pp. 305–322). Cambridge: Cambridge University Press.

Caprara, G. V., & Cervone, D. (2000). *Personality. Determinants, dynamics, and potential.* New York: Cambridge University Press

Carmona, J. E., Holland, A. K., & Harrison, D. W. (2009). Extending the functional cerebral systems theory of emotion to the vestibular modality: A systematic and integrative approach. *Psychological Bulletin, 135,* 286–302.

Carter, R., Williams, S., & Silverman, W. K. (2008). Cognitive and emotional facets of test anxiety in African American school children. *Cognition and Emotion, 22,* 539–551.

Cartwright-Hatton, S., & Wells, A. (1997). Beliefs about worry and intrusions: The meta-cognitions questionnaire and its correlates. *Journal of Anxiety Disorders, 11,* 279–296.

Cartwright-Hatton, S., Tschernitz, N., & Gomersall, H. (2005). Social anxiety in children: Social skill deficits, or cognitive distortion? *Behaviour Research and Therapy, 43,* 189–201.

Carver, S. (1996). Cognitive interference and the structure of behavior. In I. G. Sarason, G. R. Pierce, & B. R. Sarason (Eds.), *Cognitive interference: Theories, methods, and findings* (pp. 25–45). Mahwah, NJ: Erlbaum.

Carver, C. S., & Scheier, M. F. (1984). Self-focused attention in test anxiety: A general theory applied to a specific phenomenon. In H. M. Van der Ploeg, R. Schwarzer, & C. D. Spielberger (Eds.), *Advances in test anxiety research* (Vol. 3, pp. 3–20). Lisse, Netherlands: Swets & Zeitlinger

Carver, C. S., & Scheier, M. F. (1988a). A control-process perspective on anxiety. *Anxiety Research, 1,* 17–22.

Carver, C. S., & Scheier, M. F. (1988b). A model of behavioral self-regulation: Translating intention into action. *Advances in Experimental Social Psychology ,21,* 303–346.

Carver, C. S., & Scheier, M. F. (1989). Expectancies and coping: From test anxiety to pessimism. In R. Schwarzer, H. M. Van der Ploeg, & C. D. Spielberger (Eds.), *Advances in test anxiety research* (Vol. 6, pp. 3–11). Lisse, Netherlands: Swets & Zeitlinger.

Carver, C. S., & Scheier, M. F. (1990). Principles of self-regulation: Action and emotion. In E. T. Higgins & R. M. Sorrentino (Eds.), *Handbook of motivation and cognition: Foundations of social behavior* (Vol. 2, pp. 3–52). New York: Guilford Press.

Carver, C. S., & Scheier, M. F. (1991). A control-process perspective on anxiety. In R. Schwarzer & R. A. Wicklund (Eds). *Anxiety and self-focused attention* (pp. 3–8). Amsterdam, Netherlands: Harwood Academic Publishers.

Carver, C. S., Scheier, M. F., & Klahr, D. (1987). Further explorations of a control-process model of test anxiety. In R. Schwarzer, H. M. Van der Ploeg, & C. D. Spielberger (Eds.), *Advances in test anxiety research* (Vol. 6, pp. 15–22). Lisse: Swets & Zeitlinger.

Carver, C. S., Scheier, M. F., & Weintraub, J. K. (1989). Assessing coping strategies: A theoretically-based approach. *Journal of Personality and Social Psychology, 56*, 267–283.

Carver, C. S., Scheier, M. F., & Pozo, C. (1992). Conceptualizing the process of coping with health problems. In H. S. Friedman (Ed.), *Hostility, coping, and health* (pp. 167–199). Washington, DC: APA.

Carver, C. S., Peterson, L. M., Follansbee, D. J., & Scheier, M. F. (1983). Effects of self-directed attention on performance and persistence among persons high and low in test anxiety. *Cognitive Therapy and Research, 7*, 333–354.

Casbarro, J. (2005). *Test anxiety and what you can do about it: A practical guide for teachers, parents, and kids.* Port Chester, NY: Dude.

Caspi, A., Moffitt, T. E., Newman, D. L., & Silva, P. A. (1998). Behavioral observations at age 3 years predict adult psychiatric disorders: Longitudinal evidence from a birth cohort. In M. E. Hertzig & E. A. Farber (Eds.), *Annual progress in child psychiatry and child development* (pp. 319–331). Philadelphia: Brunner/Mazel.

Cassady, J. C. (2004). The influence of cognitive test anxiety across the learning-testing cycle. *Learning and Instruction, 14*, 569–592.

Cassady, J. C. (2010). Test anxiety: Contemporary theories and implications for learning. In J. C. Cassady (Ed.), *Anxiety in schools: The causes, consequences, and solutions for academic anxieties* (pp. 7–26). New York: Peter Lang.

Cassady, J. C., & Johnson, R. E. (2002). Cognitive test anxiety and academic performance. *Contemporary Educational Psychology, 27*, 270–295.

Chamberlain, S. T., & Hale, B. D. (2007). Competitive state anxiety and self-confidence: Intensity and direction as relative predictors of performance on a golf putting task. *Anxiety, Stress, and Coping, 20*, 197–207.

Chambless, D. L., Cherney, J., Caputo, G. C., & Rheinstein, B. J. (1987). Anxiety disorders and alcoholism: A study with inpatient alcoholics. *Journal of Anxiety Disorders, 1*, 29–40.

Choi, G., Ligon, J., & Ward, J. (2002). Computer anxiety and social workers: Differences by access, use, and training. *Journal of Technology in Human Services, 19*, 1–12.

Chorpita, B. F., & Barlow, D. H. (1998). The development of anxiety: The role of control in the early environment. *Psychological Bulletin, 124*, 13–21.

Christensen, T. C., Barrett, L. F., Bliss-Moreau, E., Lebo, K., & Kaschub, C. (2003). A practical guide to experience-sampling procedures. *Journal of Happiness Studies, 4*, 53–78.

Chua, L. S., Chen, D. T., & Wong, A. F. L. (1999). Computer anxiety and its correlates: A meta-analysis. *Computers in Human Behavior, 15*, 609–623.

Church, M. A., Elliot, A. J., & Gable, S. L. (2001). Perceptions of classroom environment, achievement goals, and achievement outcomes. *Journal of Educational Psychology, 93*, 43–54.

Clark, D. A., Beck, A. T., & Alford, B. A. (1999). *Scientific foundations of cognitive theory and therapy of depression.* Hoboken, NJ: John Wiley.

Clark, D. M., & McManus, F. (2002). Information processing in social phobia. *Biological Psychiatry, 51*, 92–100.

Clark, D. M., & Wells, A. (1995). A cognitive model of social phobia. In R. Heimberg, M. Liebowitz, D. A. Hope, & F. R. Schneier (Eds.), *Social phobia: Diagnosis, assessment and treatment.* New York: Guilford Press.

Coffin, R. J., & MacIntyre, P. D. (1999). Motivational influences on computer-related affective states. *Computer and Human Behavior, 15*, 549–569.

Cohen, F., & Lazarus, R. (1979). Coping with the stresses of illness. In G. C. Stone, F. Cohen, & N. E. Adler (Eds.), *Health psychology: A handbook* (pp. 217–254). San-Francisco: Jossey-Bass.

Cooper, S. E., & Robinson, D. A. (1989). The influence of gender and anxiety on mathematics performance. *Journal of College Student Development, 30*, 459–461.

Corr, P. J., & Perkins, A. M. (2006). The role of theory in the psychophysiology of personality: From Ivan Pavlov to Jeffrey Gray. *International Journal of Psychophysiology, 62*, 367–376.

Corr, P. J. (2009). The reinforcement sensitivity theory of personality. In P. J. Corr & G. Matthews (Eds.), *Cambridge handbook of personality* (pp. 347–376). Cambridge: Cambridge University Press.

Coryell, W., Noyes, R., & House, J. D. (1986). Mortality among outpatients with anxiety disorders. *The American Journal of Psychiatry, 143*, 508–510.

Covington, M. V. (1992). *Making the grade.* New York: Cambridge University Press.

Covington, M. V., & Omelich, C. L. (1979). Effort: The double edged sword in school achievement. *Journal of Educational Psychology, 71*, 169–182.

Craft, L. L., Magyar, T. M., Becker, B. J., & Feltz, D. L. (2003). The relationship between the Competitive State Anxiety Inventory-2 and sport performance: A meta-analysis. *Journal of Sport & Exercise Psychology, 25,* 44–65.

Crozier, W. R., & Alden, L. E. (2001). The social nature of social anxiety. In W. R. Crozier & L. E. Alden (Eds.), *International handbook of social anxiety: Concepts, research and interventions relating to the self and shyness* (pp. 1–20). New York: John Wiley.

Damasio, A. R. (1994). *Descartes' error: Emotion, reason, and the human brain.* New York: Grosset/Putnam.

Dannahy, L., & Stopa, L. (2007). Post-event processing in social anxiety. *Behaviour Research and Therapy, 45,* 1207–1219.

Darwin, C. (1965/1872). Concluding remarks and summary. In C. Darwin (Ed.), *The expression of the emotions in man and animals* (pp. 348–367). London: John Murray.

Davidson, R. J. (2002). Anxiety and affective style: Role of prefrontal cortex and amygdala. *Biological Psychiatry, 51,* 68–80.

Davis, H. A., DiStefano, C., & Schutz, P. A. (2008). Identifying patterns of appraising tests in first-year college students: Implications for anxiety and emotion regulation during test taking. *Journal of Educational Psychology, 100,* 942–960.

Dawson, M. R. W. (1998). *Understanding cognitive science.* Malden, MA: Blackwell.

Deaux, K., & Major, B. (1977). Sex-related patterns in the unit of perception. *Personality and Social Psychology Bulletin, 3,* 297–300.

Deffenbacher, J. L. (1986). Cognitive and physiological components of test anxiety in real life exams. *Cognitive Therapy and Research, 10,* 635–644.

Deffenbacher, J. L., & Deitz, S. R. (1978). Effects of test anxiety on performance, worry and emotionality in naturally occurring exams. *Psychology in the Schools, 15,* 446–450.

Deffenbacher, J. L., & Suinn, R. M. (1988). Systematic desensitization and the reduction of anxiety. *The Counseling Psychologist, 16,* 9–30.

Degnan, K. A., Almas, A. N., & Fox, N. A. (2010). Temperament and the environment in the etiology of childhood anxiety. *Journal of Child Psychology and Psychiatry, 51,* 497–517.

DeNeve, K. M., & Cooper, H. (1998). The happy personality: A meta-analysis of 137 personality traits and subjective well-being. *Psychological Bulletin, 124,* 197–229.

Depreeuw, E., & De Neve, H. (1992). Test anxiety can harm your health: Some conclusions based on a student typology. In D. G. Forgays, T. Sosnowski, & K. Wrzesniewski (Eds.), *Series in health psychology and behavioral medicine. Anxiety: Recent developments in cognitive, psychophysiological, and health research* (pp. 211–228). Washington, DC: Hemisphere.

Derakshan, N., Eysenck, M. W., & Myers, L. B. (2007). Emotional information processing in repressors: The vigilance-avoidance theory. *Cognition and Emotion, 21*, 1585–1614.

Derryberry, D., & Reed, M. A. (2002). Anxiety-related attentional biases and their regulation by attentional control. *Journal of Abnormal Psychology, 111*, 225–236.

Donnellan, M. B., Trzesniewski, K. H., & Robins, R. W. (2009). An emerging epidemic of narcissism or much ado about nothing? *Journal of Research in Personality, 43*, 498–501.

Drake, K. L., & Kearney, C. A. (2008). Child anxiety sensitivity and family environment as mediators of the relationship between parent psychopathology, parent anxiety sensitivity, and child anxiety. *Journal of Psychopathology and Behavioral Assessment, 30*, 79–86.

Dubi, K., Rapee, R. M., Emerton, J. L., & Schniering, C. A. (2008). Maternal modeling and the acquisition of fear and avoidance in toddlers: Influence of stimulus preparedness and child temperament. *Journal of Abnormal Child Psychology, 36*, 499–512.

Dunkel, C. S. (2002). Terror management theory and identity: The effect of the 9/11 terrorist attacks on anxiety and identity change. *Identity: An International Journal of Theory and Research, 2*, 281–301.

Dunn, B. D., Dalgleish, T., & Lawrence, A. D. (2006). The somatic marker hypothesis: A critical evaluation. *Neuroscience and Biobehavioral Reviews, 30*, 239–271.

Dunn, J. G. H., Dunn, J. C., Wilson, P., & Syrotuik, D. G. (2000). Reexa-mining the factorial composition and factor structure of the Sports Anxiety Scale. *Journal of Sport and Exercise Psychology, 22*, 183–193.

Ebner-Priemer, U. W., & Trull, T. J. (2009). Ambulatory assessment: An innovative and promising approach for clinical psychology. *European Psychologist, 14*, 109–119.

Edelmann, R. J. (1992). *Anxiety: Theory, research and intervention in clinical and health psychology.* Oxford, England: John Wiley.

Egloff, B., & Schmukle, S. C. (2002). Predictive validity of an implicit association test for assessing anxiety. *Journal of Personality and Social Psychology, 83*, 1441–1455.

Egloff, B., Wilhelm, F. H., Neubauer, D. H., Mauss, I. B., & Gross, J. J. (2002). Implicit anxiety measure predicts cardiovascular reactivity to an evaluated speaking task. *Emotion, 2*, 3–11.

Eley, T. C., Bolton, D., O'Connor, T. G., Perrin, S., Smith, P., & Plomin, R. (2003). A twin study of anxiety-related behaviours in preschool children. *Journal of Child Psychology and Psychiatry, 44*, 945–960.

Elliot, A. J. (2005). A conceptual history of the achievement goal construct. In A. J. Elliot & C. S. Dweck (Eds.), *Handbook of competence and motivation* (pp. 52–72). New York: Guilford Publications.

Emery, J. R., & Krumboltz, J. D. (1967). Standard versus individual-ized hierarchies in desensitization to reduce test anxiety. *Journal of Counseling Psychology, 14*, 204–209.

Endler, N. S. (2002). Multidimensional interactionism: Stress, anxiety, and coping. In L. Bäckman & C. von Hofsten (Eds.), *Psychology at the turn of the millennium, Vol. 1. Cognitive, biological, and health per-spectives* (pp. 281–305). Hove, England: Psychology Press/Taylor & Francis.

Endler, N. S., & Kocovski, N. L. (2001). State and trait anxiety revisited. *Anxiety Disorders, 15*, 231–245.

Endler, N. S., Edwards, J. M., & Vitelli, R. (1991). *Endler Multidimensional Anxiety Scales*. Los Angeles: Western Psychological Services.

Essex, J. K., Klein, M. H., Cho, E., & Kraemer, H. C. (2003). Exposure to maternal depression and marital conflict: Gender differences in children's later later mental health symptoms. *Journal of the American Academy of Child and Adoescent Psychiatry, 42*, 728–737.

Essex, M. J., Kraemer, H. C., Armstrong, J. M., Boyce, W. T., Goldsmith, H. H., Klein, M. H., et al. (2006). Exploring risk factors for the emergence of children's mental health problems. *Archives of General Psychiatry, 63*, 1246–1256.

Eysenck, H. J. (1967). *The biological basis of personality*. Springfield, IL: C. C. Thomas.

Eysenck, H. J. (1982). *Personality, genetics, and behavior,* New York: Praeger.

Eysenck, H. J., & Eysenck, M. W. (1985). *Personality and Individual Differences*. New York: Plenum Press.

Eysenck, M. W. (1992a). *Anxiety: The cognitive perspective*. Hove, England: Lawrence Erlbaum.

Eysenck, M. W. (1992b). The nature of anxiety. In A. Gayle & M. W. Eysenck, *Handbook of individual differences: Biological perspectives* (pp. 157–178). Chichester, England: Wiley.

Eysenck, M. (1997). *Anxiety and cognition: A unified perspective*. East Sussex, England: Psychology Press.

Eysenck, M. W., Derakshan, N., Santos, R., & Calvo, M. G. (2007). Anxiety and cognitive performance: Attentional control theory, *Emotion, 7*, 336–353.

Feldman, P. J., Cohen, S, Hamrick, N., & Lepore, S. J. (2004). Psycho-logical stress appraisal, emotion and cardiovascular repsonse in a public speaking task. *Psychology and Health, 19*, 353–368.

Feldner, M. T., Zvolensky, M. J., & Schmidt, N. B. (2004). Prevention of anxiety psychopathology: A critical review of the empirical litera-ture. *Clinical Psychology: Science and Practice, 11*, 405–424.

Fennema, E. (1977). *Influence of selected cognitive, affective, and educa-tional variables on sex-related differences in mathematics learning and studying. Women and mathematics: Research perspectives for change.* Washington, DC: NIE Papers in Education and Work.

Fisak, B., Jr., & Grills-Taquechel, A. E. (2007). Parental modeling, reinforcement, and information transfer: Risk factors in the development of child anxiety? *Clinical Child and Family Psychology Review, 10*, 213–231.

Fletcher, K. L., & Cassady, J. C. (2010). Overcoming academic anxieties: Promoting effective coping and self-regulation strategies. Cassady, J. C. (2010). Test anxiety: Contemporary theories and implications for learning. In J. C. Cassady (Ed), *Anxiety in schools: The causes, consequences, and solutions for academic anxieties* (pp. 177-200). New York: Peter Lang.

Flett, G. L., Hewitt, P. L., Endler, N. S., & Tassone, C. (1994/1995). Perfectionism and components of state and trait anxiety. *Current Psychology: Developmental, Learning, Personality, Social, 13*, 326–350.

Folkman, S., Lazarus, R. S., Dunkel-Schetter, C., DeLongis, A., & Gruen, R. (1986). The dynamics of a stressful encounter: Cognitive appraisal, coping, and encounter outcomes. *Journal of Personality and Social Psychology, 50*, 992–1003.

Fox, E., Russo, R., Georgiu, G. A. (2005). Anxiety modulates the degree of attentive resources required to process emotional facets. *Cognitive, Affective, and Behavioral Neuroscience, 5*, 396–404.

Fox, N. A., Nichols, K. E., Henderson, H. A., Rubin, K., Schmidt, L., Hamer, D., et al. (2005). Evidence for a gene-environment interaction in predicting behavioral inhibition in middle childhood. *Psychological Science, 16*, 921–926.

Fraley, R. C. (2002). Attachment stability from infancy to adulthood: Meta-analysis and dynamic modeling of developmental mechanisms. *Personality and Social Psychology Review, 6*, 123–151.

Freeston, M. H., Rheaume, J., Letarte, H., Dugas, M. J., & Ladouceur, R. (1994). Why do people worry? *Personality and Individual Differences, 17*, 791–802.

Freud, S. (1936/1926). *The problems of anxiety* (H. A. Bunker, Trans.). New York: Norton (original work published in 1926).

Freud, S. (1949). *Introductory lectures on psychoanalysis.* London, England: Allen & Unwin Ltd.

Freud, S. (1959/1926). Inhibition, symptoms, and anxiety. In J. Strachey (Ed.), *The standard edition of the complete psychological works of Sigmund Freud* (Vol. 20). London: Hogarth Press.

Friedland, N., & Merari, A. (1986). The psychological impact of terrorism on society: A two-edged sword. In N. A. Milgram (Ed.), *Stress and coping in time of war* (pp. 243–256). New York: Brunner/Mazel.

Funder, D. C., & Ozer, D. J. (1983). Behavior as a function of the situation. *Journal of Personality and Social Psychology, 44*, 107–112.

Gal, R., & Lazarus, R. (1975). The role of activity in anticipation and confronting stressful situations. *Journal of Human Stress, 1*, 4–20.

Galea, S., Ahern, J., Resnick, H., Kilpatrick, D., Bucuvalas, M., Gold, J., et al. (2002). Psychological sequelae of the September 11 terrorist attacks in New York City. *New England Journal of Medicine, 346,* 982–987.

Gatchel, R. J., Baum, A., & Krantz, D. S. (1989). *An introduction to health psychology.* New York: Random House.

Giga, S. I., Cooper, C. L., & Faragher, B. (2003). The development of a framework for a comprehensive approach to stress management interventions at work. *International Journal of Stress Management, 10,* 280–296.

Goetz, T., Praekel, F., Zeidner, M., & Schleyer, E. (2008). Anxiety levels of big fish swimming in big ponds: A multilevel analysis of test anxiety and achievement in special gifted classes. *Anxiety, Stress and Coping: An International Journal, 21,* 185–198.

Gosling, S. D., & Harley, B. A. (2009). Animal models of personality and cross-species comparisons. In P. J. Corr & G. Matthews (Eds.), *Cambridge handbook of personality* (pp. 275–286). Cambridge: Cambridge University Press.

Grant, D. M., & Beck, G. (2006). Attentional biases in social anxiety and dysphoria: Does comorbidity make a difference? *Journal of Anxiety Disorders, 20,* 520–529.

Gray, J. A., & McNaughton, N. (2003). *The neuropsychology of anxiety: An inquiry into the functions of the septohippocampal system.* New York: Oxford University Press.

Gray, J. A. (1990). Brain systems that mediate both emotion and cognition. *Cognition and Emotion, 4, 269–288.*

Gross, C., & Hen, R. (2004). The developmental origins of anxiety. *Nature Reviews Neuroscience, 5,* 545–552.

Grünbaum, A. (2001). A century of psychoanalysis: Critical retrospect and prospect. *International Forum of Psychoanalysis, 10,* 105–112.

Hamden, R. H. (2002). The retributional terrorist: Type 4. In C. E. Stout (Ed.), *The psychology of terrorism: Clinical aspects and response* (Vol. 2, pp. 165–192). Westport, CT: Praeger.

Hamilton, M. (1959). The assessment of anxiety states by rating. *British Journal of Medical Psychology, 32,* 50–55.

Hampson, S. E. (1988). *Introductions to modern psychology. The construction of personality: An introduction* (2nd ed.). New York: Routledge.

Hanin, Y. L. (2007). Emotions and athletic performance: Individual zones of optimal functioning model. In D. Smith & M. Bar-Eli (Eds.) *Essential readings in sport and exercise psychology* (pp. 55–73). Champaign, IL: Human Kinetics.

Hariri, A. R., & Holmes, A. (2006). Genetics of emotional regulation: The role of the serotonin transporter in neural function. *Trends in Cognitive Sciences, 10,* 182–191.

Harter, S., Whitesell, N., & Kowalski, P. (1987). *The effects of educational transitions on children's perceptions of competence and motivational orientation.* Unpublished manuscript. University of Denver.

Heerey, E. A., & Kring, A. M. (2007). Interpersonal consequences of social anxiety. *Journal of Abnormal Psychology, 116,* 125–134.

Heinssen, R. K., Glass, C. R., & Knight, L. A. (1987). Assessing computer anxiety: Development and validation of the Computer Anxiety Rating Scale. *Computers in Human Behavior, 3,* 49–59.

Hembree, R. (1988). Correlates, causes, effects, and treatment of test anxiety. *Review of Educational Research, 58,* 7–77.

Hembree, R. (1990). The nature, effects, and relief of mathematics anxiety. *Journal for Research in Mathematics Education, 21,* 33–46.

Hermans, H. J. M., ter Laak, J. J. F., & Maes, P. C. J. M. (1972). Achievement motivation and fear of failure in family and school. *Developmental Psychology, 6,* 520–528.

Higson-Smith C. (2002). A community psychology perspective on terrorism: Lessons from South Africa. In C. E. Stout (Ed.), *The psychology of terrorism: Programs and practices in response and prevention* (Vol. 4, pp. 3–22). Westport: Praeger.

Hill, K. T. (1972). Anxiety in the evaluative context. In W. Hartup (Ed.), *The young child* (Vol. 2, pp. 225–263). Washington, DC: National Association for the Education of Young Children.

Hill, K. T., & Eaton, W. O. (1977). The interaction of test anxiety and success-failure experiences in determining children's arithmetic performance. *Developmental Psychology, 13,* 205–211.

Hirshfeld-Becker, D., Biederman, J., Henin, A., Faraone, S. V., Micco, J. A., van Grondelle, A., et al. (2007). Clinical outcomes of laboratory-observed preschool behavioral disinhibition at five-year follow-up. *Biological Psychiatry, 62,* 565–572.

Hill, K. T., & Sarason, S. B. (1966). The relation of test anxiety and defensiveness to test and school performance over the elementary school years: A further longitudinal study. *Monograph of the Society for Research in Child Development, 31,* 1–76.

Hobfoll, S. E., Palmieri, P. A., Johnson, R. J., Canetti-Nisim, D., Hall, B. J., & Galea, S. (2009). Trajectories of resilience, resistance, and distress during ongoing terrorism: The case of Jews and Arabs in Israel. *Journal of Consulting and Clinical Psychology, 77,* 138–148.

Hock, M. (1992). Exchange of aversive communicative acts between mother and child as related to perceived child-rearing practices and anxiety of the child. In K. A. Hagtvet & B. T. Johnsen (Eds.), *Advances in test anxiety research* (Vol. 7, pp. 156–174). Lisse: Swets and Zeitlinger.

Hodge, K. (2004). *Sport motivation: Training your mind for peak performance.* Auckland, New Zealand: Reed Publishing.

Hodges, W. F. (1976). The psychophysiology of anxiety. In M. Zuckerman & C. D. Spielberger (Eds.), *Emotions and anxiety: New concepts, methods, and applications* (pp. 175–194). New York: Halsted Press.

Hoffman, B. (2010). "i think i can, but i'm afraid to try": The role of self-efficacy beliefs and mathematics anxiety in mathematics problem-solving efficiency. *Learning and Individual Differences, 20,* 276–283.

Holahan, C. J., & Moos, R. H. (1985). Life stress and health: Personality, coping, and family support in stress resistance. *Journal of Personality and Social Psychology, 49,* 739–747.

Holroyd, K. A., & Appel, M. A. (1980). Test anxiety and physiological responding. In I. Sarason (Ed.), *Test anxiety: Theory, research, and applications* (pp. 129–151). Hillsdale, NJ: Lawrence Erlbaum.

Hong, E. (1999). Test anxiety, perceived test difficulty, and test performance: Temporal patterns of their effects. *Learning and Individual Differences, 11,* 431–447.

Hopko, D.R., McNeil, D.W., Gleason, P.J., Rabalais, A.E. (2002) The emotional Stroop paradigm: Performance as a function of stimulus properties and self-reported mathematics anxiety. *Cognitive Therapy and Research, 26,* 157–166.

Horne, A. M., & Matson, J. L. (1977). A comparison of modeling, desensitization, flooding, study skills and control groups for reducing test anxiety. *Behavior Therapy, 8,* 1–8.

Hudson, J. L., & Rapee, R. M. (2004). From anxious temperament to disorder: An etiological model. In R. G. Heimberg, C. L. Turk, & D. S. Mennin (Eds.), *Generalized anxiety disorder: Advances in research and practice* (pp. 51–74). New York: Guilford Press.

Hull, C. (1943). *Principles of behavior.* New York: Appleton.

Ijzendoorn, M. H. v., & Bakermans-Kranenburg, M. J. (2004). Maternal sensitivity and infant temperament in the formation of attachment. In G. Bremner & A. Slater (Eds.), *Theories of infant development* (pp. 233-257). Malden: Blackwell Publishing.

Ilkowska, M., & Engle, R.W. (2010). Trait and state differences in working memory capacity. In A. Gruszka, G. Matthews & B. Szymura (Eds.), *Handbook of individual differences in cognition: Attention, memory and executive control* (pp. 295–320). New York: Springer.

Jain, S., & Dowson, M. (2009). Mathematics anxiety as a function of multidimensional self-regulation and self-efficacy. *Contemporary Educational Psychology, 34,* 240–249.

Jay, T. B. (1981). Computerphobia: What to do about it. *Educational Technology, 21,* 47–48.

Johnson, S. M., & Sechrest, L. (1968). Comparison of desensitization and progressive relaxation in treating test anxiety. *Journal of Consulting and Clinical Psychology, 32,* 280–286.

Jone, N., Greenberg, N., & Wesseley (2007). No plans survive first contact with the enemy: Flexibility and improvisation in disaster mental health. *Psychiatry, 70,* 361–365.

Kagan, J. (2007). *What is emotion?* New Haven, CT: Yale University Press.

Kagan, J., Reznick, J. S., & Snidman, N. (1988). Biological bases of childhood shyness. *Science, 240,* 167–171.

Kagan, J., Snidman, N., Arcus, D., & Reznick, S. J. (1994). *Galen's prophecy: Temperament in human nature.* New York: Basic Books.

Kahneman, D., & Triesman, A. (1983). The cost of visual filtering. *Journal of Experimental Psychology: Human Perception and Performance, 9,* 510–522.

Kalat, J. W., & Shiota, M. N. (2007). *Emotion.* Belmont, CA: Thompson.

Kaplan, A. (1964). *The conduct of inquiry.* Scranton, PA: Chandler Publishing.

Karevold, E., Roysamb, E., Ystrom, E., & Mathiesen, K. S. (2009). Predictors and pathways from infancy to symptoms of anxiety and depression in early adolescence. *Developmental Psychology, 45,* 1051–1060.

Kata, K. (1975). On anxiety in the Scandinavian countries. In I. G. Sarason & C. D. Spielberger (Eds.), *Stress and anxiety* (Vol. 2, pp. 275–302). Oxford, England: Hemisphere.

Kashdan, T. B. (2007). Social anxiety spectrum and diminished positive experiences: Theoretical synthesis and meta-analysis. *Clinical Psychology Review, 27,* 348–365.

Keltner, D., & Haidt, J. (2001). Social functions of emotions. In T. J. Mayne & G. A. Bonanno (Eds.), *Emotions and social behavior. Emotions: Currrent issues and future directions* (pp. 192–213). New York: Guilford Press.

King, N. J., & O'llendick, T. H. (1989). Children's anxiety and phobic disorders in school settings: Classification, assessment, and interventions issues. *Review of Educational Research, 4,* 431–470.

Klein, S. B., Sherman, J. W., & Loftus, J. (1996). The role of episodic and semantic memory in the development of trait self-knowledge. *Social Cognition, 14,* 277–291.

Kleine, D. (1990). Anxiety and sport performance: A meta-analysis. *Anxiety Research: An International Journal, 2,* 113–131.

Koivula, N., Hassmén, P., & Fallby, J. (2002). Self-esteem and perfectionism in elite athletes: Effects on competitive anxiety and self-confidence. *Personality and Individual Differences, 32,* 865–875.

Krohne, H. W. (1980). Parental child-rearing behavior and the development of anxiety and coping strategies in children. In I. G. Sarason & C. D. Spielberger (Eds.), *Stress and anxiety* (Vol. 7, pp. 233–245). Washington, DC: Hemisphere.

Krohne, H. W. (1992). Developmental conditions of anxiety and coping: A two-process model of child-rearing effects. In K. A. Hagtvet & B. T. Johnsen (Eds.), *Advances in test anxiety research* (Vol. 7, pp. 143–155). Lisse, Netherlands: Swets and Zeitlinger.

Krueger, R. F., Markon, K. E., & Bouchard, T. J. (2003). The extended genotype: The heritability of personality accounts for the heritability of recalled family evironments in twins reared apart. *Journal of Personality, 71,* 809–833.

Kubota, Y., Sato, W., Murai, T., Toichi, M., Ikeda, A., & Sengoku, A. (2000). Emotional cognition without awareness after unilateral temporal lobectomy in humans. *Journal of Neuroscience, 20, 1–5.*

Lacey, J. I. (1967) Somatic response patterning and stress: Some revisions of activation theory. In M. H. Appleby & R. Turnbull (Eds.), *Psychological stress* (pp. 14–42). New York: Appleton-Century-Crofts.

Lang, P. J. (1968). Fear reduction and fear behavior: Problems in treating a construct. In J. M. Shlien (Ed.), *Research in psychotherapy,* Vol. 1 (pp. 90–102). Washington, DC: American Psychological Association.

Lang, P. J., Rice, D. G., & Sternbach, R. A. (1972). The psychophysiology of emotion. In N. S. Greenfield & R. A. Sterbach (Eds.), *Handbook of psychophysiology* (pp. 90–102). New York: Holt, Rinehart, & Winston.

Laqueur, W. (1999). *The new terrorism.* New York: Oxford.

Lau, J. Y. F., Gregory, A. M., Goldwin, M. A., Pine, D. S., & Eley, T. C. (2007). Assessing gene-environment interactions on anxiety symptom subtypes across childhood and adolescence. *Development and Psychopathology, 19,* 1129–1146.

Lawyer, S. R., & Smitherman, T. A. (2004). Trends in anxiety assessment. *Journal of Psychopathology and Behavioral Assessment, 26,* 101–106.

Lazarus, R. S., & Alfert, E. (1964). Short-circuiting of threat by experimentally altering cognitive appraisal. *The Journal of Abnormal and Social Psychology, 69,* 195–205.

Lazarus R. S., & Folkman, S. (1984). *Stress, appraisal, and coping.* New York: Springer.

Lazarus, R. S. (1966*). Psychological stress and the coping process.* New York: McGraw-Hill.

Lazarus, R. S. (1990). Theory-based stress measurement. *Psychological Inquiry, 1,* 3–13.

Lazarus, R. S. (1991). *Emotion and adaptation.* New York: Oxford University Press.

Lazarus, R. S. (1999). *Stress and emotion: A new synthesis.* New York: Springer.

Leary, M. R. (2001) Shyness and the self: Attentional, motivational, and cognitive self-processes in social anxiety and inhibition. In W. R. Crozier & L. E. Alden (Eds.), *International handbook of social anxiety: Concepts, research and interventions relating to the self and shyness* (pp. 217–34). New York: Wiley.

LeDoux, J. (2006, May 4). Why is it hard to be happy?: The fearful brain is the problem and the solution. *Frontiers of Consciousness. Chichele Lectures,* All Souls College, Oxford, England.

LeDoux, J. E. (1996). *The emotional brain: The mysterious underpinnings of emotional life*. New York: Simon & Schuster.

Lee, J. (2009). Universals and specifics of math self-concept, math self-efficacy, and math anxiety across 41 PISA 2003 participating countries. *Learning and Individual Differences, 19*, 355–365.

Leech, S. L., Larkby, C. A., Day, R., & Day, N. L. (2006). Predictors and correlates of high levels of depression and anxiety symptoms among children at age 10. *Journal of the American Academy of Child & Adolescent Psychiatry, 45*, 223–230.

Leitenberg, H. (Ed.). (1990). *Handbook of social and evaluation anxiety*. New York: Plenum.

Lekarczyk, D. T., & Hill, K. T. (1969). Self-esteem, test anxiety, stress, and verbal learning. *Developmental Psychology, 1*, 147–154.

Lennon, M. C., Dohrenwend, B. P., Zautra, A. J., & Marbach, J. J. (1990). Coping and adaptation to facial pain in contrast to other stressful life events. *Journal of Personality and Social Psychology, 59*, 1040–1050.

Lesch, K., & Canli, T. (2006). 5-HT1A receptor and anxiety-related traits: Pharmacology, genetics, and imaging. In T. Canli (Ed.), *Biology of personality and individual differences* (pp. 273–294). New York: Guilford Press.

Levitt, E. E., & Hutton, L. H. (1983). Correlates and possible causes of mathematics anxiety. In C. D. Spielberger & J. M. Butcher (Eds.), *Advances in personality assessment* (Vol. 3, pp. 129–140). Hillsdale, NJ: Erlbaum.

Lewis, E. C. (1970). The ambiguous word "anxiety." *International Journal of Psychiatry, 9*, 62–79.

Lewis, M. (2001). Issues in the study of personality development. *Psychological Inquiry, 12*, 67–83.

Lowe, P. A., & Reynolds, R. (2005). Do relationships exist between age, gender, and education and self-reports of anxiety among older adults? *Individual Differences Research, 3*, 239–259.

Lucas, R. E., & Donnellan, B. (2009). Age differences in personality: Evidence from a nationally representative Australian sample. *Developmental Psychology, 45*, 1353–1363.

Ma, X. (1999). A meta-analysis of the relationship between anxiety toward mathematics and achievement in mathematics. *Journal for Research in Mathematics Education, 30*, 520–541.

Maccoby, E. E., & Jacklin, C. N. (1974). *The psychology of sex differences*. Stanford, CA: Stanford University Press.

Mandler, G., & Sarason, S. B. (1952). A study of anxiety and learning. *Journal of Abnormal and Social Psychology, 47*, 166–173.

Marcus, G. (2008). *Kluge*. New York: Houghton Mifflin Co.

Marsella, A. J., DeVos, G., & Hsu, F. (Eds.). (1985). *Culture and self: Asian and Western perspectives*. New York/London: Tavistock.

Marsh, H. W., Seaton, M., Trautwein, U., Lüdtke, O., Hau, K. T., O'Mara, A. J., et al. (2008). The big-fish-little-pond-effect stands up to critical scrutiny: Implications for theory, methodology, and future research. *Educational Psychology Review, 20,* 319–350.

Martinent, G., & Ferrand, C. (2007). A cluster analysis of precompetitive anxiety: Relationship with perfectionism and trait anxiety. *Personality and Individual Differences, 43,* 1676–1686.

Mathews, A. (2004). On the malleability of emotional encoding. *Behaviour Research and Therapy, 42,* 1019–1036.

Mathews, A., & MacLeod, C. (1994). Cognitive approaches to emotion and emotional disorders. *Annual Review of Psychology, 45,* 25–50.

Matthews, G. (2002). Towards a transactional ergonomics for driver stress and fatigue. *Theoretical Issues in Ergonomics Science, 3,* 195–211.

Matthews, G., & Gilliland, K. (1999). The personality theories of H. J. Eysenck and J. A. Gray: A comparative review. *Personality and Individual Differences, 26,* 583–626.

Matthews, G., & Campbell, S. E. (2009). Sustained performance under overload: Personality and individual differences in stress and coping. *Theoretical Issues in Ergonomics Science, 10,* 417–442.

Matthews, G., & Harley, T. A. (1996). Connectionist models of emotional distress and attentional bias. *Cognition and Emotion, 10,* 561–600.

Matthews, G., & Wells, A. (1999). The cognitive science of attention and emotion. In T. Dalgleish & M. Power (Eds.), *Handbook of cognition and emotion* (pp. 171–192). New York: Wiley.

Matthews, G., & Wells, A. (2000). Attention, automaticity and affective disorder. *Behavior Modification, 24,* 69–93.

Matthews, G., & Zeidner, M. (2004). A reappraisal of traits and states: Self-regulation, adaptation and trilogy of mind. In D. Yun Dai & R. J. Sternberg (Eds.), *Motivation, emotion, and cognition* (pp. 143–174). Mahwah, NJ: Erlbaum.

Matthews, G., Deary, I. J., & Whiteman, M. C. (2009). *Personality traits* (3rd ed.). Cambridge: Cambridge University Press.

Matthews, G., Gruszka, A., & Szymura, B. (2010). Conclusions: The state of the art in research on individual differences in executive control and cognition. In A. Gruszka, G. Matthews & B. Szymura (Eds.), *Handbook of individual differences in cognition: Attention, memory and executive control* (pp. 437–462). New York: Springer.

Matthews, G., Hillyard, E.J., & Campbell, S.E. (1999). Metacognition and maladaptive coping as components of test anxiety. *Clinical Psychology and Psychotherapy 6,* 111–125.

Matthews, G., Schwean, V. L., Campbell, S. E., Saklofske, D. H., & Mohamed, A. A. R. (2000). Personality, self-regulation, and adaptation. In M. Boekaerts, P. R. Pintrich, & M. Zeidner (Eds.), *Handbook of self-regulation* (pp. 171–207). San Diego, CA: Academic Press.

Mayer, J. D., Salovey, P., & Caruso, D. R. (2000). Competing models of emotional intelligence. In R. J. Sternberg (Ed.), *Handbook of human intelligence* (2nd ed., pp. 396–420). New York: Cambridge University Press.

McGregor, H. A., & Elliot, A. J. (2002). Achievement goals as predictors of achievement-relevant processes prior to task engagement. *Journal of Educational Psychology, 94,* 381–395.

McIlroy, D., Bunting, B., Tierney, K., & Gordon, M. (2001). The relation of gender and background experience to self-reported computing anxieties and cognitions. *Computers in Human Behavior, 17,* 21–33.

McInerney, V., Marsh, H. W., & McInerney, D. M. (1999). The designing of the computer anxiety and learning measure (CALM): Validation of scores on a multidimensional measure of anxiety and cognitions relating to adult learning of computing skills using structural equation modeling. *Educational and Psychological Measurement, 59,* 451–470.

Mcleod, B. D., Wood, J. J., & Weisz, J. R. (2007). Examining the association between parenting and childhood anxiety: A meta-analysis. *Clinical Psychology Review, 27,* 155–172.

Meece, J. L., Wigfield, A., & Eccles, J. S. (1990). Predictors of math anxiety and its influence on young adolescents' course enrollment intentions and performance in mathematics. *Journal of Educational Psychology, 82,* 60–70.

Meichenbaum, D. (1985). *Stress inoculation training.* New York: Pergamon Press.

Meichenbaum, D., & Butler, L. (1980). Toward a conceptual model for the treatment of test anxiety: Implications for research and treatment. In I. G. Sarason (Ed.), *Test anxiety: Theory, research and applications* (pp. 187–208). Hillsdale, NJ: Erlbaum.

Meichenbaum, D. (2009). Stress inoculation training. In W. T. O'Donohue & J. E. Fisher (Eds.), *General principles and empirically supported techniques of cognitive behavior therapy* (pp. 627–630). Hoboken, NJ: John Wiley.

Meijer, J., & Oostdam, R. (2007). Test anxiety and intelligence testing: A closer examination of the stage-fright hypothesis and the influence of stressful instruction. *Anxiety, Stress and Coping: An International Journal, 20,* 77–91.

Mellings, T. M. B., & Alden, L. E. (2000). Cognitive processes in social anxiety: The effects of self-focus, rumination and anticipatory processing. *Behaviour Research and Therapy, 38,* 243–257.

Messer, S. C., & Beidel, D. C. (1994). Psychosocial correlates of childhood anxiety disorders. *Journal of the American Academy of Child and Adolescent Psychiatry, 33,* 975–983.

Mineka, S., & Zinbarg, R. (2006). A contemporary learning theory perspective on the etiology of anxiety disorders: It's not what you thought it was. *American Psychologist, 61,* 10–26.

Mischel, W. (1968). *Personality and assessment.* New York: Wiley.

Mischel, W., & Shoda, Y. (1995). A cognitive-affective system theory of personality: Reconceptualizing situations, dispositions, dynamics, and invariance in personality structure. *Psychological Review, 102*, 246–268.

Mischel, W., & Shoda, Y. (1998). Reconciling processing dynamics and personality dispositions. *Annual Review of Psychology, 49*, 229–258.

Moffitt, T. E., Caspi, A., Harrington, H., Milne, B. J., Melchior, M., Goldberg, D., et al. (2007). Generalized anxiety disorder and depression: Childhood risk factors in a birth cohort followed to age 32. *Psychological Medicine: A Journal of Research in Psychiatry and the Allied Sciences, 37*, 441–452.

Moore, P. S., Whaley, S. E., & Sigman, M. (2004). Interactions between mothers and children: Impacts of maternal and child anxiety. *Journal of Abnormal Anxiety, 113*, 471–476.

Morling, B., & Evered, S. (2006). Secondary control reviewed and defined. *Psychological Bulletin, 13*, 269–296.

Munafò, M. R., Durrant, C., Lewis, G., & Flint, J. (2009). Gene × environment interactions at the serotonin transporter locus. *Biological Psychiatry, 65*, 211–219.

Nabi, R. L. (2003). Exploring the framing effects of emotion: Do discrete emotions differentially influence information accessibility, information seeking, and policy preference? *Communication Research, 30*, 224–247.

Naveh-Benjamin, M. (1991). A comparison of training programs intended for different types of test anxious students: Further support for an information processing model. *Journal of Educational Psychology, 83*, 134–139.

Neiss, R. (1988). Reconceptualizing arousal: Psychobiological states in motor performance. *Psychological Bulletin, 103*, 345–366.

Neisser, U. (1967). *Cognitive psychology.* Englewood Cliffs, NJ: Prentice-Hall.

Nicholls, J. G., Patashnick, M., & Mettetal, G. (1986). Conceptions of ability and intelligence. *Child Development, 57*, 636–645.

Noftle, E. E., & Shaver, P. R. (2006). Attachment dimensions and the big five personality traits: Associations and comparative ability to predict relationship quality. *Journal of Research in Personality, 40*, 179–208.

Nunnally, J. C. (1978). *Psychometric theory.* New York: McGraw-Hill.

Oatley, K., & Johnson-Laird, P. N. (1996). The communicative theory of emotions: Empirical tests, mental models, and implications for social interaction. In L. L. Martin & A. Tesser (Eds.), *Striving and feeling: Interactions among goals, affect, and self-regulation* (pp. 363–393). Hillsdale, NJ: Lawrence Erlbaum.

Ochsner, K. N., & Gross, J. J. (2005). The cognitive control of emotion. *Trends in Cognitive Sciences, 9*, 242–249.

O'Connor, T. G., Heron, J., Golding, J., Beveridge, M., & Glover, V. (2002). Maternal antenatal anxiety and children's behavioural/emotional problems at 4 years: Report from the Avon Longitudinal Study of Parents and Children. *British Journal of Psychiatry, 180,* 502–508.

Ohman, A. (2008). Fear and anxiety. In M. Lewis, J. M. Haviland, & Barrett-Feldman, L. (Eds.), *Handbook of emotions* (3rd ed., pp. 709–728). New York: Guilford Press.

O'Leary, K. D., & Smith, D. A. (1991). Marital interactions. *Annual Review of Psychology, 42,* 191–212.

Ouimet, A. J., Gawronski, B., & Dozois, D. J. A. (2009). Cognitive vulnerability to anxiety: A review and an integrative model. *Clinical Psychology Review, 29,* 459–470.

Panksepp, J. (1998). *Affective neuroscience: The foundations of human and animal emotions.* New York: Oxford University Press.

Parker, G. (1983). *Parental overprotection. A risk factor in psychosocial development.* Sydney, Australia: Grune & Stratton.

Paulhus, D. L., & Levitt, K. (1987). Desirable responding triggered by affect: Automatic egotism? *Journal of Personality and Social Psychology, 52,* 245–259.

Pearlin, L. I., & Schooler, C. (1978). The structure of coping. *Journal of Health and Social Behavior, 19,* 2–21.

Pekrun, R. (in press). Emotions. In T. Urdin (Ed.), *APA educational psychology handbook (Vol. 2).* Washington, DC: American Psychological Association.

Pekrun, R. (1985). Classroom climate and test anxiety: Developmental validity of expectancy-value theory of anxiety. In H. M. Van der Ploeg, R. Schwarzer, & C. D. Spielberger (Eds.), *Advances in test anxiety research* (Vol. 4, pp. 147–158). Lisse, Netherlands: Swets & Zeitlinger.

Pekrun, R. (2009a). Global and local perspectives on human affect: Implications of the control-value theory of achievement emotions. In M. Wosnitza, S. A. Karabenick, A. Efklides, & P. Nenniger (Eds.), *Contemporary motivation research: From global to local perspectives.* (pp. 97–115). Ashland, OH: Hogrefe & Huber Publishers.

Pekrun, R. (2009b). Emotions at school. In K. R. Wenzel & A. Wigfield (Eds), *Handbook of motivation at school* (pp. 575–604). New York: Routledge/Taylor & Francis Group.

Pekrun, R., Elliot, A. J., & Maier, M. A. (2009). Achievement goals and achievement emotions: Testing a model of their joint relations with academic performance. *Journal of Educational Psychology, 101,* 115–135.

Pekrun, R., Frenzel, A. C., Goetz, T., & Perry, R. P. (2007). The control-value theory of achievement emotions: An integrative approach to emotions in education. In P. A. Schutz & R. Pekrun (Eds.), *Emotion in education* (pp. 13–36). San Diego, CA: Elsevier/Academic Press.

Peleg-Popko, O., & Dar., R. (2001). Marital quality, family patterns, and children's fears and social anxiety. *Contemporary Family Therapy, 23*, 465–487.

Pervin, L. A., Cervone, D., & John, O. P. (2005). *Personality: Theory and research* (9th ed.). New York: Wiley.

Phillips, B. N., Martin, R. P., & Meyers, J. (1972). Interventions in relation to anxiety in school. In C. D. Spielberger (Ed.), *Anxiety: Current trends in theory and research* (Vol. 2, pp. 410–464). New York: Academic Press.

Posner, M. I., & DiGirolamo, G. J. (1998). Executive attention: Conflict, target detection, and cognitive control. In R. Parasuraman (Ed.), *The attentive brain* (pp. 401–423). Cambridge, MA: The MIT Press.

Powers, D. E. (2001). Test anxiety and test performance: Comparing paper-based and computer-adaptive versions of the graduate record examination (GRE) general test. *Journal of Educational Computing Research, 24*, 249–273.

Praekel, F., Zeidner, M., Goetz, T., & Schleyer, E. (2008). Female big fish swimming against the tide: The BFLPE and gender ratio in special gifted classes. *Contemporary Educational Psychology, 33*, 78–96.

Putwain, D. W. (2007). Test anxiety in UK schoolchildren: Prevalence and demographic patterns. *British Journal of Educational Psychology, 77*, 579–593.

Putwain, D. W. (2008). Deconstructing test anxiety. *Emotional and Behavioral Difficulties, 13*, 145–155.

Pylyshyn, Z. W. (1984). *Computation and cognition. Toward a foundation of cognitive science*. Cambridge, MA: MIT Press.

Rachman, S. (2003). *The treatment of obsessions*. Oxford, UK: Oxford University Press.

Rachman, S. (2004). *Anxiety* (2nd ed.). Oxford, England: Blackwell.

Rachman, S., & Hodgson, R. (1980). *Obsession and compulsions*. Englewood Cliffs, NJ: Prentice-Hall.

Raglin, J. S., & Hanin, Y. (2000). In Y. Hanin (Ed.), *Emotions in sport* (pp. 93–111). Champaign, IL: Human Kinetics.

Ramirez, O. M., & Dockweiler, C. J. (1987). Mathematics anxiety: A systematic review. In R. Schwarzer, H. M. Van der Ploeg, & C. D. Spielberger (Eds.), *Advances in test anxiety research* (Vol. 5, pp. 157–175). Lisse: Swets & Zeitlinger.

Rapee, R. M. (1997). Potential role of childrearing practices in the development of anxiety and depression. *Clinical Psychology Review, 17*, 47–67.

Rapee, R. M. (2001). The development of generalized anxiety. In M. W. Vasey & M. R. Dadds (Eds.), *The developmental psychopathology of anxiety* (pp. 481–503). New York: Oxford University Press.

Raphael, B. (2007). The human touch and mass catastrophe. *Psychiatry, 70*, 329–336.

Reeve, C. L., Bonaccio, S., & Charles, J. E. (2008). A policy-capturing study of the contextual antecedents of test anxiety. *Personality and Individual Differences, 45*, 243–248.

Regner, I., Escribe, C., & Dupeyrat, C. (2007). Evidence of social comparison in mastery goals in natural academic settings. *Journal of Educational Psychology, 99*, 575–583.

Reiss, S. (1997). Trait anxiety: It's not what you think. *Journal of Anxiety Disorders, 11*, 201–214.

Rende, R. D. (1993). Longitudinal relations between temperament traits and behavioral syndromes in middle childhood. *Journal of the American Academy of Child & Adolescent Psychiatry, 32*, 287–290.

Resnick, H., Viehe, J., & Segal, S. (1982). Is math anxiety a local phenomenon? A study of prevalence and dimensionality. *Journal of Counseling Psychology, 29*, 39–47.

Richardson, F. C., & Woolfolk, R. L. (1980). Mathematics anxiety. In I. G. Sarason (Ed.), *Test anxiety: Theory, research, and applications* (pp. 271–287). Hillsdale, NJ: Erlbaum.

Riskind, J. H., & Alloy, L. B. (2006). Cognitive vulnerability to psychological disorders: Overview of theory, design, and methods. *Journal of Social and Clinical Psychology, 25*, 705–725.

Riskind, J. H., Williams, N. L., & Joiner, T. E., Jr. (2006). The looming cognitive style: A cognitive vulnerability for anxiety disorders. *Journal of Social and Clinical Psychology, 25*, 779–801.

Rolls, E. T. (1999). *The brain and emotion*. Oxford, England: Oxford University Press.

Rosen, J. B., & Schulkin, J. (1998). From normal fear to pathological anxiety. *Psychological Review, 105*, 325–350.

Rosen, J. B., & Schulkin, J. (2004). Adaptive fear, allostasis, and the pathology of anxiety and depression. In J. Schulkin (Ed.), *Allostasis, homeostatis, and the costs of physical adaptation* (pp. 164–227). Cambridge: Cambridge University Press.

Rosen, L. D., & Maguire, P. (1990). Myths and realities of computerphobia: A meta-analysis. *Anxiety Research, 3*, 175–191.

Rosenthal, M. J. (1990). Inconsistent parenting and anxiety in the child. *Anxiety Research, 3*, 61–63.

Rosenthal, T. L. (1980). Modeling approaches to test anxiety and related performance problems. In I. G. Sarason (Ed.), *Test anxiety: Theory, research and applications* (pp. 245–270). Hillsdale, NJ: Erlbaum.

Rothbart, M. K., & Bates, J. E. (1998). Temperament. In W. Damon & N. Eisenberg (Eds.), *Handbook of child psychology: Vol. 3. Social, emotional, and personality development* (5th ed., pp. 105–176). New York: Wiley.

Rothbart, M. K., Sheese, B. E., & Conradt, E. D. (2009). Childhood temperament. In P. Corr & G. Matthews (Eds.), *Cambridge handbook of personality* (pp. 177–190). New York: Cambridge University Press.

Rothbaum, F., Weisz, J. R., & Snyder, S. S. (1982). Changing the world and changing the self: A two-process model of perceived control. *Journal of Personality and Social Psychology, 42,* 5–37.

Rowe, D. C. (1990). As the twig is bent? The myth of child-rearing influences on personality development. *Journal of Counseling & Development, 68,* 606–611.

Russo, R., Whittuck, D., Roberson, D., Dutton, K., Georgiou, G., & Fox, E. (2006). Mood-congruent free recall bias in anxious individuals is not a consequence of response bias. *Memory, 14,* 393–399.

Rutter, M., Moffitt, T. E., & Caspi, A. (2006). Gene-environment interplay and psychopathology: Multiple varieties but real effects. *Journal of Child Psychology and Psychiatry, 47,* 226–261.

Safina sorry for final flop. (2009, February 2). *The Dominion Post,* New Zealand, p. D3.

Salovey, P., Mayer, J. D, Goldman, S., Turvey, C., & Palfai, T. (1995). Emotional attention, clarity, and repair: Exploring emotional intelligence using the Trait Meta-Mood Scale. In J. W. Pennebaker (Ed.), *Emotion, disclosure, and health* (pp. 125–154). Washington, DC: American Psychological Association.

Santos, R., Wall, M. B., & Eysenck, M. W. (2010). *Anxiety and processing efficiency: fMRI evidence.* Working paper. University of London.

Sapolsky, R. M. (1992). *Stress, the aging brain, and the mechanisms of neuron death.* Cambridge, MA: MIT Press.

Sarason, I. G. (1980). Introduction to the study of test anxiety. In I. G. Sarason (Ed.), *Test anxiety: Theory, research and applications* (pp. 3–14). Hillsdale, NJ: Erlbaum.

Sarason, I. G. (1984). Stress, anxiety, and cognitive interference: Reactions to tests. *Journal of Personality and Social Psychology, 46,* 929–938.

Sarason, I. G. (1986). Test anxiety, worry, and cognitive interference. In R. Schwarzer (Ed.), *Self-related cognitions in anxiety and motivation* (pp. 19–35). Hillsdale, NJ: Erlbaum.

Sarason, I. G. (1988). Anxiety, self-preoccupation and attention. *Anxiety Research, 1,* 3–7.

Sarason, I. G., & Sarason, B. R. (1990). Test anxiety. In H. Leitenberg (Ed.), *Hand-book of social and evaluative anxiety* (pp. 475–496). New York: Plenum Press.

Sarason, I. G., & Stoops, R. (1978). Test anxiety and the passage of time. *Journal of Consulting and Clinical Psychology, 1,* 102–109.

Sarason, I. G., Sarason, B. R., & Pierce, G. R. (1990). Anxiety, cognitive interference, and performance. *Journal of Social Behavior and Personality, 5,* 1–18.

Sarason, I. G., Sarason, B. R., & Pierce, G. R. (1995). Cognitive interference: At the intelligence-personality crossroads. In D. Saklofske & M. Zeidner (Eds.), *International handbook of personality and intelligence* (pp. 285–296). New York: Plenum.

Sarason, S. B., Davidson, K. S., Lighthall, F. F., Waite, R., & Ruebush, B. K. (1960). *Anxiety in elementary school children*. New York: Wiley.

Scherer, K. (2009). Component models of emotion can inform the quest for emotional competence. In G. Matthews, M. Zeidner, & R. Roberts (Eds.), *The science of emotional intelligence: Knowns and unknowns*. New York: Oxford University Press.

Schlenker, B. R., & Leary, M. R. (1982). Social anxiety and self-presentation: A conceptualization and model. *Psychological Bulletin, 92*, 641–669.

Schnabel, K., Asendorpf, J. B., & Greenwald, A. G. (2008). Understanding and using the implicit association test: V. measuring semantic aspects of trait self-concepts. *European Journal of Personality, 22*, 695–706.

Schwarzer, R., & Lange, B. (1983). Test anxiety development from grade 5 to grade 10: A structural equation approach. In H. M. Van der Ploeg, R. Schwarzer, & C. D. Spielberger (Eds.), *Advances in test anxiety research* (Vol. 2, pp. 147–157). Lisse: Swets & Zeitlinger.

Schwarzer, R., Seipp, B., & Schwarzer, C. (1989). Mathematics performance and anxiety: A meta analysis. In R. Schwarzer, H. M. Van der Ploeg, & C. D. Spielberger (Eds.), *Advances in test anxiety research* (Vol. 6, pp. 105–119). Lisse: Swets & Zeitlinger.

Seaton, M., Marsh, H. W., & Craven, R. G. (2009). Earning its place as a pan-human theory: Universality of the big-fish-little-pond effect across 41 culturally and economically diverse countries. *Journal of Educational Psychology, 101*, 403–419.

Seipp, B., & Schwarzer, C. (1996). Cross-cultural anxiety research: A review. In C. Schwarzer & M. Zeidner (Eds.), *Stress, anxiety, and coping in academic settings* (pp. 13–68). Tubingen, Germany: Francke-Verlag.

Selye, H. (1956). Stress and psychobiology. *Journal of Clinical and Experimental Psychopathology, 17*, 370–375.

Shaver, Ph. R., & Mikulincer, M. (2009). Attachment theory: I. Motivational, individual-differences, and structural aspects. In P. Corr & G. Matthews (Eds.), *Cambridge handbook of personality* (pp. 228–246). Cambridge: Cambridge University Press.

Shoda, Y., Mischel, W., & Wright, J. C. (1994). Intraindividual stability in the organization and patterning of behavior: Incorporating psychological situations into the idiographic analysis of personality. *Journal of Personality and Social Psychology, 67*, 674–687.

Sieber, J. E., O'Neil Jr., H. F., & Tobias, S. (1977). *Anxiety, learning and instruction*. Hillsdale, NJ: Erlbaum.

Siegle, G. J., & Hasselmo, M. E. (2002). Using connectionist models to guide assessment of psychological disorder. *Psychological Assessment, 14*, 263–278.

Siegle, G. J., Ghinassi, F., & Thase, M. E. (2007). Neurobehavioral therapies in the 21st century: Summary of an emerging field and an extended example of cognitive control training for depression. *Cognitive Therapy and Research, 31,* 235–262.

Silver, R. C., Holman, E. A., McIntosh, D. N., Poulin, M., Gil-Rivas, V., & Pizarro, J. (2006). Coping with a national trauma: A nationwide longitudinal study of responses to the terrorist attacks of September 11. In Y. Neria, R. Gross, R. D. Marshall, & E. S. Susser (Eds.), *9/11: Mental health in the wake of terrorist attacks* (pp. 45–70). New York: Cambridge University Press.

Simon, J. A., & Martens, R. (1979). Children's anxiety in sport and nonsport evaluative activities. *Journal of Sport Psychology, 1,* 160–169.

Skinner, E. A., Edge, K., Altman, J., & Sherwood, H. (2003). Searching for the structure of coping: A review and critique of category systems for classifying ways of coping. *Psychological Bulletin, 129,* 216–269.

Slapion, M. J., & Carver, C. S. (1981). Self-directed attention and facilitation of intellectual performance among persons high in test anxiety. *Cognitive Therapy and Research, 5,* 115–121.

Smith, B., & Caputi, P. (2001). Cognitive interference in computer anxiety. *Behaviour and Information Technology, 20,* 265–273.

Smith, B., & Caputi, P. (2007). Cognitive interference model of computer anxiety: Implications for computer-based assessment. *Computers in Human Behavior, 23,*1481–1498.

Smith, R. E., & Smoll, F. L. (1990). Sport performance anxiety. In H. Leitenberg (Ed.), *Handbook of social and evaluative anxiety* (pp. 417–453). New York: Plenum.

Smith, R. E., Smoll, F. L., & Schutz, R. W. (1990). Measurement and correlates of sport-specific cognitive and somatic trait anxiety: The Sport Anxiety Scale. *Anxiety Research, 2,* 263–280.

Smoller, J. W., Paulus, M. P., Fagerness, J. A., Purcell, S., Yamaki, L. H., Hirshfeld-Becker, D., . . . Stein, M. B. (2008). Influence of RGS2 on anxiety-related temperament, personality, and brain function. *Archives of General Psychiatry, 65,* 298–308

Sowa, C. J., & Lafleur, N. K. (1986). Gender differences within test anxiety. *Journal of Instructional Psychology, 13,* 75–80.

Spangler, G., Pekrun, R., Kramer, K., & Hofmann, H. (2002). Students' emotions, physiological reactions, and coping in academic exams. *Anxiety, Stress & Coping: An International Journal, 15,* 413–432.

Spence, J. T., & Spence, K. W. (1966). The motivational components of manifest anxiety: Drive and drive stimuli. In C. D. Spielberger (Ed.), *Anxiety and behavior* (pp. 291–326). New York: Academic Press.

Spielberger, C. D. (1966). Theory and research on anxiety. In C. D. Spielberger (Ed.), *Anxiety and behavior* (pp. 3–20). New York: Academic Press.

Spielberger, C. D. (1972a). *Anxiety: Current trends in theory and research.* New York: Academic Press.

Spielberger, C. D. (1972b). Conceptual and methodological issues in anxiety research. In C. D. Spielberger (Ed.), *Anxiety* (Vol. 2, pp. 481–493). New York: Academic Press.

Spielberger, C. D. (1972c). Current trends in theory and research on anxiety. In C. D. Spielberger (Ed.), *Anxiety: Current trends in theory and research* (Vol. 1, pp. 3–19). New York: Academic Press.

Spielberger, C. D. (1973). *Manual for the State-Trait Anxiety Inventory for Children*. Palo Alto, CA: Consulting Psychologists Press.

Spielberger, C. D. (1983). *Manual for the State-Trait Anxiety Inventory (STAI)*. Palo Alto, CA: Consulting Psychologists Press.

Spielberger, C. D. (1989). *The State-Trait Anxiety Inventory: A comprehensive bibliography* (2nd ed.). Palo Alto, CA: Consulting Psychologists Press.

Spielberger, C. D., & Vagg, P. R. (1987). The treatment of test anxiety: A transactional process model. In R. Schwarzer, H. M. Van der Ploeg, & C. D. Spielberger (Eds.), *Advances in test anxiety research* (Vol. 5, pp. 179–186). Berwyn, PA: Swets North America.

Spielberger, C. D., & Vagg, P. R. (1995a). *Test anxiety: Theory, assessment, and treatment*. Philadelphia: Taylor & Francis.

Spielberger, C. D., & Vagg, P. R. (1995b). *Test anxiety: A transactional process model*. In C. D. Spielberger & P. R. Vagg (Eds.), *Test anxiety: Theory, assessment, and treatment*. Series in clinical and community psychology (pp. 3–14). Philadelphia: Taylor & Francis.

Spielberger, C. D., Anton, W. D., & Bedell, J. (1976). The nature and treatment of test anxiety. In M. Zuckerman & C. D. Spielberger (Eds.), *Emotions and anxiety: New concepts, methods, and applications* (pp. 317–344). New York: Erlbaum/Wiley.

Spielberger, C. D., Gonzales, H. P., Taylor, C. J., Algaze, B., & Anton, W. D. (1978). Examination stress and test anxiety. In C. D. Spielberger & I. G. Sarason (Eds.), *Stress and anxiety* (Vol. 5, pp. 167–191). New York: Wiley.

Spielberger, C. D., Gorsuch, R. L., & Lushene, R. E. (1970). *Manual for the State-Trait Anxiety Inventory*: Palo Alto, CA: Consulting Psychologists Press.

Spielberger, C. D., & Reheiser, E. C. (2004). Measuring anxiety, anger, depression, and curiosity as emotional states and personality traits with the STAI, STAXI and STPI. In M. J. Hilsenroth & D. L. Segal (Eds.), *Comprehensive handbook of psychological assessment, Vol. 2. Personality assessment* (pp. 70–86). Hoboken, NJ: John Wiley.

Stein, D. J. (2006). Advances in understanding the anxiety disorders: The cognitive-affective neuroscience of 'false alarms.' *Annals of Clinical Psychiatry, 18*, 173–182.

Stelmack, R. M., & Rammsayer, T. H. (2008). Psychophysiological and biochemical correlates of personality. In G. J. Boyle, G. Matthews,

& D. H. Saklofske (Eds.), *The SAGE handbook of personality theory and assessment, Vol. 1. Personality theories and models* (pp. 33–55). Thousand Oaks, CA: Sage Publications.

Stetz, M. C., Wildzunas, R. M., Wiederhold, B. K., Stetz, T. A., & Hunt, M. P. (2006). The usefulness of virtual reality stress inoculation training for military medical females: A pilot study. *Annual Review of CyberTherapy and Telemedicine, 4*, 51–58.

Stevens, S. S. (1946). On the theory of scales of measurement. *Science, 105*, 677–680.

Stewart, R. E., & Chambless, D. L. (2009). Cognitive-behavioral therapy for adult anxiety disorders in clinical practice: A meta-analysis of effectiveness studies. *Journal of Consulting and Clinical Psychology, 77*, 595–606.

Stieger, S., Göritz, A. S., & Burger, C. (2010). Personalizing the IAT and the SC-IAT: Impact of idiographic stimulus selection in the measurement of implicit anxiety. *Personality and Individual Differences, 48*, 940–944.

Stone, A. A., Helder, L., & Schneider, M. M. (1988). Coping with stressful events: Coping dimensions and issues. In L. H. Cone (Ed.), *Life events and psychological functioning: Theoretical and methodological issues* (pp. 182–210). Newborn Park, CA: Sage.

Strahan, E. Y. (2003). The effects of social anxiety and social skills on academic performance. *Personality and Individual Differences, 34*, 347–366.

Suinn, R. M. (1990). *Anxiety management training.* New York: Plenum Press.

Suls, J., & Wheeler, L. (Eds.) (2000). *Handbook of social comparison.* New York: Kluwer Academic/Plenum.

Suls, J., Martin, R., & Wheeler, L. (2002). Social comparison: Why, with whom, and with what effect? *Current Directions in Psychological Science, 11*, 159–163.

Taylor, J. A. (1953). A personality scale of manifest anxiety. *Journal of Abnormal and Social Psychology, 48*, 285–290.

Tenenbaum, G., & Bar-Eli, M. (1995). Personality and intellectual capabilities in sport psychology. In D. H. Saklofske & M. Zeidner (Eds.), *International handbook of personality and intelligence* (pp. 687–710). New York: Plenum.

Thayer, R. E. (1996). *The origin of everyday moods: Managing energy, tension, and stress.* New York: Oxford University Press.

Thorpe, S. J., & Brosnan, M. J. (2007). Does computer anxiety reach levels which conform to DSM IV criteria for specific phobia? *Computers in Human Behavior, 23*, 1258–1272.

Tobias, S. (1985). Test anxiety: Interference, defective skills and cognitive capacity. *Educational Psychologist, 3*, 135–142.

Tobias, S. (1992). The impact of test anxiety on cognition in school learning. In K. A. Hagtvet & B. T. Johnsen (Eds.), *Advances in test anxiety research* (Vol. 7, pp. 18–31). Lisse, Netherlands: Swets and Zeitlinger.

Trzesniewski, K. H., Donnellan, M. B., & Robins, R. W. (2003, April). *Integrating self-esteem into a process model of academic achievement.* Paper presented at the Biennial meeting of the Society for Research on Child Development, Tampa, Florida.

Trzesniewski, K. H., Donnellan, M. B., & Robins, R. W. (2008). Is "generation me" really more narcissistic than previous generations? *Journal of Personality, 76,* 903–918.

Turner, S. M., Beidel, D. C., & Roberson-Nay, R. (2005). Offspring of anxious parents: Reactivity, habituation, and anxiety-proneness. *Behaviour Research and Therapy, 43,* 1263–1279.

Twenge, J. M. (2000). The age of anxiety? The birth cohort change in anxiety and neuroticism, 1952–1993. *Journal of Personality and Social Psychology, 79,* 1007–1021.

Twenge, J. M., & Campbell, W. K. (2008). Increases in positive self-views among high school students: Birth-cohort changes in anticipated performance, self-satisfaction, self-liking, and self-competence. *Psychological Science, 19,* 1082–1086.

Twenge, J. M., Gentile, B., DeWall, C. N., Ma, D., Lacefield, K., & Schurtz, D. R. (2010). Birth cohort increases in psychopathology among young Americans, 1938–2007: A cross-temporal meta-analysis of the MMPI. *Clinical Psychology Review, 30,* 145–154.

Tyrer, P. J. (1999). *Anxiety: A multidisciplinary review.* London: World Scientific Publications.

van Beijsterveldt, C. E. M., Verhulst, F. C., Molenaar, P. C. M., & Boomsma, D. I. (2004). The genetic basis of problem behavior in 5-year-old Dutch twin pairs. *Behavior Genetics, 34,* 229–242.

Van den Bergh, B. R., Mulder, E. J., Mennes, M., & Glover, V. (2005). Antenatal maternal anxiety and stress and the neurobehavioural development of the fetus and child: Links and possible mechanisms: A review. *Neuroscience and Biobehavioral Reviews, 29,* 237–258.

Van der Kolk, B. A., & McFarlane, A. C. (1996). The black hole of trauma. In B. A. van der Kolk, A. C. McFarlane, & L. Weisaeth (Eds.), *Traumatic stress: The effects of overwhelming experience on mind, body, and society* (pp. 3–24). New York: Guilford Press.

Van Yperen, N. W. (2007). Performing well in an evaluative situation: The roles of perceived competence and task-irrelevant interfering thoughts. *Anxiety, Stress, and Coping, 20,* 409–419.

Vasey, M.W., El-Hag, N., & Daleiden, E.L. (1996) Anxiety and the processing of emotionally threatening stimuli: Distinctive patterns of selective attention among high- and low-test-anxious children. *Child Development, 67,* 1173–1185.

Vassilopoulos, S. P. (2008). Coping strategies and anticipatory processing in high and low socially anxious individuals. *Journal of Anxiety Disorders, 22,* 98–107.

Victor, A. M., Bernat, D. H., Bernstein, G. A., & Layne, A. E. (2007). Effects of parent and family characteristics on treatment outcome of anxious children. *Journal of Anxiety Disorders, 21,* 835–848.

Voight, M. R., Callaghan, J. L., & Ryska, T. A. (2000) Relationship between goal orientation, self-confidence, and multidimensional anxiety among Mexican-American female youth athletes. *Journal of Sport Behavior, 23,* 271–288.

Voncken, M. J., & Bögels, M. (2008). Social performance deficits in social anxiety disorder: Reality during conversation and biased perception during speech. *Journal of Anxiety Disorders, 22,* 1384–1392.

Webb, E. J., Campbell, D. T., Schwartz, R. D., & Sechrest, L. (1966). *Unobtrusive measures: A survey of nonreactive research in social science.* Skokie, IL: Rand McNally.

Weidner, G., & Collins, R. L. (1993). Gender, coping, and health. In H. W. Krohne (Ed.), *Attention and avoidance: Strategies in coping with aversiveness* (pp. 241–265). Gottingen, Germany: Hogrefe & Huber.

Weil, M. M., & Rosen, L. D. (1995). The psychological impact of technology from a global perspective: A study of technological sophistication and technophobia in university students from twenty-three countries. *Computers in Human Behavior, 11,* 95–133.

Weil, M. M., Rosen, L. D., & Wugalter, S. (1990). The etiology of computer phobia. *Computers in Human Behavior, 6,* 361–379.

Wells, A. (2000). *Emotional disorders and metacognition: Innovative cognitive therapy.* New York: John Wiley & Sons.

Wells, A. (2008). Metacognitive therapy: Cognition applied to regulating cognition. *Behavioural and Cognitive Psychotherapy, 36,* 651–658.

Wells, A. (2010). Metacognitive therapy: Application to generalized anxiety disorder. In D. Sookman & R. L. Leahy (Eds.), *Treatment resistant anxiety disorders: Resolving impasses to symptom remission* (pp. 1–29). New York: Routledge/Taylor & Francis Group.

Wells, A., & Matthews, G. (1994) *Attention and emotion: A clinical perspective.* Hove, England: Lawrence Erlbaum.

Wells, A., & Matthews, G. (2006). Cognitive vulnerability to anxiety disorders: An integration. In L. B. Alloy & J. H. Riskind (Eds.), *Cognitive vulnerability to emotional disorders* (pp. 303–325). Mahwah, NJ: Lawrence Erlbaum.

Wenzel, A., & Finstrom, N. (2005). Cognitive biases associated with social interaction fears and anxiety. In P. L. Gower (Ed.), *New research on the psychology of fear* (pp. 1–23). Hauppauge, NY: Nova Science.

Whaley, S. E., Pinto, A., & Sigman, M. (1999). Characterizing inter-actions between anxious mothers and their children. *Journal of Consulting and Clinical Psychology, 67*, 826–836.

Widiger, T. A., & Lowe, J. R. (2007). Five-factor model assessment of personality disorder. *Journal of Personality Assessment, 89*, 16–29.

Wigfield, A., & Eccles, J. S. (1989). Test anxiety in elementary and secondary school students. *Educational Psychologist, 24*, 159–183.

Wigfield, A., & Eccles, J. S. (1990). Test anxiety in the school setting. In M. Lewis & S. M. Miller (Eds.), *Handbook of developmental psychopathology: Perspectives in developmental psychology* (pp. 237–250). New York: Plenum Press

Wigfield, A., & Meece, J. L. (1988). Math anxiety in elementary and secondary school students. *Journal of Educational Psychlogy, 80*, 210–216.

Williams, J. M. G., Watts, F. N., MacLeod, C., & Mathews, A. (1997). *Cognitive psychology and emotional disorders* (2nd ed.). Chichester: Wiley.

Wills, T. A. (1986). Stress and coping in early adolescence: Relationships to substance use in urban high schools. *Health Psychology, 5*, 503–529.

Wilson, E. J., MacLeod, C., Mathews, A., & Rutherford, E. M. (2006). The causal role of interpretive bias in anxiety reactivity. *Journal of Abnormal Psychology, 115*, 103–111

Wine, J. D. (1971). Test anxiety and the direction of attention. *Psychological Bulletin, 76*, 92–104.

Wine, J. D. (1980). Cognitive-attentional theory of test-anxiety. In I. G. Sarason, (Ed.), *Test anxiety: Theory, research, and applications* (pp. 349–385). Hillsdale, NJ: Erlbaum.

Wolpe, J. (1958). *Psychotherapy by reciprocal inhibition*. Stanford, CA: Stanford University Press.

Wong, S. S. (2008). The relations of cognitive triad, dysfunctional attitudes, automatic thoughts, and irrational beliefs with test anxiety. *Current Psychology, 27*, 177–191.

Woodman, T., & Hardy, L. (2001) Stress and anxiety. In R. Singer, H.A. Hausenblas, & C.M. Janelle (Eds.), *Handbook of research on sport psychology* (pp. 290–318). New York: Wiley.

Wren, D. G., & Benson, J. (2004). Measuring test anxiety in children: Scale development and internal construct validation. *Anxiety, Stress, and Coping: An International Journal, 17*, 227–240.

Zayas, V., Whitsett, D. D., Lee, J. J. Y., Wilson, N., & Shoda, Y. (2008). From situation assessment to personality: Building a social-cognitive model of a person. In G. J. Boyle, G. Matthews, & D. H. Saklofske (Eds.), *The SAGE handbook of personality theory and assessment, Vol. 2. Personality measurement and testing* (pp. 377–401). Thousand Oaks, CA: Sage Publications.

Zeidner, M. (1998). *Test anxiety: The state of the art*. New York: Plenum Press.

Zeidner, M. (2006). Stress, anxiety, and coping with terror: The Israeli experience. In P. Buchwald (Ed.), *Stress and anxiety: Applications to health, work place, community, and education* (pp. 263–291). Newcastle, Australia: Cambridge Scholar Press.

Zeidner, M. (2007). Test anxiety: Conceptions, findings, conclusions. In P. Schutz & R. Pekrun (Eds.), *Emotions in education*. Beverly Hills, CA: Sage.

Zeidner, M. (2008). Anxiety revisited: Theory, research, applications. In G. Boyle, D. Saklofske, & G. Matthews (Eds.), *Handbook of personality assessment, Vol. 1* (pp. 423–446). Beverly Hills, CA: Sage.

Zeidner, M. (2010). Test anxiety. In I. B. Weiner & E. Craighead (Ed.), *Corsini's encyclopedia of psychology* (4th ed., pp. 1766–1768). New York: Wiley.

Zeidner, M., & Ben-Zur, H. (1994). Individual differences in post-traumatic stress, anxiety, and coping in the aftermath of the Persian Gulf War. *Personality and Individual Differences, 16*, 459–476.

Zeidner, M., & Hammer, A. (1990). Life events and coping resources as predictors of stress symptoms in adolescents. *Personality and Individual Differences, 11*, 693–703.

Zeidner, M., & Matthews, G. (2005). Evaluation anxiety: Current theory and research. In A. J. Elliot & C. S Dweck. (Eds), *Handbook of competence and motivation* (pp. 141–163). New York: Guilford Publications.

Zeidner, M., & Matthews, G. (2000). Intelligence and personality. In R. J. Sternberg (Ed.), *Handbook of intelligence* (pp. 581–610). New York: Cambridge University Press.

Zeidner, M., & Nevo, B. (1992). Test anxiety in examinees in a college admission testing situation: Incidence, dimensionality, and cognitive correlates. In K. A. Hagtvet & B. T. Johnsen (Eds.), *Advances in test anxiety research* (Vol. 7, pp. 288–303). Lisse: Zeitlinger.

Zeidner, M., & Saklofske, D. (1996). Adaptive and maladaptive coping. In M. Zeidner & N. S. Endler (Eds.), *Handbook of coping: Theory, research, applications* (pp. 505–531) New York: Wiley.

Zeidner, M., & Schleyer, E. (1999). The big-fish-little-pond effect for academic self-concept, test anxiety, and school grades in gifted children. *Contemporary Educational Psychology, 24*, 305–329.

Zeidner, M., Klingman, A., & Papko, O. (1988). Enhancing students' test coping skills: Report of a psychological health education program. *Journal of Educational Psychology, 80*, 95–101.

Zeidner, M., Matthews, G. M., & Roberts, R. D. (2009). *What we know about emotional intelligence: How it affects learning, work, relationships, and mental health*. Cambridge, MA: MIT Press.

REFERENCES

Ziemke, T., & Lowe, R. (2009). On the role of emotion in embodied cognitive architectures: From organisms to robots. *Cognitive Computation, 1,* 104–117.

Zuckerman, M. (1994). *Behavioral expressions of biosocial bases of sensation seeking.* New York: Cambridge University Press.

Zuckerman, M. (2005). *Psychobiology of personality* (2nd ed.). New York: Cambridge.

Zung W. W. K. (1971). A rating instrument for anxiety disorders. *Psychosomatics, 12,* 371–379.

Index

Note: Page numbers followed by "*f*" and "*t*" denote figures and tables, respectively.